Research Competency in Higher Education

About the Editors

Prof. S.C. Panigrahi, M.A., M.Phil., Ph.D. in Education, is a Professor of Education and Head, Department of Education, Centre of Advanced Study in Education (CASE), Faculty of Education & Psychology, The Maharaja Sayajirao University of Baroda, Vadodara. He has more than 23 years of teaching and research experience. He has worked extensively in the area of Qualitative Research, Sociology of Education, Constructivism, Tribal Education, Special Education and Teacher Education.

Prof. H.J. Patadia, M.Sc., M.Ed., Ph.D. in Education, is a Professor of Education, Department of Education, Centre of Advanced Study in Education (CASE), Faculty of Education and Psychology, The Maharaja Sayajirao University of Baroda, Vadodara. She has more than 20 years of teaching and research experience. She has worked extensively in the area of Research Methodology, Mathematics Teaching, ICT in Education, and Teacher Education.

Dr. H.S. Mistry, M.A., M.Ed., UGC-NET (Education), Ph.D. (Education) is a Research Assistant, NCTE, New Delhi. He has more than 8 years of teaching and research experience. He has published 6 books and 18 papers as an article/research paper in different journals and as chapters in different books. He has also completed 7 Research Projects funded by IASE, GCERT, Gandhinagar. He has worked extensively in the area of Special Education, Teacher Education, Science and Mathematics Teaching.

Research Competency in Higher Education

Mapping and Management

Editors
Prof. S.C. Panigrahi
Prof. H.J. Patadia
Dr. H.S. Mistry

CONCEPT PUBLISHING COMPANY PVT. LTD.
NEW DELHI-110059

ISBN-13: 978-93-5125-184-2

First Published 2015

Published and Printed by

Concept
Since 1974

Concept Publishing Company Pvt. Ltd.
Regd. Office:
A/15-16, Commercial Block, Mohan Garden,
New Delhi-110059 (INDIA)
Phones : 25351460, 25351794, *Fax* : 091-11-25357109
Email : publishing@conceptpub.com
Website: www.conceptpub.com

Editorial Office:
H-13, Bali Nagar, New Delhi-110 015, India.

Cataloging in Publication Data--Courtesy: D.K. Agencies (P) Ltd. <docinfo@dkagencies.com>

National Seminar on 'Research Competency: Mapping and Management' (2014 : Centre for Advanced Study in Education, Maharaja Sayajirao University of Baroda)
Research competency in higher education : mapping and management / editors, Prof. S.C. Panigrahi, Prof. H.J. Patadia, Dr. H.S. Mistry.
pages cm
Papers presented at the National Seminar on 'Research Competency: Mapping and Management' held at Centre of Advanced Study in Education, Faculty of Education and Psychology, Maharaja Sayajirao University of Baroda, Vadodara, during 24-25 March, 2014.
Includes bibliographical references and index.
ISBN 9789351251842
1. Education, Higher—Research—India—Congresses. 2. Universities and colleges—India—Administration—Congresses. 3. Dissertations, Academic—India—Congresses. I. Panigrahi, S. C., editor. II. Patadia, H. J., editor. III. Mistry, H. S. (Hemendra S.), editor. IV. Maharaja Sayajirao University of Baroda. Centre for Advanced Study in Education.host institution. V. Title.

LB2341.8.I5N38 2014 DDC 378.072054 23

Preface

It is of utmost importance that young minds be attracted to doctoral research, as it holds promise for the development of the nation. There is evident upsurge in enrolment of Ph.D. Programmes. Does it really hold a promise for development? The reason for unproductive research in education in India is the easy going tendency of most of the researchers. Our only trend seems to be to get the Ph.D. degree or a book published, at the earliest. Above all, the mindset of the researchers needs to be oriented towards research rigour. Recently a doctoral thesis was adjudicated for the award of the Ph.D. degree, wherein, the text was found to be its own testimony. A section of the concluding paragraph reads—*It is an interesting study on the academic performance of the elementary level school students in the context of their family size and the SES. The research rigour has been observed throughout the study. It is immense peace to experience this unique quality research. The testimony of this research work is fully established through each and every bit of the scholarly text. The emerging theses are marvelous. The investigator has satisfyingly sought the reality with respect to many a questions which keep lurking with us, such as, "The Social Status of the students has been found affecting their academic performance, more significantly, than their Economic status.." The meaningful continuous flow of findings has immediate message for our Nation and Globe at large.*

The above paragraph presents a mixed scenario of research expectation, researchers' competency and research quality. Many universities in India have started pre-Ph.D. tests to search for competent researchers, concurrently, with SLET and NET, and tests for JRF. Do all these tests assure and ensure competent researchers? Over and above these the UGC has imposed Ph.D. Course Work and Academic Performance Indicators. No intensive research is required to test the validity of these. But, all this is acceptable, because, the intent is fair and genuine. Can we do away with this vicious polygon, rather, circle and search for some foolproof strategies to approach the genuine, competent, dedicated, simple, honest, cultured scholars?

The present volume is the result of the National Seminar on 'Research Competency: Mapping and Management' held at Centre of Advanced Study in Education, Faculty of Education and Psychology, The Maharaja Sayajirao University of Baroda, Vadodara, Gujarat, India, during 24th-25th March, 2014 with the following sub-themes.

1. Status of Extant Research

The intent is to produce a prologue of Educational Research in India. The research demands perspective, passion, dedication and culture. But, the Educational Research is largely wanting. It is more or less surviving on the borrowed methodology from other disciplines. It is more of descriptive and evaluative than suggestive. Most of it is quantitative than qualitative. Most of it is based on borrowed methodology than indigenous. There is a need to explore:

(a) How the Educational Researchers are registered?
(b) Who are the Research Guides?
(c) Who decides the research agenda?
(d) How a research problem is identified and formulated?
(e) How the research work is conducted?
(f) What is the relevance and quality of research guidance?
(g) Which problems are faced by the researchers?
(h) How much financial support is there for research?
(i) What per cent of GDP is invested on research?
(j) What is the nature and relevance of Ph.D. course work?
(k) How a Ph.D. thesis is evaluated?
(l) What are the emerging research trends? Any many more

2. Planning of Educational Research

There is very little planning for educational research. The evident truth is that it is going on arbitrarily. There is more focus on soft skills than hard skills. There is more focus on applied research than fundamental research. There is methodology based problem than problem demanded methodology. The Research Methodology is being employed mechanically. The Policy Perspective Part has been dislocated. Earlier, the research agenda was decided by the apex agencies, namely, NIEPA (Now NUPEA), NCERT, ICSSR, CASE and TIFR. Where has their vision gone? Could we reflect on:

(a) Developmental challenges and research agenda,
(b) Factors for examining feasibility of educational research,
(c) Criteria for financial support for educational research by the education institutions, apex agencies and community,
(d) Relative focus on various types of research, and
(e) Formulating policy research.

3. Administration of Educational Research

Almost all apex agencies, such as, UGC, ICSSR and NCERT play a dual role of granting funds and monitoring. These agencies are evidently wanting in playing a dual role. For example, grants from these bodies are released towards the end of the financial year, when not much time is left. Universities do not provide permission unless the grant is received. Then the utilization certificate is required in the form of certified statement of receipt and expenditure. Indifferent agencies, unripe educational administration, and helpless committed researchers play mercilessly with the public exchequer and capital. We are a witness to many universities, where emerging theses, rest on floors of confidential halls, before those are dispatched. Then these rest on the cots, carols, and cupboards of the external referees, indefinitely, many a times without a genuine cause. What is the resolution?

(a) What should be the mechanisms of funding research by the apex agencies?
(b) What should be the criteria for qualifying PG Teachers as Research Guides?
(c) How should the external referees be appointed for examining the Ph.D. Thesis?
(d) What should be the approaches for bringing out timely surveys on educational research?
(e) How to address the developmental challenges through educational research?

4. Educational Research: What Next?

With all the ifs and buts, educational research in India has its own ethos and grace. But, who will synthesize educational research? We all need to awaken our sensitivities to education. Let us learn to value the indigenous. Do all the stakeholders know why the brains and souls of the Indian scholars are flying to Cambridge Press, Oxford Press, and other International Presses grossly neglecting the Indian Press and Publishers? No research rigour is required to reach the causes. It is because of the relative value attributed to foreign (international) publications under the Academic Performance Indicators. What is published is not that important as where it is published.

(a) How long will we compromise with the fragmented research? Should not it be wholistic related to the ground realities, which are, very often, rather always, multi-parametric?
(b) Should not the educational research be collective and collaborative: Formal-informal-non-formal?
(c) Why have the social scientists not come out of their dummy laboratories? Is there not a need to conduct naturalistic situational research through deep observation, reflection and intuition and construct grass root theories, addressing our problems, through our tools, through our sources and resources, to better our quality of life and living?

The present volume on Mapping and Management of Researchers' Competency includes the expressed opinions of the scholars from different parts of the country on these sub-themes. Although no definite answer could be arrived at the basic issues but, the guidelines provided by them will be helpful to the researchers, teacher educators, university education departments, research organizations, higher education authorities and policy-makers.

We are thankful to each and everyone who help directly or indirectly resulted in bringing out the present volume.

Place: Vadodara, Gujarat, India **Editors**
Date: 13.11.2014

Preface

SECTION TWO
Planning of Educational Research

SECTION THREE
Administration of Educational Research

List of Contributors

Baliya, J.N., Department of Educational Studies, Central University of Jammu, Jammu, Jammu & Kashmir.

Barve, Minakshi (Retd), Professor, School of Education, Yashwantrao Chavan Maharashtra Open University, Nasik, Maharashtra.

Behera, Biswajit, Ph.D. Student, Department of Education, Faculty of Education & Psychology, The M.S. University of Baroda, Vadodara-390002, Gujarat.

Bhagwat, Minaxi S., Ph. D. Student, Department of Education, Faculty of Education & Psychology, The M.S. University of Baroda, Vadodara-390002, Gujarat.

Bhatti, Arti, Research Scholar, Department of Education, Faculty of Education & Psychology, The M.S. University of Baroda, Vadodara-390002, Gujarat.

Biswal, Bibhuti Narayan, Principal, Sri Sathya Sai Vidyaniketan, Near Tata SSL, N.H. No. 8, Ganeshvad, Sisodra, Navsari-396463, Gujarat.

Chandrakar, Mukesh, Assistant Professor, Department of Education, Guru Ghasidas Vishwavidyalaya, Bilaspur, Chhattisgarh.

Deka, Mouchumi, Ph.D. Research Scholar, Department of Education, A.M. School of Educational Sciences, Assam University, Silchar, Assam.

Deota, Nilambar P., Professor, Department of Education, Faculty of Education & Psychology, The M.S. University of Baroda, Vadodara-390002, Gujarat.

Dharankar, Madhavi, Assistant Professor, School of Education, Yashwantrao Chavan Maharashtra Open University, Nasik, Maharashtra.

Ganiger, Bharathi, UGC-JRF, Department of Education, Faculty of Education & Psychology, The M.S. University of Baroda, Vadodara-390002, Gujarat.

Goel Devraj, Professor Emeritus, Department of Education, Faculty of Education & Psychology, The M.S. University of Baroda, Vadodara-390002, Gujarat.

Goel, Chhaya, Professor, Department of Education, Faculty of Education & Psychology, The M.S. University of Baroda, Vadodara-390002, Gujarat.

Gulhane, G.L., Head, Post Graduate Department of Education, Sant Gadge Baba Amravati University Amravati, Maharashtra.

Gururajan, Pramila, Ph.D. Student, Department of Education, Faculty of Education & Psychology, The M.S. University of Baroda, Vadodara-390002, Gujarat.

Helaiya, Sheetal, Assistant Professor, Waymade College of Education, Vallabh Vidyanagar, Anand

Khedekar, Sandhya Milind, Assistant Professor, Thakur Shyamnarayan College of Education and Research, Kandivali-East, Mumbai, Maharashtra.

Kothari, R.G., Professor, Department of Education, Faculty of Education & Psychology, The M.S. University of Baroda, Vadodara-390002, Gujarat.

Madhavi, R.L., Temporary Teaching Assistant, Department of Education, Faculty of Education & Psychology, The M.S. University of Baroda, Vadodara-390002, Gujarat.

Mahale, Sanjivani R., Assistant Professor, School of Education, Yashwantrao Chavan Maharashtra Open University, Nasik, Maharashtra.

Mani, R.S., Professor, Department of Education, Faculty of Education & Psychology, The M.S. University of Baroda, Vadodara-390002, Gujarat.

Oza, Dipti, Professor, Department of Education, Faculty of Education & Psychology, The M.S. University of Baroda, Vadodara-390002, Gujarat.

Padhi, Sambit Kumar, Assistant Professor, Department of Education, Guru Ghasidas Vishwavidyalaya, Bilaspur, Chhattisgarh.

Panigrahi, S.C., Professor & Head, Department of Education, Faculty of Education & Psychology, The M. S. University of Baroda, Vadodara-390002, Gujarat.

Patadia, Harsha J., Professor, Department of Education, Faculty of Education & Psychology, The M.S. University of Baroda, Vadodara-390002, Gujarat.

Patel, Dhirendra, Lecturer, H.R. Gajwani, B.Ed. College, Gandhidham, Kutch, Gujarat

Pathania, Sudershan Kumar, Research Scholar, P. G. Department of Education, University of Jammu, Jammu, Jammu & Kashmir.

Patted, L.B., Principal, University College of Education, Dharwad-580001, Karnataka.

Patted, Nataraj B., Research Scholar, Dept of Agri Business Management, University of Agriculture Science, Dharwad-580001, Karnataka.

Priyadarshini, Ekta, Research Scholar, Department of Education, Faculty of Education & Psychology, The M.S. University of Baroda, Vadodara-390002, Gujarat.

Rai, Dona, Research Scholar, Department of Education, NEHU, Shillong-22.

Ramesh, M., UGC Research Fellow, Department of Education, Faculty of Education & Psychology, The M.S. University of Baroda, Vadodara-390002, Gujarat.

Sahasrabuddhe, Milind, Associate Professor, Department of Educational Administration, Faculty of Education & Psychology, The M.S. University of Baroda, Vadodara-390002, Gujarat.

Santwani, Sarla A., Principal, H.R. Gajwani B.Ed. College, Gandhidham, Kutch, Gujarat.

Sethi, Aradhana, Research Scholar, Banastali Vidyapeeth, Rajasthan.

Sharma, Pushpalata, Associate Professor, Kalyan P.G. College, Bhilai, Chhattisgarh.

Shoket, Mohd, P.G. Department of Education, University of Jammu, Jammu, Jammu & Kashmir.

Sindhi, Swaleha, Temporary Teaching Assistant, Department of Educational Administration, Faculty of Education & Psychology, The M.S. University of Baroda, Vadodara-390002, Gujarat.

Singh, Harishankar P.P. College of Education, Gondia, Maharashtra.

Talesra, Hemlata, Director, Professor & Head, Smt. K.B. Dave College of Education, Pilvai, Mehsana, Gujarat.

Thumar, P.B., Professor & Director, Physical Education Department, The M.S. University of Baroda, Vadodara-390002, Gujarat.

Varghese, Mary George, Assistant Professor, MES's Pillai College of Education and Research, Chembur, Mumbai, Maharasthra.

Vithalrao, Magre Sunita, Associate Professor, Department of Education, University of Mumbai, Mumbai, Maharashtra.

Vyas, Pranav, Professor, Department of Micro Biology, Faculty of Science, The M.S. University of Baroda, Vadodara-390002, Gujarat.

SECTION ONE
Status of Extant Research

SECTION ONE

Status of Extant Research

1

Competencies in Doing Educational Research

S.C. Panigrahi and *Biswajit Behera*

Social Science Research

Fundamentally social science research is concerned with people and their life contexts which underpin human activities. It involves a range of methods which is borrowed from various disciplines such as anthropology, sociology, psychology and history. Anthropology contributes techniques of participant observation, interviews and field note-taking. From sociology, we learn how social relationships are formed and psychology provides an understanding of human behaviour. Research involves the collection of data through above range of methods.

Social science research differs from research in the natural sciences because of its focus on individuals and groups and their behaviour within cultures and organizations. There is unpredictability in the behaviour of human beings, so it cannot develop powerful solutions to social problems.

Quality in social science research depends on power of its outcomes and therefore, its quality rests upon how language is used to interpret meaning. Further, ethical issues are centrally important in social science research as its focus is on human beings.

Social science research is an art as well as a science. The skills and knowledge needed to be a researcher can only be acquired through experiences over a period of time. There are always judgements to be made. Researcher should be prepared to critique his work and reflect on how it could have been done differently.

Educational Research

Educational research comes under social science research. It is extensively based on the disciplines of sociology and psychology. So, it is not a discrete discipline. It is concerned not only with activities of teachers and students in schools, but includes all life-long learning. The purposes of education are based on different ideological factors. So, research has to work within and around the different views of education. Key organizing concepts for education are those of curriculum and pedagogy. Its meanings are different to different people. For example, to Bruner, it is understood as students' experiences in the classroom; Piaget suggested that learning is dependent upon the child's development where as Vygotsky viewed that the development of mind is the process of interaction between the child and adults or peers.

Educational research can also be understood as 'school effectiveness' research and 'school improvement 'research. These researches used wide range of data and placing more emphasis on trends and changes over time.

Paradigm of Research

There are two main paradigms that form the basis of research in the social sciences. The paradigm that is rooted in the physical sciences is called the systematic, scientific or positivist approach. The opposite paradigm has come to be known as qualitative approach. The two opposing sides have their own values, terminology, methods and techniques to understand social phenomenon in research methodology.

No matter what paradigm the researcher works within, he has to adhere to certain values regarding the control of bias, maintenance of objectivity during research process and the conclusions drawn. It is the application of these values to the process of information gathering, analysis and interpretation that enables it to be called a research process.

Research as Process

Research is an academic activity. In a technical sense, it is an act of scientific investigation. It is a systematized effort to gain new knowledge. So, the method which man employs for obtaining the knowledge of whatever the unknown can be called as research. Research is a process which comprises defining the problem, formulating hypothesis, collecting, organizing and evaluating data, making deductions and reaching conclusions.

So, research involves determining:

- What we want to study? (The research question)
- How do we want to study it? (The design)
- Whom we want to study? (The sample or the case)
- How best to acquire information (data collection techniques)
- How best to analyze or interpret the information (data analysis)
- How to confirm the findings (verification process)

To accomplish these tasks an educational researcher needs to possess certain competencies. These **competencies** are illustrated below:

1. **How to decide upon a methodology?**
The first thing the researcher needs to do research is to think about research methodology. Before choosing a right type of methodology, one should know the differences between quantitative and qualitative research. Qualitative research attempts to get an in-depth opinion for participants. Quantitative research generates statistics through the use of large-scale survey research. It is not that quantitative research is better than qualitative research or *vice-versa*. Neither is better than the other. So, the researcher needs to know the type of qualitative research methodologies like action research, ethnography, grounded theory, etc., and the type of quantitative research methodologies like experimental and survey.
2. **How to choose the research methods?**
Research methods are the tools for collecting data. The

researcher must know about these tools to find the most appropriate methods. Some of tools are interview, questionnaire, observation, focus group and etc.

It is not necessary to use only one research method. A combination of methods can be desirable in order to overcome the different weaknesses inherent in all the methods. In order to choose the method(s) researcher should consider the followings:

- What is the purpose of the research?
- What is the time scale?
- Whether is it collaborative or individual?
- What is the budget?

For example, the researcher aims to find out the attitude of teachers towards educational T.V programme. In this case, focus group setting of teachers can be the appropriate method

3. **How to conduct focus groups?**

The focus group is coordinated by a facilitator who asks questions, probes for more detail, scaffolds the things and tries to ensure that everybody is participating and no one dominates the discussion.

(i) It is very important to understand how people interact in a group setting. It is therefore, necessary to hold pilot focus group with participants.

(ii) Another requirement is video tape of this focus group. The video recordings will help the researcher to assess body language, analyze the asking of questions etc.

(iii) It is also extremely important to make sure that the right type of venue for the focus group is chosen in order to facilitate discussion and the standard of recording.

(iv) It is essential to select potential participants for the group.

4. **How to Conduct Interviews?**

There are three main types of interview which tend to be used in social research:

Unstructured interview semi-structured and structured interview.

The most important competencies of a researcher during conduct of interviews are:

(a) How to record it? (Tape recorder, video recorder, note taking)
(b) What type of questions he needs to ask (constructing interview schedule)
(c) How to establish rapport (firm eye contact, body language, treating interviewees with respect)
(d) How can he probe for more information (obtain clarification, elaboration, explanation and understanding through questioning)

5. **How to construct questionnaires?**

When the researcher is sure that questionnaire is the most appropriate method for his research, he needs to decide to construct a close-ended, open ended or combination questionnaire:

(i) Deciding which questionnaire to use (open questions where respondents use their own words to answer a question, closed questions where pre written response categories are provided),
(ii) Administering the questionnaire (self administered),
(iii) Piloting the questionnaire (in order to see if it is obtaining the results that is required by the researcher),
(iv) Getting a high response.

Researcher can take following measures to try to ensure a high response rate

- Any learning issues?
- Is it relevant to the respondents lives, attitudes and beliefs
- Is clear, concise and uncultured?
- Are instructions straight forward?
- Reassure any problems?

6. **How to carry out participant observation?**

In participant observation, the researcher immerses himself into the situation. The action is deliberate and intended to add to knowledge. It is a procedure for generating understanding about the way of life of others. The researcher participates in the community. It is important to

(i) Gain access to the community (level of negotiation required),

(ii) Collecting information (preparing field notes),
(iii) Analyzing information (Analysis in the field so that hypotheses can be discussed with key informants).

7. **How to analyze the data?**

The researcher has chosen to conduct qualitative or quantitative research by methodological preference and educational background.

(i) Deciding which approach to use:
For quantitative, issues of validity and reliability are important and qualitative data analysis is a very personal process and particularly a transcript is analyzed.

(ii) Analyzing data:
For quantitative data, the statistics is the most efficient method to use. Transcript analysis, focus group analysis, interview summary form, content analysis, discourse analysis, thematic and comparative analysis are some of the types of analysis.

(iii) Processing the data:
The different processes involved in qualitative data analysis are:

(a) The researcher needs to ***think*** about the data when data collection starts,
(b) He needs to ***judge*** the value of data,
(c) As the research progresses, he needs to ***interpret*** the data to gain understanding of what is going on,
(d) Finally, he needs to undertake the process to ***generate*** meanings and findings.

But, in quantitative data analysis, many complex statistical techniques are to be used.

8. **How to report your findings?**

Once, the research is completed and data is analyzed, the task of reporting the findings is needed. It is in the form of written reports and journal articles which can be reproduced on line and oral presentations. So, the researcher should:

(a) Remember the audience,
(b) Style of writing,
(c) Do the audiences understand statistics?

(d) Have they the time to read?
(e) Are they interested in methodology?
(f) Are they interested in conclusions and recommendations?
(g) Does a researcher need to write using complex terminology?
(h) Does he need to keep language as simple as possible?

Conclusion

Becoming a successful researcher is a continual learning process in which we all make mistakes. Researchers should be open and honest what they are doing. But it should be remembered that undertaking a research can be fascinating, rewarding and exciting!

References

Best, J.W. and Khan, J.V. (1986), *Research in Education,* Prentice-Hall of India, New Delhi.

Denzin, N.K. and Lincoln, Y.S. (2000), *Handbook of Qualitative Research,* Sage, London.

Gay, L.R. and Airasian, P. (2000), *Educational Research: Competencies for Analysis and Application,* Prentice Hall, New Jersey.

Hancock, D. and Algozzine, Bob (2006), *Doing Case-study Research: A Practical Guide for Beginning Researchers,* Teachers College Press, New York.

Kumar, R. (2007), *Research Methodology: A Step-by-Step Guide for Beginners,* Pearson Education, New Delhi.

Somekh, B. and Lewin, C. (2007), *Research Methods in the Social Sciences,* Vistar Publications, New Delhi.

2
Research: A Holistic Insight

Dipti Oza

To synthesize educational research there is a need to develop an insight, a holistic mapping of its need and prevalence. The seminar note has very rightly raised the issues related to it. Why do we do research?, How is it relevant? Is it only to satisfy our personal need and requirement or wish to contribute in a field of discipline or help to formulate functional policies and programmes for national educational status?

Truly speaking any educational institution does not have a very clear research policy, neither for students, research programmes nor projects. All are individualistic and scattered attempts which in turn fail to generalize and contribute to develop insight. Autonomy is essential but discipline is much more meaningful and purposeful.

While planning the strategies it is very important to keep in mind who does the research, why the research, what is its utility—personal and national? What are the incentives to do research? What are the essential competencies required? How to nurture? In this chapter an attempt is made to think loud on various strategies to do research, with a holistic insight and contributing both the researcher in person and the nation in general.

What is the researcher's purpose to do the educational researches? When it was asked to students who are pursuing their Ph. D, almost in one voice said it is for gaining degree and this degree may help them in entering into teaching profession. Very few (less than 3 per cent) said for gaining knowledge, because they wish to develop insight into subject/topic, nothing else to do, adding one more degree, etc.(This is true for all the discipline not only in Education).

How do you select the topic for research? The answers are varied in nature like personal interest, guide's choice, material available, convenience for data collection, etc. In the absence of clear policy for conducting research most of the researches are taken either on personal interest or guide's choice. The researches done may be having high research value still either the researches go unnoticed or do not hold relevance or connection with current needs in education. This is a point where there is need to think and develop vision/insight.

What is the need of doing research? To widen the knowledge of discipline, updating the knowledge of discipline and study its current relevance etc. It needs to do for providing significant direction to framing important policy, programme which requires data base. Even at times of implementation the data base helps for its effectiveness.

For doing the research do the researchers have the required competencies? What are the competencies we are looking for? Right from childhood if you observe the child, one can notice that as a innate trait the child is curious, information explorer, hard worker has perseverance, passion is creative,….. etc. All these traits need to be nurtured by providing experiences and opportunities right from the childhood to growing up stages. Today the scenario is that very few researchers are groomed with competencies, others are not even prepared for nurturing it as wish to complete it at the earliest. Most of them are full time employee and if they get time then they wish to spare time for the research. Will these type of mindset prepare them for good research? They have proved that the era in which we are living is the era of smart working rather than hard working.

Now in this situation if one thinks to improve the status of research one has to make strategies. Most of the policy decisions or implementation in education is not coming from education but largely imposed by the social work or other field. Instead let us try to identify the trends, issues on demands, out-side/in-side class-room but relevant to students and their growing up. The strategies could be as follows:

1. Identification of Thrust areas (National/State/Region/ University/College or Department level). Every university/ college can work on various aspects of one area. All students can work on it and there are by and large, details covering various aspects of the topic and the data can be gathered. By compiling these it can prove to be very valuable information for making recommendations, action to be taken or any implementation purpose. It also helps in obtaining a deep understanding of concepts and theoretical understanding.
2. Working in each area at least for three to five years at all levels like Post Doctoral, Doctoral, Master level thesis or at projects (e.g. Adolescents, disadvantage groups, how to improve researches by doing meta analysis of existing done researches, etc.).
3. Identification of two or three areas.
4. Design Projects in team. Working in teams results in many values essential for mankind like cooperation, collaboration, sharing—etc., and escape from prey of unhealthy competition and other evils, instead we can prove to be complementary and develop mutual respect and dignity.
5. Action research at UG level/community work.
6. Research based assignments/time bound projects at PG level.
7. Community linkage, educational relevance projects and action researches.
8. Development of social sensitivity and really preparing research minded teacher at any or all level of education.

There can be many strategies to up-grade the status of research, enriching knowledge, improving quality of research and grooming our youth for doing research competencies, ultimately gain at all level, national, institutional and personal too.

3

Some Neglected Areas in Qualitative Research

Nilambar P. Deota

India's Legacy in Education

India is a land of learning. This is quite true with reference to Ancient India—Bharat—India which has served as a beacon light to the entire world. Sanskrit literature is very rich in its contents in almost all the disciplines and the slogan is very apt when it is said that व्यासोच्छिष्टं जगत् सर्वं ।

The foundation of India culture is based on the Sanskrit language. There is a **misconception about the Sanskrit** language that it is only a language for chanting mantras in temples or during religious ceremonies. However, that is less than 5 per cent of the Sanskrit literature. More than 95 per cent of the Sanskrit literature has nothing to do with religion, and instead it deals with philosophy, law, science, literature, grammar, phonetics, interpretation etc.

Sanskrit as a Language of Science

We have got a long scientific heritage and the great scientific achievements of our ancestors are recorded in the Mahabharata. and Ramayana. In particular, Sanskrit was the language in which all our great scientists in ancient India wrote their works. It is because of two reasons.

1. Sanskrit was the Language of Free Thinkers

Sanskrit was the language of free thinkers, who questioned everything, and expressed the widest spectrum of thoughts on various subjects. Today, no doubt, we are behind the Western countries in science, but there was a time when India was leading the whole world in science. Knowledge of the great scientific achievements of our ancestors and our scientific heritage will give us the encouragement and moral strength to once again take India to the forefront of science in the modern world.

In ancient India there were everywhere **debates or Shashtrarthas** which permitted free discussion of ideas, criticism of one's opponent and free dissent in the presence of a large gathering. Such freedom of thought and expression led to great development of science, since science also requires freedom, freedom to think, freedom to express one's ideas, and freedom to dissent. The great scientist Charak has mentioned in his book *Charak samhita* that debating is necessary for the development of science, particularly debating with one's mental equals.

In the earliest *Nyaya* text, which is the *Nyaya Sutras of Gautam*, several categories of debate are mentioned e.g. *vad, jalp, vitanda,* etc. These were further developed by the subsequent writers of *Nyaya.*

2. The Word 'Sanskrit' Means "Prepared, Pure, Refined or Perfect"

It was not for nothing that it was called the 'evavani' (language of the Gods). It has an outstanding place in our culture and indeed was recognized as a language of rare sublimity by the whole world.

Sanskrit was the language of our philosophers, our scientists, our mathematicians, our poets and playwrights, our grammarians, our jurists, etc. who have made their contribution in the fields of Mathematics, Astronomy, Medicine, Engineering, etc. The Classical Sanskrit enabled scientific ideas to be expressed with great precision, logic and elegance. Science requires precision. Also, science requires a written language in which ideas can be written with great precision and logic. The sole credit of it goes to the great grammarian Panini for creating a standard language. This provided for uniformity and it systematized the language so that scholars could easily express and communicate their ideas with great precision which was a necessary requirement for the development of science.

The Vedic literature is only about 1 per cent of the entire Sanskrit literature. (the Vedic literature is not in accordance with the Panini's grammar.) About 99 per cent of Sanskrit literature is non-vedic Sanskrit literature. For instance, the Ramayana, the Mahabharata, the Puranas, the works of Kalidas etc., are no doubt highly respected but they are not part of the Vedic literature and hence they are now almost all existing in accordance with Panini's grammar.

The spoken language no doubt is very useful, but the spoken dialects change every 50 or 100 kilometers, and hence there is no uniformity in them. A written language like Classical Sanskrit in which scholars could express and communicate ideas to other scholars living far away with great precision and clarity was thus absolutely necessary for the development of science, and this is the great achievement of Panini.

3. *Contribution of Sanskrit in Various Disciplines*

In fact each scripture is a research work par excellence in India. It presents certain profound and sound principles reflecting the truth. Most of these books are in the form of Fundamental Research.

Sanskrit language has contributed in the following disciplines profusely. To just refer the few:

Disciplines	*Works*
1. Medicine & Surgery & Animal Husbundary	Vaagbhat, Charak and Sushrut
2. Engineering	Taksha shastras.
3. Astronomy and mathematics	Aryabhatta, Brahmagupta, Varahamihira and Bhaskar, numbers in the decimal system, invention of zero
4. Economics	Chanakya's Arthashastra
5. Education & Linguistics	Rig Praatishakhyas, Taittiriya Upanishad-Shikshaa Valli,
6. Sex education	Vaatsyaayana's Kamasutras and other allied authors

Disciplines	Works
7. Management	Chanakya's Arthashastra, Mahabharata, Ramayana and *Bhagawad Gita*
8. Grammar/Etymology	Panini and Patanjali (authors of *Ashtadhyayi* and the *Mahabhashya*) and the works of Nighantu and Yaska's Nirukta
9. Aeronautics	Sage Bhardvaaja's Vaimanika Shastras
10. Yoga-Physical education	Patanjali's Yogasutras, Hathayoga Pradipikaa, Shiva Samhita, Gheranda Samhita
11. Psychology	Saankhya system
12. Logic	Tarkashaastra of Gautama, Nyaya Philosophy, Vaisheshika Darshana of Kanaada and Poorva Mimamsaa of sage Vyasa.
13. Philosophy	Gautam (founder of the Nyaya system), Ashvaghosha (author of *Buddha Charita*), Kapila (founder of the Sankhya system), Shankaracharya, Brihaspati, etc.
14. Science of Interpretation	Jaimini's *Mimansa Sutras*—laid the foundation of a whole system of rational interpretation of texts which was used not only in religion but also in law, philosophy, grammar, etc. In literature, the contribution of Sanskrit is of the foremost order.
15. Physiognomy	Samudrika Shastra in relation to Greek Physiognomy-a science of body signs and prediction of the future tense.
16. Embryology	Garbhopanishad and Bhagvad

4. About Indian Philosophy

Shatdarshana or six classical (orthodox) schools of Indian philosophy.

The development of sciences and scientific philosophy in ancient India owes much more to the development of Indian philosophy.

The generally accepted view is that there are six systems of Classical (orthodox) Indian philosophy (Shat Dharshana) and three non-classical (unorthodox) systems. The six classical (orthodox) systems are Nyaya, Vaisheshik, Sankya, Yoga, Purva Mimansa and Uttar Mimansa (also known as Vedanta). The non-classical, heterodox or Nastika (unorthodox) systems are Buddhism, Jainism and Charvak.

1. *Nyaya*—presents the scientific outlook. It insists that nothing is acceptable unless it is in accordance with reason and experience. It was subsequently distorted by the later Nyayayiks.
2. *Vaisheshik*—presents the atomic theory—the physics of ancient India.
3. *Sankhya*—Probably presents the materialist ontology of the Nyaya Vaisheshik system. However, very little of the original literature on Sankhya has survived, and there is some controversy about its basic principles, some saying that it is dualistic and not monistic because it has two entities, purush and prakriti, in it.
4. Yoga—presents a method of physical and mental discipline.
5. Purva mimansa (or briefly mimansa)—lays emphasis on the performance of the yagya for attaining various spiritual and worldly benefits. Hence, relies on the Brahmana part of the Vedas.
6. Uttar Mimansa (or Vedanta)—lays emphasis on brahmagyan, hence relies on the Upanishad part of the Vedas.

It is necessary to mention about the Nyaya and Vaisheshik systems, which represent the scientific outlook. Nyaya philosophy states that nothing is acceptable unless it is in accordance with reason and experience, and this is precisely the scientific approach (see in this connection D.P. Chattopadhyaya's *What is Living and What is Dead in Indian Philosophy* which is a seminal work on Indian Philosophy).

Vaisheshik is the atomic (parmanu) theory, which was originally the physics of ancient India. Nyaya and Vaisheshik were regarded as one system, but since physics is the most fundamental of all sciences, the Vaisheshik system was later separated from Nyaya and made as a separate system of philosophy.

The Sankhya philosophy certainly seems to have given the materialist ontological foundation on which the later Nyaya-Vaisheshik scientific philosophy was built, and hence we can broadly call the Indian philosophy representing the scientific approach as the Sankhya-Nyaya-Vaisheshik system.

The Nyaya Vaisheshik system is (1) realist, and (2) pluralistic. This is in contrast to Advaita Vedanta of Shankaracharya which is monastic and monistic, regards the world as illusion or maya in the ultimate analysis. The word 'pluralistic' is in contrast to the word 'monistic'. The word 'monistic' means that there is only one entity in the world.

It may be mentioned that the Nyaya philosophy developed logic to an extent even beyond what Aristotle and other Greek thinkers did (see D.P. Chattopadhyaya's books in this connection), and logical thinking is necessary for science.

Thus the Nyaya philosophy gave great support and encouragement to science in ancient India. It must be mentioned that the Nyaya philosophy is one of the Shat Darshanas i.e. one of the six orthodox systems in Indian philosophy, and not an unorthodox system like the Charvaks. Hence, our great scientists could not be persecuted by the orthodox people since they could say that they were relying on an orthodox philosophy, namely, the Nyaya. This was unlike in Europe where some of the greatest scientists like Galileo were persecuted by the Church for preaching ideas inconsistent with the Bible.

Shankaracharya's Advaita philosophy says that there is only one entity in the world i.e. Brahman whereas the various objects like table, glass, pen, room etc. are not different from each other, and their difference is only an illusion. On the other hand, the Nyaya Vaisheshik systems says that there are several real entities and the world comprises of not just one entity, but a large number of entities which are different e.g. table, book, room, human bodies etc. Hence, the Nyaya philosophy is pluralistic and not monistic.

5. *The Real Research Problems in Philosophy*

The two most important branches of philosophy are *ontology and epistemology.* Ontology is the study of existence. In other words, in ontology the questions asked are what really exists? Does God exist? Does the world exist or is it illusion (maya)? What is real, and what is only apparently real?

Epistemology is the study of the means of valid knowledge. For instance, how do I know that this object in front of me exists? The answer is that it is **Pratyaksha**—the knowledge which we derive from the five senses, and *pratyaksha pramana* is regarded as the *pradhan pramana* or the most basic of all the means of valid knowledge.

Pratyaksha pramana may not necessarily lead to truthful knowledge in all cases. For instance, we see the sun rising from the east in the morning, going up above us in the mid-day, and setting in the west. If we rely only on *Pratyaksha Pramana* we would conclude that the sun goes around the earth. However, the great mathematician and astronomer Aryabhata in his book *Arybhatiya* wrote that the same visual impression will be created if we assume that the earth is spinning on its axis. In other words, if the earth is rotating on its axis it will appear that the sun rises from the east and sets in the west. Hence, along with *Pratyaksha Pramana* we have also to apply reason, as observation alone may not always lead to truthful knowledge.

However, there are other *pramanas* e.g. ***anuman*** **(inference),** *shabda* (statement of some expert or authoritative persons) etc. Thus, much of scientific knowledge comes from *anuman pramana.* For instance, **Rutherford** never saw an atom with his eyes, but by studying the scattering of alpha rays (which are positively charged helium ions) he used *anuman praman* (inference) to deduce that there was a positively charged nucleus around which negatively charged electrons were orbiting. Similarly, black holes cannot be known by *pratyaksha pramana* (since light cannot escape from them), but we can infer their existence by the movement of some nearby heavenly bodies on which an invisible body (the black hole) is exercising a gravitational pull. (Though this too may sometimes *be deceptive* e.g. a *mirage)*. This is also the approach of science because in science we largely rely on observation, experiment and logical inferences.

The third *Pramana* in the epistemology of the *Nyaya* system is **Shabda Pramana,** which is the statement of an expert or a person having great reputation in a particular field. We often accept such statements to be correct, even though we may not understand the proof, because the person making it has a reputation of an expert.

For instance, we accept that $e = mc^2$ as *Shabda pramana* since Einstein has a great reputation as a theoretical physicist, although we ourselves may be unable to understand how he reached that equation (as that will require a knowledge of higher mathematics and physics which we may not possess). Similarly, we accept what our doctor tells us about our ailment, as he is an expert.

There is another *pramana* called ***upaman*** (analogy) in the *Nyaya* system.

Thus, these two factors which gave great encouragement to the development and progress of science we may now come to the specific subjects of science dealt with by our ancient scientists.

6. Contribution in Other Disciplines

Condition of Science in Modern India

At one time India was leading the world in science. Scholars from Arabia and China would come to India to learn from us in our great universities at Taxila, Nalanda, Ujjain etc. as our disciples. However, it must be regrettably stated that today we are lagging far behind the West in modern science. We have no doubt produced great scientists and mathematicians like C.V. Raman, Chandrashekhar, Ramanujan, S.N. Bose, J.C. Bose, Meghnad Saha etc., but these belong to the past. In fact, much of Silicon Valley in California is today manned by the Indian scientists, particularly in information technology. In most of the science and mathematical faculties in American Universities there are a large number of Indian professors. Hence, it is not due to any inherent inferiority that India has not progressed as much as Westerners in science in modern times, but due to certain other reasons.

The reason is in the third phase which begins with the Indian mutiny of 1857 and its suppression by the British

> rulers. After 1857, the British were determined that there should not be any such outbreak against their rule. For this purpose they did two things: (a) they increased their army in India and particularly the number of Europeans in the Indian Army, and also placed the artillery completely in the hands of Europeans artillery and (b) they started a policy of deliberately demoralizing the Indian people by spreading the propaganda that Indians were only a race of fools and savages before the British came into India and there was nothing worthwhile in Indian culture as it was the culture of fools and savages. This was deliberately done so that the Indian people may themselves start believing that they were an inferior race and should gladly accept the Britishers as their masters. It is because of the third phase that we had forgotten the great achievements of our ancestors, including their achievements in science.

a. Mathematics

The decimal system was perhaps the most revolutionary and greatest scientific achievement in the ancient world in mathematics. The numbers in the decimal system were called Arabic numerals by the Europeans, but surprisingly the Arab scholars called them Hindu numerals. Were they really Arabic or Hindu? In this connection it may be mentioned that the languages Urdu, Persian and Arabic are written from right to left but if you ask any speaker of these languages to write any number e.g. 257 he will write the number from left to right. This shows that these numbers were taken from a language which was written from left to right and not from right to left. It is accepted now that these **numbers came from India and they were copied by the Arabs from us.**

To illustrate the revolutionary significance of the decimal system. Ancient Rome was a great civilization, the civilization of Caesar and Augustus, but if one would have asked an ancient Roman to write the number one million he would have almost gone crazy because to write one million he would have to write the letter M which stands for millennium (or one thousand) one thousand times. In the Roman numerals there is no single number greater than M, which stands for one thousand. To write 2000 we have to write MM, to write 3000 we have to write MMM, and to write one million one has to write M one thousand times.

On the other hand, under our system to express one million we have just to write the number one followed by six zeros.

In the Roman numerals there is no zero. Zero was an invention of ancient India and progress was not possible without this invention. Think about the great contributions of our great mathematicians like Aryabhatta, Brahamgupta, Bhaskar, Varahamihira etc. See the two simple illustrations in this connection.

The number 1,00,000 is called a lakh in the Indian numeral system. 100 lacs is called one crore, 100 crores is called one arab, 100 arabs is called one kharab, 100 kharabs is called one neel, 100 neels is called one padma, 100 padmas is called one shankh, 100 shankh is called one mahashankh, etc. Thus one mahashankh will be the number 1 followed by 19 zeros (for further details you may see V.S. Apte's Sanskrit English Dictionary on the internet by using Google). On the other hand the ancient Romans could not express any number larger than one thousand except by repeating M and the other numerals again and again.

Take another illustration. According to the *Agni Purana*, the Kaliyuga in which we are living consists of 4, 32, 000 years. The preceding Yuga is known as the Dwapar Yuga and is twice as long as the Kaliyuga. Preceding the Dwapar Yuga, is the Treta Yuga which is thrice the duration of the Kaliyuga. The Yuga preceding Treta Yuga is the Satyuga which was said to be four times longer than the Kaliyuga. One Kaliyuga, one Dwapar Yuga, one Treta Yuga and one Satyuga are collectively known as one **Chaturyugi** (or 43 lacs 20 thousand years). Fifty Six Chaturyugis are known as one **Manvantar**. Fourteen Manvantars is known as one **Kalpa.** Twelve Kalpas make **one day of Brahma**. Brahma is believed to have lived for billions or trillions of years.

One may or may not believe the above system, but one can only marvel at the flight of imagination of our ancestors who could conceive of billions or trillions of years in history.

Aryabhatta in his famous book called the *Aryabhatiya* wrote about algebra, arithmetic, trigonometry, quadratic equations and the sine table. He calculated the value of Pi at 3.1416, which is close to the actual value which is about 3.14159. Aryabhatta's works were later adopted by the Greeks and then the Arabs.

We can think about the contribution of the other mathematicians e.g. Brahmagupta, Bhaskar, Varahamihira etc. in this regard.

Ref. Hanuman Chalisa, Pushpak Vimana in Ramayana, Science of embryology, Vedic Mathematics

b. Astronomy

In ancient India, Aryabhata in his book *Aryabhatiya* presented a mathematical system that postulated that the earth rotated on its axis. He also considered the motion of the planets with respect to the sun (in other words there was a hint in Aryabhat's system of the heliocentric theory of Copernicus, though there is a debate about it). The other famous astronomers of that time were Brahma Gupta who headed the astronomical observatory at Ujjain and wrote a famous text on astronomy, and Bhaskara, who also was a head of the astronomical observatory at Ujjain. Varahamihira presented a theory of gravitation which suggested that there is a force due to which bodies stuck to the earth, and also kept the heavenly bodies in their determined places. We are giving the unnecessary credit to Newton.

I am not going into detail into these theories of these great astronomers, but I would certainly like to say that it is remarkable that *even today predictions can be made about the time and date of solar and lunar eclipses on the basis of calculations made by the ancient astronomers thousands of years ago, and that too at a time when there were no modern instruments like telescopes etc. and observations had to be made with the naked eye.*

c. Medicine

The names of Sushruta and Charaka are the most famous in ancient Indian medicine. Sushruta is regarded as the father of Indian surgery and he invented **cataract surgery, plastic surgery, artificial foot**, replacement of embryo from one womb to another, a good knowledge of anatomy etc. many centuries before it was invented by the westerners. In his book *Sushruta Samhita* he has mentioned in great detail about the medicines and surgeries, including dozens of instruments used in surgeries.

Charaka Samhita is an ancient Indian Ayurvedic text on internal medicine written by Charaka and it is central to the modern day practice of Ayurvedic medicine. Both *Sushruta Samhita* and *Charak Samhita* were written in Sanskrit. In this connection it may be mentioned that in the London Science Museum in one floor relating to medicine, there is mention of the various achievements in medicine in ancient India including the surgical instruments used by Sushruta.

It is thus evident that India was far ahead of all countries in medicine in ancient times.

d. Engineering

In Engineering, too, we have made great progress as is evident from the great South Indian temples in Tanjore, Trichy, Madurai, etc. as also the temples in Khajuraho, Orissa, etc. It is said that there was an institute in Aihole in Karnatka in the 6th Century A.D. which developed structural mechanics. The principles developed by this institute e.g. sloped roofs were applied to structures built in Kerala, eastern Andhra Pradesh and Tamilnadu. See the works on architectures and house building called *Vastushastras*.

e. Literature

In literature, the contribution of Sanskrit is of the foremost order. The works of Kalidas (*Shakuntala, Meghdoot, Malavikagnimitra*, etc.), Bhavabhuti (*Malti Madhav, Uttar Ramcharit*, etc.) and the epics of Valmiki, Vyas, etc. are known all over the world. These and countless other Sanskrit works kept the light of learning ablaze in our country upto modern times.

To Conclude

1. In fact each scripture is a research work par excellence in India. It presents certain profound and sound principles reflecting the truth. Most of these books are in the form of FUNDAMENTAL RESEARCH. Now the time has come to put to test the principles recorded in these scriptures either by having action research or experimental research.

There is now a need to synthesise past and present knowledge for the benefit of future generations.

2. The present higher education needs to *unearth the secrets from the ancient* scriptures which are in Sanskrit language and needs to place them before the world with pride. Of course, the only difficulty is, those who have knowledge of Sanskrit lack the knowledege of modern disciplines and *vice-versa.*
3. For that matter each discipline must have some *orientation courses* with regard to the contents which are stored in Sanskrit texts and an attempt has to be made to incorporate the worthy literature of it in the present curriculum so that the present courses of HE will become rich in contents and will have a holistic touch.
4. Today India is facing huge problems, and these can only be solved by science. We have to spread the scientific outlook to every nook and corner of our country, if we are to progress. And by science I mean not just physics, chemistry and biology but the entire scientific outlook. We must develop the rational and questioning attitude in our people, and abolish superstitions and empty rituals.
5. Hence, it is not due to any inherent inferiority that India has not progressed as much as Westerners in science in modern times, but due to certain other reasons. We have a powerful *scientific heritage and knowledge of it would give us the moral courage and strength* once again to come in the forefront of science in the modern world.

To solve our massive problems today we must quickly catch up with the West in science. Only with the help of science can we abolish poverty, unemployment etc. which are our major social problems today.

References

Full text of the speech delivered by Justice Markandey Katju, Judge, Supreme Court of India on 13.10.2009 in the Indian Institute of Science Bangalore

Deota, N. P. (2012). *Effective Leadership Qualities.* Germany: Lambert Academic Publishing. ISBN No. 978-3-659-13518-7.

Deota, N.P. (2012). *An Insight into Educational Philosophy*. Germany: Lambert Academic Publishing. ISBN No. 978 -3-659-17077-5.

Deota, N.P. (2012). *Kaliedoscopic Views on Education*. Germany: Lambert Academic Publishing. ISBN No.978-3-659-23958-8.

Deota, N.P. (2012). *Linguistic Analysis of Sanskrit Selections—Xith Std of Gujarat*. Germany: Lambert Academic Publishing. ISBN No. 978-3-659-25713-1.

Deota, N.P. (2013). *Footprints of Modern Management in Valmiki Ramayana*. Germany: Lambert Academic Publishing. ISBN No. 978-3-659-44791-4.

4

Relevant Canons of Quality Research

G.L. Gulhane

Introduction

Research is an essential and powerful tool in leading man towards progress. Only research can provide laudable support in formulation of policies related to education, generate new knowledge, solve problems and facilitate decision-making in educational processes and thereby improve quality of education (Tuli: 2011). By seeking and blundering we learn. Enough research will tend to support researchers' conclusions. The opposite of a correct statement is a false statement. But the opposite of a profound truth may well be another profound truth (Niels Bohr). Therefore, to present the profound truth about the conclusions, systematic rules play an important role.

Present Scenario of Research in Education

The level of research in Indian universities is on decline day-by-day barring a few exceptions. Yet there seems to be a growing concern among academicians about the quality of research that takes place in Indian universities. It seems that the rapid, exploding, escalating number of doctoral theses granted by universities in a year is not indicative of the quality of work. Researches in universities tend to be confined within the safe walls of respective disciplines. An interdisciplinary approach is rarely followed. No research proposal or report is presented before a group of experts for critical evaluation. There are very few agencies offering grants for research projects in education. Many of the researchers get discouraged by the formalities and procedures. Even research fellowships don't serve the purpose of quality. Educational research is often undertaken for the sake of degree and not with a goal to make a significant discovery.

Quality Research

Quality in higher education is an indefinable notion. Its attributes are complex and intangible. It remains highly resistant to assessment by means other than judgements that represent personal values, as much as professional standards. To set into the framework of well thought definition would be: Quality is the degree of excellence of the entire educational experience. (Doherty-Delmore: 2002). The quality of any product can be measured and compared with other products. But it is difficult to measure the quality of education, as it is service. Quality is a multiple concept in higher education. It embraces the quality of input such as students, faculty members, the infrastructure and the teaching-learning process including extra-curricular activities etc., and the quality of output, in terms of students who obtained their degrees. But quality of all these input and output components of higher education depends upon quality of research being done in the field of higher education relating to its input and output components. A research providing solutions to the problems contributing in the domain of knowledge is called quality research (Gupta: 2009).

Guidelines for the Presentation of Numbers in the Research Report

The purpose of research is not well served unless the findings are made known to others. The people other than researchers are curious to know the findings of a research problem without having any contact with the research process. After completing the research, a researcher presents the outcome of the study in a systematic way in the form of a research report.

Every research report requires that the manuscript be typed in the format of the professional association representing the discipline of the research report. For example, in a department of education, it is likely that the report will present tables and figures and describe these in the text using guidelines presented by American Psychological Association (APA). This section describes the rules that one is likely to encounter when discussing numbers in text. Numbers may be expressed as words (six) or as figure 6, but when should a word be used as opposed to a figure? Hence, here dawns eight canons that would be the light of the day based on APA.

(A) Expressing Numbers as Figures

Rule No. 1: Use figures to express numbers 10 and above and words to express numbers below 10 (American Psychological Association):

For example:

Correct	*Incorrect*
only about 12%	only about twelve percent
a 26 mm line	a twenty-six millimeter line
six subjects	6 subjects
three out of five group	3 out of 5 groups

Exceptions

(i) Numbers below 10 that are grouped for comparison with numbers 10 and above, and appear in the same paragraph, are also expressed as figures.

Correct	*Incorrect*
6 of 32 groups	Six of 32 groups, 6 of thirty two Six of thirty-two groups
When ranked, the 3rd and 12th	When ranked, the third and twelfth When ranked, the third and 12th

(ii) Numbers that represent statistical or mathematical

function, fractional or decimal quantities, percentages, ratios, and percentiles and quartiles are expressed as figures, regardless of size.

Correct	*Incorrect*
a mean of 3.54	a mean of three point fifty four a mean of three and fifty-four one hundredths
subtracted from 5	subtracted from five
4 3/4 times as many	four and three fourths times as many
0.44	point forty-four .44 (must precede a decimal with 0)
a 5 kg weight	a five kilogram weight
scored in the 4th percentile	scored in the fourth percentile

(iii) Numbers that immediately precede a unit of measurement are expressed as figures, regardless of size.

Correct	*Incorrect*
a 6 mm line	a six millimeter line a six mm line
a mean of 36.22 cm	a mean of thirty-six and twenty-two one hundredths centimeters

(iv) Numbers that denote a specific place in a numbered series, parts of books and tables, and each number in a list of four or more numbers are expressed as figures, regardless of size.

Correct	*Incorrect*
sample 4	sample four
figure 1	figure One
page 60	page sixty
chapters 2, 5, 6, 8, and 23	chapters two, five, six, eight, and 23

(v) Numbers that represent time, dates, ages, sample or population size, scores and points on a scale, exact sums of money, and numerals as numerals are expressed as figures, regardless of size.

Correct	*Incorrect*
4 persons in each sample	four persons in each sample
seven 9-year-old children	seven nine-year-old children 7-9 year-old children
in 7 years	in seven years
study began in 1984	study began in nineteen eighty-four
prior to April 1	prior to April first
no group lasted longer than 3.5 hours	no group lasted longer than three and one half hours
a score of 6 or greater	a score of six or greater
each subject was paid $7.50	each subject was paid seven dollars and fifty cents

(B) Expressing Numbers as Words

Rule No. 2: Use words to express numbers below 10 that do not represent precise measurements and that are not grouped for comparison with numbers 10 and above:

Correct	*Incorrect*
about seven or eight	about 7 or 8
one of the first	1 of the first 1 of the 1st
only two persons	only 2 persons
two surveys	2 surveys
one-way ANOVA	1-way ANOVA
two-tailed *F* test	2-tailed *F* test

Exceptions

(i) The numbers *zero* and *one* when the words would be easier to comprehend than the figures, or when the words do not appear in context with numbers 10 above, are expressed in words.

Correct	*Incorrect*
one-on-one session	1 on 1 session
only one subject	only 1 subject
the concept of zero	the concept of 0

(ii) Any number that begins a sentence, title, or heading should be expressed in words. (whenever possible, reword the sentence to avoid beginning with a number.)

Correct	*Incorrect*
Five studies support	5 studies support
Twenty-six percent of.....	26% of
	Twenty-six % of ...

(iii) Common fractions are expressed as words.

Correct	*Incorrect*
one half the sample	1/2 the sample
	1 half the sample
exactly one fifth	exactly 1/5

(iv) Honour universally accepted usage.

Correct	*Incorrect*
the Twelve Apostles	the 12 Apostles
the Ten Commandments	the 10 Commandments
the Fourth of July	The 4th of July

(C) Combining Figures and Words to Express Numbers

Rule No. 3: Use a combination of figures and words to express rounded large numbers and back-to-back modifiers.

Example: Rounded large numbers:

Correct	*Incorrect*
About 3 thousand	About 3,000
	About three thousand
A net loss of $1 billion	A net loss of one-billion dollars
	a net loss of $1,000,000

Example: Back-to-Back modifiers:

Correct	*Incorrect*
3 one-way interactions	Three one-way interaction
2 two dollar bills	2 $2.00 bills, 2 2 dollar bills

(D) Ordinal Numbers

Rule No. 4: Treat ordinal numbers (except percentile and quartiles) as you would cardinal numbers:

Example:

Correct	*Incorrect*
the first sample	the 1st sample
the 11th grade	the eleventh grade
the 2nd and 12th	the second and 12th
	the second and twelfth
the second	the 2nd
the 12th	the twelfth

(E) Decimal Fractions

Rule No. 5: Place the decimal point on the line, not above the line. Use a zero before the decimal point when numbers are less than 1:

Correct	*Incorrect*
0.45 mm	point forty-five millimeters
	.45
a 0.2 s interval	a .2 second interval

Exception: Do not use a zero before a decimal fraction when the number cannot be greater than 1, as in correlations, probability values, proportions, and levels of statistical significance, e.g. $r = .44$, $p < .01$.

(F) Arabic or Roman Numerals

Rule No. 6: Use Arabic, not Roman, numerals, whenever possible:

Exception: If roman numerals are part of an established terminology, do not changes to Arabic numbers, for example, "type II error".

(G) Commas

Rule No. 7: Use commas between groups of three digits in most figures of 1,000 or more:

Exceptions

Page numbers	page 2134
Binary digits	001101010
Serial numbers	571606999
Degrees of temperature	2349° F
Acoustic frequency designations	3000 Hz
Degrees of freedom	F (35, 1100)
Numbers to the right of a decimal point	6,750.0748

(H) Plurals of Numbers

Rule No. 8: To form the plurals of numbers, whether expressed as figures or as words, add "s" or "es" alone, without an apostrophe:

Correct	*Incorrect*
the early 1960s	the early 1960's
from the 30s and 40s	form the 30's and 40's

The above are the eight canons that would become a key and significant feature for writing a quality research report.

Conclusion

Research is the most effective instrument for ensuring quality in education. It is justifiably hoped that quality of research would substantially be improved in the whole country in general and the sample in particular. Application of relevant basic rules would indeed enrich and enhance not only the research scholars, educationalists, experts, guides and research innovators, but it is the need of the hour for any and everyone who writes to top in the basics of language and research applications: A solution to relevant canons of quality research.

References

Alstete, J.W. (1995). *Benchmarking in Higher Education: Adapting Best Practices to Improve Quality*, ASHE-ERIC-HE Report No.5. Washington: the George Washington University.

Gupta, P. (2009). *Quality Research: A Potent Key to Quality Higher Education*. New Delhi: University News, pp. 13-20.

Kjell, Erik Rudestam and Rae R. Newton. (2007). Surviving Your Dissertation, California: Sage Publications.

Khamkar, S.B. (2011). *Doctoral theses in Education 2005-2008*, Mumbai: Bharateeya Shikshan Mandal.

Kumar, Ranjit (2007). Research *Methodology*, Delhi: Pearson Education.

Mikkelsen, Britha (2009). *Methods for Development Work And Research*. London: Sage Publications.

Powar, K.B. (2005). *Quality in Higher Education*. New Delhi: Anamaya Publishers.

Rai, B.C. (1992). *Problems of Indian Education*. Lucknow: Prakashan Kendra.

Sridevi K.V. (2008). Attitude of M.Ed. Students towards Research. *Journal of AIAER Bhubaneswer*, pp. 73-75.

Tahkur, Devedra and Thakur D. N. (1997). *Tribal Education*. New Delhi: Deep & Deep Publishing. p. 153.

Tuli, P.K. (2011). Research at crossroads: A critique of master's level research in education. *MIER Journal of Educational Studies Trends and Practices Jammu*, pp. 67-77.

Websites visited

- www.reflectiveaction.com.
- www.tttjournal.co.uk
- www.education.indiana.edu.
- www.viking.coe.uh.edu
- www.aiuweb.org

5

Knowledge and Use of Internet by Research Scholar

Magre Sunita Vithalrao

Introduction

Today, the internet is a public, cooperative and self-sustaining facility accessible to hundreds of millions worldwide. The internet is presently being used as a source for teaching, learning and research material. Information and communication technologies for doing research processes will have some advantages: students will play a more active role, discussions of courses will contain more detail, students will become more independent, communication between researcher and supervisors will become level and direct, research skills will increase, and the hierarchical structure between researcher and supervisors will be more flexible. Accessing, using and sharing knowledge via the internet and other communication technologies lies in the interest of the researcher, primarily those in the university level; those with the power for social change and development. For those university researchers carrying out this change, it could be said they have an obligation to be equipped with qualified cognitive, affective, and psychomotor proficiency during their studies. Producing knowledge and turning this knowledge into use of technology to increasing quality of research and the researcher ability to access and use this knowledge purposefully while sharing it at a high level is a requirement of the globalization era. Internet knowledge has been defined as a set of individual characteristics or qualities that develop over time and that generalize from one set of tasks or uses involving the internet to another (Potosky 2007). It is what people know about the internet, both Internet terminology and internet skills.

Consequently, the purpose of this study is to develop a measure of internet knowledge and use of internet by research scholar.

Need and Significance of the Study

Use of internet is occupying a big place in each and every individual's life. Supervisors and researchers are conducting research to increase the knowledge of information technologies. The use of internet has changed the concept of traditional process of research.

Review of Related Research

In relation to gender, a common finding is that there are significantly more males who are addicted to the internet than females (Brenner 1997; Chen *et al.* 2007; Ko *et al.* 2006; Leung 2004). Differences in internet use were also found according to age, gender, and socio-economic status (Mesch 2001; Shaw and Gant 2002). Jagboro (2003) carried out a study of internet usage in Nigerian universities where the opinion of 73 respondents was sought. On specific uses of internet, two-third of the respondents indicated that they used it for e-mail, to get research materials followed while course materials had 39.73 per cent. The recorded low level of utilization of the internet was attributed to the low level of connectivity and the high cost of cybercafé facilities. Moreso, Hanaur *et al.* (2004) surveyed a diverse community college to assess the use of the internet by the students of health—related information. The internet is acknowledged globally as a technology dominated by young people, and particularly students who are more inclined to exploit internet resources for education, social interaction and entertainment (Salako and Tiamiyu, 2007). Kumar and Kaur (2005) conducted a research on internet and its use in the engineering colleges of Punjab. A majority of the respondents used the internet located at the college, use internet for education and research purposes, while half of them use it for communication purpose. More than half of the students use the internet for consulting technical reports. Salako and Tiamiyu (2007) surveyed the use of search engines for research by postgraduate students of the University of Ibadan, Nigeria. Copies of 327 questionnaires were analysed and it was found that most of the responding postgraduate students were aware of, and had become familiar with the internet before the start of their postgraduate courses. On how they learnt to use search engine, more than half of the respondents were taught by friends, less than half learnt to use it by trial and error while a few were taught at a computer school.

Statement of the Problem

- Knowledge and Use of Internet by Research Scholar: A Study
- Operational Definition
- Knowledge and Use of Internet

For the present study the knowledge and use of internet means the direct experience about internet, internet facilities, comparisons of other tools and use of internet and obstacles about internet which was measured and constructed and validated by the researcher.

Research Scholar

In this study the research scholars means the persons doing M.Ed., M.Phil. and Ph.D.in the subject of Education studying in the Research Centres of Colleges of Education and University Department.

Aim

To study the Knowledge and Use of Internet by Research Scholar

Objectives

1. To study the Knowledge and Use of Internet by Research Scholar on the basis of
   (a) Educational Qualification (M.Ed., M.Phil. and PhD),

(b) Gender,
(c) Faculty (Arts and Science) and
(d) Part time and full time Research Scholar.

2. To compare the Knowledge and Use of Internet by Research Scholar on the basis of
   (a) Educational Qualification (M.Ed., M.Phil. and Ph.D.),
   (b) Gender,
   (c) Faculty (Arts and Science) and
   (d) Part time and full time Research Scholar.
3. To compare different factors of Knowledge and Use of Internet (Direct Experience about Internet, Internet Facilities, Comparisons of other Tools andUse of Internet and lastly Obstacles about Internet) by Research Scholar on the basis of
   (a) Educational Qualification (M.Ed., M.Phil. and Ph.D.),
   (b) Gender,
   (c) Faculty (Arts and Science), and
   (d) Part time and full time Research Scholar.

Hypotheses

1. There is no significant difference between the overall Knowledge and Use of Internet by Research Scholar on the basis of
   (a) Educational Qualification (M.Ed., M.Phil. and PhD),
   (b) Gender,
   (c) Faculty (Arts and Science), and
   (d) Part time and full time Research Scholar.
2. There is no significant difference between the different dimensions of Knowledge and Use of Internet (Direct Experience about Internet, Internet Facilities, Comparisons of other Tools and Use of Internet and lastly Obstacles about Internet) by Research Scholar on the basis of
   (a) Educational Qualification (M.Ed., M.Phil. and Ph.D),
   (b) Gender,
   (c) Faculty (Arts and Science) and
   (d) Part time and full time Research Scholar.

Limitation

There are several limitations to this research. First, only one university and researchers from the faculty of education were included in the research population. This population might have been extended to include universities at different development levels and within different geographic regions.

The study is limited to research scholars of M.Ed., M.Phil. and Ph.D. in the subject of Education in Mumbai University only.

Methodology

The present study employed descriptive method of the comparative type. It aimed at studying the Knowledge and use of internet by Research Scholar. It aimed to compare variables Direct Experience about Internet, opinion of Internet Facilities, Comparisons of other Tools and Use of Internet and lastly Obstacles about Internet and overall Knowledge and use of internet by Research Scholar on the basis of their Educational Qualification (M.Ed., M.Phil. and Ph.D), Gender (male and female), Faculty (arts and science) and d) Part time and full time Research Scholar.

Sample

For the present study 115 Research Scholar were selected with stratified random sampling from the Research Centres of Colleges of Education and Department of Education of Mumbai University.

Tool

In order to study the Knowledge and use of internet by Research Scholars tools were constructed by the researcher. Five point Rating Scale having options: Strongly Agree (5), Agree (4), Neutral (3), Disagree (2) Strongly Disagree (1). The Tool is consisting of 75 statements about four dimensions—Direct Experience about Internet (23 statements), opinion about Internet Facilities (27 statements), Comparisons of other Tools and Use of Internet (11statements) and lastly Obstacles about Internet (14statements). Validity and reliability of the tool were established using split-half reliability method. The split-half reliability for the whole tool was calculated and Cronbach's alpha is 0.86 and Spearman-Brown Prophecy is 0.69. Minimum score was 75 and maximum score was 375.

Analysis of Data

The researcher had used '*t*' test and ANOVA for analyzing the data.

Table 5.1: Showing F ratio for the Overall Knowledge and Use of Internet by Research Scholar on the basis of their Educational Qualification M.Ed., M.Phil. and Ph.D.

Source of Variance	*Sum of Squares*	*df*	*Mean sum of Squares*	*F ratio*	*Level of Significance (0.05 level)*
Between groups	3786.92	2	1893.46	2.91	Not Significant
Within groups	72953.74	112	651.37		

Table 5.1 indicates that F ratio is ($F = 2.91$) which is less than the table value ($F = 3.07$) therefore, the null hypothesis is accepted. It can be concluded that there is no significant difference in the Overall Knowledge and Use of Internet by research scholar on the basis of their Educational Qualification M.Ed., M.Phil. and Ph.D.

Table 5.2: Showing F ratio for Direct Experience about Internet by Research Scholar on the basis of their Educational Qualification M.Ed., M.Phil. and Ph.D.

Source of Variance	*Sum of Squares*	*df*	*Mean sum of Squares*	*F ratio*	*Level of Significance (0.05 level)*
Between groups	734.70	2	367.34	3.83	Significant
Within groups	10453.48	112	93.01		

Table 5.2 indicates that F ratio is significant (F=3.83) and which is greater than table value (F = 3.07) therefore the null hypothesis is rejected. It can be concluded that there is significant difference in Direct Experience about Internet by Research Scholar on the basis of their Educational Qualification M.Ed., M.Phil. and Ph.D.

Table 5.3: Showing F ratio for the Opinion about Internet Facilities by Research Scholar on the basis of their Educational Qualification M.Ed., M.Phil. and Ph.D.

Source of Variance	*Sum of Squares*	*df*	*Mean sum of Squares*	*F ratio*	*Level of Significance (0.05 level)*
Between groups	619.18	2	309.59	2.70	Not Significant
Within groups	12851.55	112	114.47		

Table 5.3 indicates that F ratio is (F = 2.70) and which is less than the table value (F = 3.07) therefore the null hypothesis is accepted. It can be concluded that there is no significant difference in the opinion about Internet Facilities by research scholar on the basis of their Educational Qualification M.Ed., M.Phil. and Ph.D.

Table 5.4: Showing F ratio for the Comparisons of other Tools and Use of Internet by Research Scholar on the basis of their Educational Qualification M.Ed., M.Phil. and Ph.D.

Source of Variance	*Sum of Squares*	*df*	*Mean sum of Squares*	*F ratio*	*Level of Significance (0.05 level)*
Between groups	297.02	2	148.51	3.76	Significant
Within groups	4425.73	112	39.51		

Table 5.4 indicates that F ratio is significant (F = 3.76) and which is greater than table value (F = 3.07) therefore the null hypothesis is rejected. It can be concluded that there is significant difference in the opinion about Internet Facilities by Research Scholar on the basis of their Educational Qualification M.Ed., M.Phil. and Ph.D.

Table 5.5: Showing F ratio for the Obstacles about using Internet by Research Scholar on the basis of their Educational Qualification M.Ed., M.Phil. and Ph.D.

Source of Variance	*Sum of Squares*	*df*	*Mean sum of Squares*	*F ratio*	*Level of Significance (0.05 level)*
Between groups	573.74	2	286.87	4.49	Significant
Within groups	7158.99	112	63.92		

Table 5.5 indicates that F ratio is significant (F = 4.49) and which is greater than table value (F = 3.07) therefore the null

hypothesis is rejected. It can be concluded that there is significant difference in the Obstacles about using Internet by Research Scholar on the basis of their Educational Qualification M.Ed., M.Phil. and Ph.D.

Table 5.6: Showing the Mean and S.D. of Dimensions of Knowledge and use of internet by Research Scholar on the basis of Gender

Area/Total	*No.*	*Gender*	*Mean*	*S.D.*	*t-value*	*Significance level*	Hypothesis
DEI	49	Male	93.69	11.23	0.50	0.05 (N.S.)	Accepted
	66	Female	94.68	9.11			
IF	49	Male	113.85	10.38	–1.01	0.05 (N.S.)	Accepted
	66	female	111.81	11.21			
CT and UI	49	Male	45.97	7.56	0.72	0.05 (N.S.)	Accepted
	66	female	46.89	5.48			
OI	49	Male	50.85	7.85	0.52	0.05 (N.S.)	Accepted
	66	female	51.65	8.55			

Gender and Knowledge and Use of Internet by Research Scholar

There is no significant difference between the dimensions of Knowledge and Use of Internet (Direct Experience about Internet, Internet Facilities, Comparisons of other Tools andUse of Internet and lastly Obstacles about Internet) by Research Scholar on the basis of gender this hypothesis is accepted.

Table 5.7: Showing the Mean and S.D. of Dimensions of Knowledge and use of internet by Research Scholar on the basis of Faculty

Area/Total	*No.*	*Faculty*	*Mean*	*S.D.*	*t-value*	*Significance level*	*Hypothesis*
DEI	75	Arts	94.46	10.14	0.30	0.05 (N.S.)	Accepted
	40	Science	93.87	9.94			
IF	75	Arts	112.24	11.75	–0.65	0.05 (N.S.)	Accepted
	40	Science	113.52	9.07			
CT and UI	75	Arts	46.73	6.71	0.54	0.05 (N.S.)	Accepted
	40	Science	46.07	5.94			
OI	75	Arts	53.30	7.83	1.72	0.05 (N.S.)	Accepted
	40	Science	49.45	8.74			

Faculty and Knowledge and Use of Internet by Research Scholar

There is no significant difference between the dimensions of

Knowledge and Use of Internet (Direct Experience about Internet, Internet Facilities, Comparisons of other Tools and Use of Internet and lastly Obstacles about Internet) by Research Scholar on the basis of faculty this hypothesis is accepted.

Table 5.8: Showing the Mean and S.D. of Dimensions of Knowledge and use of internet by Research Scholar on the basis of working time

Area/Total	*No.*	*Working Time*	*Mean*	*S.D.*	*t-value*	*Significance level*	*Hypothesis*
DEI	99	Part time	94.40	10.06	0.37	0.05 (N.S.)	Accepted
	16	Full time	93.37	10.19			
IF	99	Part time	113.24	10.60	1.23	0.05 (N.S.)	Accepted
	16	Full time	109.25	12.20			
CT and UI	99	Part time	46.66	6.54	0.73	0.05 (N.S.)	Accepted
	16	Full time	45.5	5.78			
OI	99	Part time	51.26	8.08	-0.14	0.05 (N.S.)	Accepted
	16	Full time	51.62	9.43			

Working Time and Knowledge and use of Internet by Research Scholar

There is no significant difference between the different factors of Knowledge and Use of Internet (Direct Experience about Internet, Internet Facilities, and Comparisons of other Tools and Use of Internet and lastly Obstacles about Internet) by Research Scholar on the basis of working time this hypothesis is accepted.

Table 5.9: Mean and S.D. of Overall score and Dimension wise score about Knowledge and use of internet by Research Scholar

Dimensions	*Mean*	*Neutral Point*
Direct Experience about Internet (DEI)	94.46	69
Internet Facilities (IF)	112.68	81
Comparisons of other Tools and Use of Internet CT&UI	46.50	33
Obstacles about Internet (OI)	51.31	42
Total	**304.76**	**225**

It could be seen from Table-D the Knowledge and use of internet rating scale contain 75 statements with the score on each statement ranging between 1 to 5, the total score of the instrument could range between 75 to 375 with the neutral point of 225. A mean score above the neutral point indicates more amount of knowledge and use of internet by research scholar, while a mean score below the neutral point shows less amount of knowledge and use of internet by research scholar. The obtained mean overall score about knowledge and use of internet by research scholar is (304.76) which is above the neutral point (225). This indicates that the research scholars have more amount of knowledge and use of internet. The dimension-wise score is also above the neutral point. Hence it may be concluded that the research scholars have more amount of knowledge and use of internet in the research.

Findings

- There is no significant difference in the Overall Knowledge and Use of Internet by Research Scholar on the basis of their Educational Qualification M.Ed., M.Phil. and Ph.D.
- There is no significant difference between the dimensions of Knowledge and Use of Internet by Research Scholar on the basis of gender.
- There is no significant difference between the dimensions of Knowledge and Use of Internet by Research Scholar on the basis of faculty.
- There is no significant difference between the dimensions of Knowledge and Use of Internet by Research Scholar on the basis of working time.

Conclusion

All the relations were positive in direction. A present study of the subject of research does not make a difference in the Knowledge and Use of Internet by Research Scholar on the basis of educational qualification, gender, faculty and working time of research.

Research Scholars have more amount of knowledge and use of internet in the research.

References

Jagboro (2003). A Study of Internet Usage in Nigerien Universities.

Joseph Kehinde Fasae and Fasa Rachael Aladeniyi (2012). Internet Use by students of Faculty of Science in two Nigerian Universities, *Library Philosophy and Practice.*

Kian-Sam Hong Abang Ahmad Ridzuan Ming-Koon Kuek (2009). Students' Attitudes toward the Use of the Internet for Learning: A study at a university in Malaysia.

Kumar and Kaur (2005). Internet and Its Use In the Engineering College Student.

S. Francisca, Mary Rani (2010). Internet Knowledge of Research Scholars and their Usage, Edutracks, 38-41.

Salako, Tiamiyu (2007). Use of Search Engines for Research *by Postgraduate Students of the University of Ibadan.*

6
Research Competency of Scholars in Sikkim University

Dona Rai

Introduction

Research in a general term means collecting information by observing, asking questions, making experiments etc., about something to reach a valid decision in a certain matter. In a scientific terminology *'research is an endeavour to discover facts by scientific method and is a course of a critical investigation'*. Every research has its own premises and perspectives, and research arises due to curiosity and aims at discovering truth and resolving contradictions in the area of study. Thus, research is the search for knowledge or as any systematic investigation to establish novel facts, solve new or existing problems, prove new ideas, or develop new theories, usually using a scientific or a systematic approach. The primary objective of the research is discovering, interpreting and developing methods and systems for the advancement of human knowledge on a wide variety of scientific matters of our world and the universe.

Research involves the mastery of skills needed to design and conduct a systematic, empirical, objective, public and critical investigation of an identified problem or an issue. Research may be descriptive, designed to develop a theory, or intended to test a hypothesis. For a successful research, researcher should have the ability to conduct independent research and to make appropriate use of quantitative, qualitative, or mixed methods of analytical techniques. One must also be able to produce reliable observations, make sound inferences, and offer reasonable hypotheses. Finally one must have the disposition to think productively and critically about issues. A researcher has to be competent in critically reviewing the literature, developing comprehensive theoretical knowledge and indepth understanding, framing research questions, developing effective tools/instruments for effective research, collecting data, and analysing data.

Significance of the Study

Ph.D is seen as a kind of diploma that certifies one's competence to carry out independent and original research. Some believe that the thesis is the ultimate evidence for being a researcher, whereas some argue that the researcher, not the thesis should be the product of the process. This chapter is an attempt to recognize the competency of researches persuing their research in Sikkim University.

As Sikkim University came into being in the year 2007, along with Masters programme it also introduced PhD programme and MPhil/PhD integrated programme in various fields. Being a newly established university, no such research has been done in this area. Hence, an utmost urge was felt to conduct a research on this issue and the present paper is an outcome.

Operational Definition of the Keywords Used

1. **Research Competency:** It means the ability of researcher to conduct research in their respective field. They have to be competent in critically reviewing the literature, developing comprehensive theoretical knowledge and in depth understanding, framing research questions, developing tools/instruments for effective research, collecting data, and analysing data.
2. **Scholars:** In this study it means those students who are pursuing their PhD or integrated MPhil/PhD programme in Sikkim University.
3. **Sikkim University:** Sikkim University, a Central University, established and fully funded by the

Government of India under an Act of Parliament of India came into existence on 2 July, 2007.

Objectives of the Study

The objectives are:

1. To find out the process of registration in PhD.
2. To study the competency of scholars pursuing research in Sikkim University.
3. To find out the kind of funding, scholarship/fellowship or any monetary grant availed by the scholars.

Methodology

A self-constructed questionnaire consisting of open-response and closed-response questions, was utilized to collect data from scholars. Data was collected from 15 scholars who are registered and pursuing PhD or MPhil/PhD (integrated) programme in various areas in Sikkim University.

Findings and Discussions

Registration

The process includes successful completion of 6 months' coursework which is followed by writing of synopsis. This synopsis has to go through Board of Studies and then Board of School before registration.

Course Work

In Sikkim University, as per the UGC norms six months course work is included in all Ph.D. work except in M.Phil.-Ph.D. integrated programme where course work is not needed. Scholars believe that course work helps in better understanding of research methodology.

Selection of Guide/Supervisor

Selection of guide/supervisor depends on the area of interest. First the draft synopsis is made followed by a discussion between the expertise and the scholar. If the draft is satisfying to the expertise then the scholar is assigned under the specific expertise. The selection is based on research area wise.

Further, the research problem is formulated after discussion between the scholar and his/her guide/supervisor.

Research Ethics

Scholars are aware of research ethics. Ethics are standards of professional behaviour. These ethical standards are: seeking permission to research, responsibility as a researcher to the community, confidentiality about private information, feedback to the people among whom the research has been done.

They believe that a researcher has to maintain professional and scientific responsibility, maintain confidentiality and privacy, respect of participants, avoidance of deception and foremost maintain avoidance of plagiarism.

Research Method

Formulation of problem is done after scrutinizing the general area of study and then narrowing down the problem so that it can be completed in the given time of period. After this, reviewing of available literatures is done and for this they use the university library, internet and other resources. Literature review make them aware of what has been done on the area they have undertaken and what still needs to researched. This also helps them in formulation of hypothesis. Research hypothesis guides them in their entire research programme; methods, data collection, and analysis of data. Data is collected from primary as well as secondary sources. Methods of data collection include case study, survey, experimental method, available data, observation, interviews, questionnaires, and tests.

Problems Faced by Scholars during Field Work

Most of the scholars have stated that they face financial problem during their field work. Some of them have stated that getting acquainted with the local people in the field is a problem, inadequacy of data, poor infrastructure (library etc.), climate/weather problem.

Financial Assistance

Scholars in Sikkim University are availing financial aids from UGC NET-JRF, project fellowship, Non-NET fellowship, University fellowship. Those who are availing Non-NET or University fellowship have commented that the amount is not sufficient for their research work whereas other who are availing UGC NET-JRF and project fellowship have stated that the amount they are availing is adequate to meet their requirements.

Suggestions

- The root problems that this paper came up with are: inadequacy of data and poor infrastructure of library in Sikkim University. The university library should keep updating its intake of materials (books, journals, periodicals, reports etc.) regularly. A well equipped library is a must for successful research.
- Scholars should keep themselves updated with grant aids so that they facilitate themselves.

References

Critical thinking in Education: A Review. (2000). *Educational Research, II* (3). Retrieved from http://www.tandfonline.com/doi/pdf/10.1080/001318800440579#.UwjHu3_9ZNA

Ford, Emma, Dr. Nicola Barrett and Dr Tristram Hooley. (2009). Researchers' Skills and Competencies. UK: Research Councils UK (RCUK) Careers Research and Advisory Centre (CRAC) Limited.

Meline, G., and Janson, K. (2006). *What Skills and knowledge should a PhD have? Changing preconditions for PhD education and post doc work.* Portland Press.

Morrow, V., and Richards, M. (1996). The Ethics of Social Research with Children: An Overview. *Children and Society, X*, 90-105.

Norris, S.P. (1985). *Synthesis of Research on Critical Thinking.* Canada: Educational Leadership.

Onwuegbuzie, A.J., and Collins, K.M. (2007). A Typology of Mixed Methods Sampling Designs in Social Science Research. *The Qualitative Report, XII* (2), 281-316.

Swain, A.K. (2009). *A text book of Research Methodology.* New Delhi: Kalyani Printers.

7
Importance of Course Work in Educational Research

Milind Sahasrabuddhe and *Swaleha Sindhi*

Introduction

Importance of Ph.D. Degree: it is not of any doubt that a Ph.D. degree will be an addition to the social status of any person. When one is serving somewhere in an institution for school/higher education or when one wants to join any institution for higher education, this degree will be an addition to one's professional as well as economic growth. However, these benefits are not confined to micro level only; when one works at macro level it is beneficial to an institution/society/economy/nation. Thus, benefits of this degree are spread over micro and macro level.

It is known to all that this particular degree is the highest one for any discipline/subject. One can pursue a Ph.D. degree after completion of M.Phil or getting master degree with some minimum percentages. Now a days, one may have to pass the Ph.D. Eligibility Test (PET) or NET/SLET examination which was not there earlier. From the year, 2009 whether one wants to get Ph.D. degree as fulltime student or as part time student one has to pass these examinations. Those who have an M.Phil. degree or have passed NET/SLET examination are exempted from this. However, it is of utmost importance that one needs to have mastery over all those things which are needed for a researcher.

Necessities for a Researcher

Common things are needed to be a good researcher such as

1. Fluency over a language
2. Knowledge about subject in which Ph.D. is to be obtained.
3. Mastery over some statistical techniques required for research.
4. Computer application knowledge
5. Ability of data collection
6. Collection of review of literature.

Finally, mastery over a language is required for analyzing data with qualitative techniques. Knowledge of English is helpful in collecting data and correcting information recommendations of various committees/commissions. It is also important for qualitative techniques of data analysis as in absence of it, one cannot interpret and analyze reports.

Similarly, a researcher needs proven knowledge about chapterterization scheme otherwise one can't present the research report in a data perspective. One needs to know where and which statistical techniques should be used, if necessary. They should be in accordance with objectives of a study and therefore, only if they are necessary but a true researcher needs to have knowledge about usability of various statistical measures. Hence, a researcher can use them.

One should also have knowledge about modern terminologies and one must not maintain any distance from technology. Computers which are a part of a modern technology have proven their utility in the field of research. Researchers, by their proper use, can bring knowledge at their home. They can obtain knowledge at time, place and pace of their own convenience. They can get knowledge about a concept from various dimensions, recommendations of various educational committees and commissions, can get knowledge about related literature and past researches, can also analyze data when statistical formulas are to be used and last but not least, they can present a final report with the necessary modification.

Present Inputs of Ph.D. Course Work

In light of above facts, when one has a look at the inputs of Ph.D. course work, one gets the following information. Those who have obtained an M.Phil degree are exempted from this course work. Those who have to undergo this course work, this is one of the requirement which they have to complete. In absence of completing this course, they cannot submit the synopsis of their research work. It is conducted every Saturday and Sunday. Inputs for this course consist of knowledge of various topics related to research methodology, knowledge about applications of computers.

When one makes a detailed analysis of the contents of this course one will instantly raise his/her eyebrows about utility of topics related to research methodology. This is because in a discipline like education one is expected to have full knowledge about research methodology from various books on the iron, similarly they have to complete a direction of work which requires the application of various techniques of data analysis. Hence, this course work does not provide anything new to them. Similarly, mere quantitative knowledge does not serve the purpose of research especially in social science. In fact, students should be made aware about various qualitative techniques for data analysis—especially content analysis. Because in the absence of this knowledge, they would not be able to note different important things from their responses. In case of execution of questionnaires, interview schedules as well as observation schedules content analysis is a very important technique. Similarly, students should be trained for shadowing observation. They would learn to take note of important matters as well as they would also know the other side of the coin. While interviewing, any educational leader would tell that he/she is adopting democratic style of leadership. But how he/she deals with students, teachers, parents, government officials, media persons etc., one can know in reality the extent to which one is adopting a democratic style of leadership with different persons in different situations.

Conclusion

Knowledge about various qualitative techniques is very vital in research on Social Sciences. This is because one can understand the factors responsible for the present situation and from that, remedial action plan can be put in to practice e.g. factors related to job satisfaction, organizational climate, phenomenon of low enrollment and high rate of wastage as well as stagnation related to a particular level and section of society. They should also be told how effectively one can collect required data and one can take needed resources or needed information from books, internet etc.

Bibliography

Bryk, A.S. (2009). Support a science of performance improvement. *Phi Delta Kappa,* April 2009, pp. 597-600.

Burkhardt H. and Schoenfeld, A. (2003). Improving educational research: Toward a more useful, more influential and better-funded enterprise. *Education Researcher,* 32 (9), 3-14. DOI: 10.3102/0013189X032009003

Clements, D.H. and Sarama, J. (2009). *Learning and Teaching Early Math: The Learning Trajectories Approach*. NY: Routledge.

Cochrane Collaboration (2007). *The Cochrane Collaboration: The Reliable Source of Evidence in Health Care*. Retrieved from http://www.cochrane.org

8

Framework of Researcher Competencies

Need of the Hour

Bharati Ganiger and *Ramesh M.*

Introduction

Human beings are always curious about nature and its structure and function. To satisfy this curiosity we are always trying to find out the cause and effect of natural phenomenon through research. Research in any area should always be the highest priority of any nation. This is true even in the Education system. Any changes that need to be brought, the effectiveness of the present method, resource, infrastructure on any other facility, innovative ideas can be seen only through research. The ultimate aim of research is to find new knowledge, it requires a systematic plan of action and scientific thinking. Research in any discipline needs certain competencies which includes knowledge, skills and attitudes. Researchers will have acquired some competencies during their period of research. The basic competencies in research are required for acquiring higher level competencies. Competencies are acquired, developed, practiced and further sharpened to become proficient. Competent researcher builds competencies relevant to the range of research. A researcher needs enough competencies to carry out research from the selection of topics to dissemination of research reports. There are different competencies such as knowledge, skills, attitude. All these competencies do not stand in isolation and are not developed in an isolation manner. Each and every competency support for acquiring the other competencies.

Research and Researcher

Research is search for knowledge, and it is a careful, scientific and systematic effort of gaining new knowledge and applying it to new situations. Research is an orderly investigation of a subject matter for creation of new knowledge and also to add to the existing knowledge. It is mere 're-search' implying that the subject matter already exists, because of one or the other reason due to changes, it needs to be studied again. It is observable, testable, verifiable and replicable. Various researchers opine differently about research. Wikipedia states that Research comprises "creative work undertaken on a systematic basis in order to increase the stock of knowledge, including knowledge of man, culture and society, and the use of this stock of knowledge to devise new applications. Martyn Shuttleworth— "In the broadest sense of the word, the definition of research includes any gathering of data, information and facts for the advancement of knowledge". Another definition of research is given by Creswell who states that— "Research is a process of steps used to collect and analyze information to increase our understanding of a topic or issue". It consists of three steps: Pose a question, collect data to answer the question, and present an answer to the question.

In the realm of Education, in the education system many of the things are always subjected to change, the structure, curriculum, management, syllabus, textbooks, and methods of teaching, evaluation process, infrastructure and what not in the system. The research in all these sub areas may lead to bring the expected changes, and improve the quality of the educational system. According to John Dewey (1938), the process of research has following steps

- Reviewing the literature studies
- Identification and definition of the problem
- Formulation of a hypotheses
- Collection, organization and analysis of data
- Formulation of conclusions
- Verification, rejection or modification of the hypothesis

by the test of its sequences in a specific situations reports
- Dissemination of research report

Types of Research

There are different types of research but research has three fundamental types:

- Basic research/Fundamental research
- Applied research
- Action research

Types of Educational Research:

- Historical research
- Descriptive research
- Correlation research
- Experimental research
- Case study research
- Ethnographic research

Researcher

Researcher is one who is never satisfied with the knowledge gained. He is always interested in finding new knowledge and comparing with it the existing one. Self-motivated, he possesses inquisitiveness, commitment, sacrifice, excellence, knowledge, recognition, scholarly approach, and integration. For a researcher the process of research must be never ending journey to the frontiers of knowledge. In depth research builds competencies within the researcher which leads to the development of sound theory. In depth research depends upon the researcher's abilities and intellect.

Principles Underlying the Development of Competencies

Competencies can be acquired through multiple means. Knowledge alone is not enough for an individual to attain competency, there are other experiences. Skills, attitudes, application and evaluation also complement the acquisition of competencies. Individual researchers should experience the opportunities to acquire competencies and monitor one's own competencies.

Principles of Competencies for Researchers

- The researcher must open-minded and must be a critical and creative thinker,
- Hard working, diligent, focused and devoted to the specific area of interest.
- Must be updated in the present era of research
- Self-confident and optimistic
- Capable of SWOT analysis
- Scientific knowledge
- Ability to learn and adapt
- Ability to formulate a research issue
- Ability to use ICT tools
- Ability to work in interdisciplinary environment
- Ability to incorporate the advancements in the research
- Ability to work in team
- Ability to develop network
- Communication skills
- Ability to ask questions
- Ability of accessing
- Language skills
- Leadership skills
- Creativity
- Open-mindedness
- Self-motivation
- Adaptability
- Self-assessment

Required Research Competencies

To be competent in any of the areas requires having the knowledge and the ability or skills to complete a task perfectly. This knowledge and skill may be acquired through training, or work or life experience. Researchers need a required number of competencies for doing research. The researcher requires the competencies from idea inception and the review of the literature to dissemination of research findings. Breadth and depth of knowledge is needed.

Researchers need to understand and have knowledge of the breadth of literature, and possible research designs and analyses available, while also having specific knowledge in the particular topic they are researching, as well as the design, procedures, and analyses selected. Competency is more than just knowledge and skill but also includes attributes. More specifically, competent researchers should be curious and perseverant, and in addition, should engage in life-long learning and continuing education related to research development. The competencies in research is very important and inevitable; researcher should research the knowledge competently. Different competencies are required for the researcher. All the competencies are broadly categorised into five competencies which are as follows:

- Knowledge
- Skills
- Attitudes
- Application
- Evaluation

Knowledge

- Ground knowledge of various theories and conceptual models which will provide basis for the further research.
- Researcher should have the knowledge of the field in he/ she is interested.
- Understand the value of research to the field.
- Knowledge of research designs, and skill of selecting the appropriate design for the present study undertaken.
- Knowledge of programme development, development of measurement tools and techniques. Sampling procedure, skill of selecting proper sample and sampling procedure.
- Identifying the threats (both internal and external) of the research design.
- Establishing the validity, reliability and credibility of the programme and research tools.
- Knowledge of basic statistical procedures for data analysis and interpretation.
- Knowledge of appropriate professional guidelines in writing for e.g.: APA.

- Knowledge of professional ethical codes.
- Understands the strength and limitation of qualitative and quantitative research designs.
- Understand the differences among qualitative and quantitative designs.
- Understands the different purposes of qualitative and quantitative designs.
- Identify a best method to formulate research questions and find answers for the questions.

Skills

- Skill of retrieving the related studies and use existing research as foundation for the study.
- Drawing the ground ideas from the literature and integrate existing relevant literature into further research.
- Skill of logical argumentation through writing.
- Skill of synthesizing the results within existing literature.
- Skill of presenting the qualitative results using graphs, metaphors, models and relevant depictions.
- Skill of communicating the research work through graph, tables etc.
- Presenting the research report skilfully in a seminar conferences etc. also prepare a scholarly manuscript for publication.

Application

- Determine which literature is relevant to include for the present study.
- Integrate results from multiple sources and build a strong rationale for a study.
- Ability to use available resources in an effective way.
- Identifying relevant problem.
- Build a conceptual framework on one's own.
- Understanding of the research theoretical paradigm.
- Understanding the connection between data collection techniques and research methodology.
- Understands how to apply various research design for the present study.

- Knowledge of instrumental development.
- In-depth knowledge of the selected methodology for a particular study.
- Connect the existing literature to the research questions.
- Employing appropriate sampling techniques for the present study.
- Applying appropriate statistical tools for analysing and interpreting the data.

Evaluation

- One of the most important core competencies is evaluation and feedback.
- Researcher should evaluate his competencies through multiple means.
- Researcher should identify the strength and weakness in the area research, accordingly he should act further.
- Researcher needs to assess his research competencies in terms of knowledge and skill and attitudes.
- Competency to evaluate thesis, research projects etc.

All the competencies are of utmost importance and could be accomplished in several ways, like attending seminars, conferences, exchanging ideas, being with virtual community, integrate results from multiple sources (e.g: literature, articles, presentation, data) etc.

Conclusion

A structured strategy in all the research institutions including Universities should be made for developing and managing essential researcher competencies. Education system needs to focus on the research and development not only of the discipline but also provide concern for researcher competencies development and encouragement.

- Identify your Core Competencies
- Match your Interest with your competencies
- Work out your competencies
- Never give up when faced with problems

- Be fast and consistent, fast and consistent will always beat the slow and steady.

References

Best J.W. and Kahn J.V. (2010). *Research in Education,* New Delhi: PHI Learning Private Limited.

Creswell, J.W. (2008). Educational Research: Planning, conducting, and evaluating quantitative and qualitative research (3rd ed.). Upper Saddle River: Pearson.

Dewey, J. (1938). *Logic: The theory of Inquiry,* New York: Holt, Rinehart & Winston.

Shuttleworth, Martyn (2008). "Definition of Research", *Explorable,* Explorable.com. Retrieved 14 August 2011.

9

Research Competencies According to Neo-Researchers of (AT) Case

Ramesh M. and *Bharati Ganiger*

Introduction

Research in education is for dissemination of knowledge, skills, attitudes which can develop the nation's whole education system. Research is for searching for new knowledge; researchers should possess competencies in order to carry out research. The following are competencies such as review and synthesis, the literature, studies in a focussed area of research, finding out the area of research, identifying recent trends and formulating the research problem and its purpose. Based on the formulated research problem, the researcher prepares a comprehensive theoretical/ conceptual framework which includes outline of entire study by the one who going to carry it out. While preparing the conceptual framework, the researcher should chose the appropriate methodology and design of the study. According to the methodology, data needs to be collected through various tools and techniques. Researchers should possess enough competencies to gather and organise the data, analysing and interpret the data in a scientific way of writing a report. It is not enough to prepare a good research report, it must also be disseminated through publication, abstract etc. All the competencies are very essential for all researchers, all these scientific way of writing helpful for the future researcher. In these perspectives present research study focussed expected research competencies for neo researcher of

Centre of Advanced Study in Education (CASE) the Maharaja Sayajirao University of Baroda. CASE has a unique academic culture in India from the time of inception to till now. CASE contributed more for the growth of educational research that cuts across all the areas. CASE acts as a pioneer of all researchers who are pursuing research in education. From the past to the present CASE follows the Saturday forum and Tuesday forum pattern for the one who wish to pursue Doctoral study in the field of education. Researchers are very active and innovative in doing research. Being the researcher of CASE, some of the competencies which are expected are possessed. In this direction present research paper focussed expected research competencies of neo-researchers of CASE.

Title of the Study

Research Competencies of Neo-Researchers of CASE

Objective

To study the expected Research Competencies of Neo-Researchers of CASE

Delimitation of the Study

The study was delimited to present regular Ph.D. Research Scholars of CASE

Methodology

Research Design

Descriptive Survey Method used for the present study.

Sample of the Study

Regular Ph.D. Research Scholars at CASE, Faculty of Education and Psychology. The M.S. University of Baroda, Vadodara.

Tool for the Data Collection

Questionnaire

The investigators constructed the open ended questionnaire. The items included in the questionnaire vary from simple basic research skills to complex competencies required for the researcher.

Data Collection

The investigators personally administered the questionnaire to all the Ph.D. regular research scholars to write their views on Research Competencies. 10 research scholars have responded to the questionnaire.

Data Analysis

The collected open ended questionnaires were analysed through content analysis.

Findings

The competencies explored for different phases of the process of research. Like—

- **The competencies required to locate the research problem:** The researchers at CASE are of the opinion that, to locate the research problem knowledge of the subject matter, knowledge of current trends in education, zeal to discover the hidden, identifying the lacunae in the process of education, understanding the present needs of the society, accordingly thinking about thc changes about the changes to be made and attitude to bring that change, confidence to begin with the change. Researcher should read, view and review various related literature to identify the gap and to locate a research problem, knowledge of info savvy skills to get updates regarding the field of research. Competency of introspection regarding the naturally occurred incidence i.e., why and how it has happened, and trying to locate here exactly where the problem lies and competency of analysing that.

- **The key components should reflect in the title of the study:** The researchers viewed that the specific area of the study could be mentioned, the title should reflect the intention of the research as the key words, may cover the variables and geographical area to be considered for the study.
- **Competencies to find and establish the research gaps:** The researcher should review the related studies rigorously, should have the ability of finding out what has already been researched and developed in the area of interest and what needs to be done further to fulfil the needs of the society.
- **Establishing the rationale of the study:** The researchers should have the competency of knowing and drawing out the need of the study, researchers should understand the importance and future benefits of the study and should convince society about the importance of the study. Researcher should really contribute the piece of research to the field.
- **Competency to draw implications from reviews:** The researcher should review the studies thoroughly then should find the important contribution of the studies, the objectives, the research methodologies, data collection process and data analysis process, potentials and limitations of the studies, Competency of differentiating different studies with similar and contradictory findings. Identifying the gaps between them and hypothesizing that the researcher present efforts to minimise or bridge the gap. Researcher should have the competency to compare all these ideas to own research process for its support and improvement.
- **Competencies to frame research questions:** Here the researcher should be very thorough on the reviews studied and should come out with certain questions, which could be solved through the present study undertaken. Critical thinking is needed to how to frame the research questions.
- **Differentiation between research questions and objectives:** The researcher should differentiate between

the research questions and objectives, that the research questions are broad enough and need not be attainable but may lead the researcher to frame proper objectives for the study. Researcher should have the competency to frame clear, concise and attainable objectives which show the proper way and exact need to the do the research.

- **Competency to generalize the research results to a larger population:** The researcher should be intelligent enough in selecting the sample which is a representative sample of the population, thereby helps in generalizing the results to the population. Competency of the researchers in knowledge and understanding of population, sample and sampling techniques. Competencies of selecting the sample, using proper sampling techniques are highly important for the researchers.
- **Deciding that the study would be Quantitative or Qualitative:** The researcher should be competent enough to decide the method of the study, whether Qualitative, Quantitative or Mixed method. To go by any method, researcher should have the understanding of all the research methods. The method is totally depend on the nature of the study, nature of data collection, tools, nature of data. Here the researcher should think and forecast his whole study pattern before deciding the method.
- **The competencies required for selecting the sample and sampling techniques in the research field:** Thorough knowledge and deep understanding of the selection of the sample and sampling techniques, critical thinking, and divergent thinking is needed for the researcher to select the sample and sampling technique.
- **What are the competencies required for collecting the research data:** Honesty, sincerity, self-involvement, self-motivation, patience, accepting the challenges, risk-taking ability, self-confidence, problem solving ability, decision making ability, potential for communication, knowledge of the sources of the data and ability of accessing the data from the source.
- **The rationale of establishing the Validity, Reliability and Credibility:** The researcher should be competent enough to establish the validity, reliability and credibility

of the research tools and programmes. It strengthens the study. It would be a real contribution of the researcher if one could establish all these. The quality of a research is related to its utility and generalizability of the results of the study, the researcher needs to take care of these factors.

- **How do you judge the appropriate data collection method according to the research methodology?:** The researcher should be competent to judge the appropriate data collection methods according to the study undertaken; this could be achieved through reviewing the studies, referring to books, discussion with experts, attending brain storming sessions at Tuesday Seminar, Saturday Researchers Forum and other discussions.
- **Competency to select research methodology that best matches to research questions and objectives:** It is based on the nature of the study, the objectives of the study, and again the researcher interest of working out with certain designs. Researcher should go through the theory of the research that undertaken, accordingly, review the studies of similar interest, find out the common ideas of the study, discussing with the experts may lead to proper selection of the best design for the study.
- **The competencies required constructing the tools for data collection:** Analysing the kind of data to be collected is desirable for the researcher. Accordingly construct the items clearly, precisely and meaningfully. Researcher should consider the sample characteristics before construction of tools, the language competency is equally important. Capacity to construct different tools for different kind of data, and different tools for similar interest also. Knowledge of validating the tools is also required. After constructing the tools one should discuss with the experts for improvements. Competency of communication is needed to discuss research tools with the experts.
- **How much the researcher should competent enough to analyse data manually and by the use of Statistical Softwares:** The researcher should be competent enough to analyse the research data; knowledge of statistics is a

must, knowledge and understanding of mathematical operations and computer skills, info-savvy skills are very basic for the researcher. Knowledge of statistical softwares has become need of the hour. Researchers are of the view that they are not competent and they need training in the use of statistical softwares. Some researchers opined that after undergoing the Ph.D. course work the competency in manually analysing the data has been developed.

- **The competencies required to analyze and interpret the research data collected:** The researcher should have the competency of analysing, classification, tabulation, organization and interpreting the data very clearly. Researcher should be unbiased. Interpretation should reflect the research results that have come out. Deeper understanding of the data is required in analysing the qualitative data.
- **The competencies required to write a research report:** Command over the language is very important. Researcher should be competent to organise the content, critically and logically interconnecting the variables is a must also as well as competency of discussing the research process and findings very logically. The research paper should follow the guidelines required i.e., researcher should be updated in his knowledge regarding the writing and publication of the research paper. Knowledge and skills of formatting the text, drawing charts and graphs, working with MS office, writing the reference according the APA guidelines, and the research report should include the discussion wherein the researcher should discuss about the finding and their contribution, and why the finding are in this way, identification of the potential advantages and limitations of the study, should have competency of summarising concisely the principal implications of the findings, concluding with providing further suggestions for conducting research.
- **Competencies to work in Interdisciplinary environment:** Researcher should have interest and positive attitude towards their mother discipline and should value other disciplines. Extensive knowledge in the relevant areas while working with interdisciplinary environment, open

mindedness to accept the episteme of other disciplines is also necessary. Researcher may interconnect the findings with other disciplines for drawing the implications.

- **Competencies required to work in a team:** Human being ought to be social in nature, irrespective of their working professions, team mind is always better than single. Researcher should have competency of good communication with the team. Hardworking, leadership qualities, motivation, co-ordination, co-operation and collaboration and networking among researchers is highly valued. Delegation of responsibility, motivating self and others, monitoring, working with diverse researchers are appreciable in researchers.
- **Competencies required for Communication**
  1. *Writing:* The researcher should have writing abilities for writing applications, knowledge of grammar, vocabulary, sequencing the contents logically in the research report.
  2. *Speaking:* The researcher should have the ability of speaking confidently, presentation skills, teaching competencies, facing the interviews confidently, discussing the research ideas with the groups and experts.
- **Ethical Competencies required for a researcher:** The researcher should always be honest in conducting the research process, prevent plagiarism, be unbiased with respect to research, positive attitude towards the nation, respect the truth, and respect the diversity. Respect the other research and researcher, consideration of mentioning the original author's details when referenced.

Conclusion

Researchers needs training in developing the research competencies; in Ph.D course work it has helped the research to develop the competencies to some extent. The discussions in the Tuesday seminars and Saturday researcher forums, national seminars, workshops conduction in CASE are really helping the research scholars to develop the research competencies.

References

Best, J.W. and Kahn, J.V. (1993), *Research in Education,* (7th ed.) New Delhi: Prentice Hall of India Private Ltd.

NPA Core Competencies Committee (2007-2009), *NPA Postdoctoral Core Competencies,* http://postdoc.siqmaxi.org/results.

Research Competency Committee (2011), Research Competencies for the Counselling Profession.

Saunders, J.P., Monty, A., Tajalli, E. (2003). Educational researchers' use of information services on the World Wide Web: a first report on the PERINE survey of educational researchers in 8 European nations during 2001 and 2002. In *European Conference on Educational Research, University of Hamburg, 17-20 September 2003*. Retrieved February 23.

Tautkeviciene *et al.* (n.d.) Demand for and Practice of Developing information competencies among Researchers, Kauna University of Technology, Lithuania.

10

A Critical Look at the Doctoral Research Programme in the Institutions of Higher Education

Dr. Sambit Kumar Padhi and *Dr. Mukesh Chandrakar*

Introduction

In developing countries like India where a large chunk of population remains not only below poverty line, but also backward in several aspects of quality life, higher education system assumes an important role in contributing significantly to better living standard. Over the last few decades, the higher education system of India has witnessed an amazing development reflecting a contradictory/fluctuating trend of quantitative expansion and qualitative deterioration. Basically, higher education in India is imparted through universities and colleges. Quality of higher education has been an issue of global concern in recent years. It is directly linked with the economic development, skill and knowledge generation over the various subjects. It has substantial role to play in developing skills and preparing intellectual manpower for catering the needs of society as well as creation of knowledge through research. Since, a long time institutions of higher education such as universities have been entrusted with two major functions i.e., teaching and research. Third dimension of the university function extension was added to the university with community affairs. The prime objective function of the university is to ensure teaching research and extension activities simultaneously. Universities are expected to carryout research with a greater magnitude. The key function of the university is not only teaching but also creating academically acceptable and high quality research workers. It is well accepted phenomena that without quality research a university is just another under graduate college.

Research refers to the activities related to the acquisition of knowledge or information. It is an activity seeking to gain greater understanding of a phenomenon and is directed towards the solution or elucidation of a problem. Research in the field of higher education is the demand of the day because it is directly linked with social and economic development, skill and knowledge generation over various subjects. It has been felt that without proper research, it will be difficult for a country to stand on its own feet in the arena of globalization and internationalization. Change in every aspect of human life has posed serious questions on the relevance of research in higher education and its ability to cater to the multifaceted needs of the society as of today. Problems and difficulties in the field of higher education necessitate purposeful and sustained research efforts. Reforms, progress and excellence in research require competent and dedicated team of researchers. In addition to that, proper and systematic planning, actions according to the plan, review and feed-back time to time for minimizing the errors are some of the important facts for ensuring quality research in the field of higher education.

Making the student/researcher self-reliant and country self-reliant is the need of the time. University should not focus much on the number of Ph.D. produced rather its prime objective needs to be creation of a knowledgeable and skilled person who can meet the need of the society and strengthen the research output of the society/ country. Interdisciplinary research needs to be encouraged, which is felt as the core of university research at the present time. Learner and supervisor should not be very sceptical towards adopting of interdisciplinary kind of learning and research. No doubt university is a place for both teaching and research. Research should be in such a manner which can make a person viable for the society.

In order to attain that the following parameters are very important

- Curriculum to be designed looking at the local and global needs.

- Teaching learning environments needs to be created.
- Research culture should be developed and promoted.

Some Observations on Doctoral Research Programme

- Research is not prime focus in majority of the institutions of higher education till date. Orientation and creation of awareness towards research in these institutions are very rare, rather they are busy in generating educated young unemployed workers who run after the government and the public services like postal, railway, land surveys etc.
- Though research has been a part of the mandate of the university, a critical look reveals that most of the Indian universities are not bestowing adequate attention to it.
- Very less number of students engaged themselves in order to pursue quality researches where as many of them are pursuing to get a degree.
- Not only the researchers only, but also very few research supervisors pay right attention, and ample time to their research scholars.
- Lack of research minded students in the campus as research is a collaborative, cooperative activity which requires rigorous discussion, interactions etc.
- The traditional mind set of senior faculty members seldom allow a student time for inter-faculty interaction and inter-disciplinary research.
- Misconception towards use of Information and Communication Technology
- Lack of autonomy, accountability is primarily responsible for poor research.
- Time and freedom to the researcher is another important factor

It is a common observation that the demand and production for Ph.D. degrees has been exponentially increased over the last few decades because Ph.D/research degree is now linked with appointment and promotion (CAS) in the institutions of higher education. In response to the general demand, many universities increased their Ph.D. production without being sufficiently ambitious about the quality bench marks. There was a time when rarest of the rare used to pursue a Ph.D. Degree even if the procedure for getting admission was not much complicated like to day. In the meantime, UGC regulation made either NET/SLET/ SET or Ph.D. as the minimum eligibility condition for requirement of teachers/Lectures, especially in the colleges and universities. Again a new resolution was passed by UGC 2009 where in those who pursue Ph.D. as per (UGC Ph.D. regulation -2009) is exempted from the said examination.

Analysis and Discussion

Entry of Students

There is no uniform rule followed in different universities for selection of Ph.D. students. No doubt entrance test is being conducted in all the universities as per UGC Regulation-2009 but it is not uniform in terms of syllabi covered, types of questions, weightage to the questions, number of questions, total marks and total time allocated for the test. In addition to that some universities prepared merit list on the basis of scores obtained in the entrance test only while in other cases entrance test is followed by research proposal presentation and personal interview. It is worthwhile to mention that very few private universities follow genuine admission procedure mentioned in new UGC guidelines.

Result

Some universities do not declare the date of examination and conduct pre-Ph.D. course work examination at right time. Declaration of course-work examination result is another big issue as a result of which students are always at the state of dilemma. Long awaited result, and equally long awaited calls for presentation of seminars and research proposals leave aspirants confused and perplexed many a time.

Quality Research Work

Points such as quality of research work, its originality, method of data collection, analysis and interpretation of data and so on matters many a time.

Time Related Indicators

This is a known fact that very few research scholars are engaged in full time research work. The Ph.D. ordinance at any Indian universities normally expects the candidate to complete Ph.D. work in 2-5 years, even for part time candidate.

Students

It is very well known fact that ideas rule the world. Most of the students do not try to generate their own ideas and usually leave the responsibility on the supervisor. Therefore they confuse many a time and do not know what they exactly want to do up to the last moment.

Ph.D. Ordinance

Ph.D. ordinances in of many universities are not very clear and not uniform throughout the country. In this connection many a decision has been left to the disposal of Heads of the department. Therefore lack of uniformity in taking many decisions is observed within the universities. Even it is also found that after going through the same line different interpretations are made among faculty members of a single department.

Supervisor and Resources

So far the selection of supervisor for guiding scholars is concerned, it mostly depends on the university's internal policy. That means there is no uniform policy adopted by all the universities for selecting the supervisors. It is a common observation that most of the time supervisors are selected/approved either on the basis of their seniority or on the basis of the number of research papers published. In both the cases quantity matters instead of quality.

Another problem is that paucity of supervisors and dearth of resources is a pertinent issue. Year after year students aspiring for Ph.D. are increasing, but the number of supervisors are not increasing with equal proportion.

Evaluation

The most serious loophole found in the system is its evaluation system. The most interesting matter is that the internal examiner decides the probable list of external examiners. It is an indication that the secrecy of the names of the external examiners as prescribed in the UGC regulation has simply remained on paper. In addition to that can the research a work of 4-5 years be evaluated within 30-40 minutes? Does not it mean that the formalities are done simply for the name sake?

Relevance and Practical Applicability

How many of the theses have practical applicability, beneficial for society at a large?. Most of them are no doubt increasing the data of Ph.D. production but how many of them are fulfilling the primary objectives of research is matter of great question.

Pursuing Ph.D. is no doubt a long journey. One needs to sustain perseverance and endurance throughout the journey instead of taking it as a burden. The nature and structure of Indian Doctoral programme is quite different from other stages of education including the post graduate level of education. In such a situation, it will be quite wise to work with positive aspirations, interest, punctuality, sincerity and commitment. A researcher will only excel in his research, when he takes it as a challenge and move with good academic morality

References

Agarwal, P. (2009). *Indian Higher Education: Envisioning the Future*, New Delhi: Sage Publication India Pvt. Ltd.

Attar, Rabbanni (2010). Universities in Need of Reform, *Economic and Political Weekly*, Vol. XLV (17), April 24.

Draftaur, C.N. (2001). Indian Universities: Temple of Learning or Warehouse, University News, Vol. 39 (07), February 1-7.

Ganam, A. (2013). *Overview of Research and Development of India*, University News, New Delhi, Vol. 15(17), April 29-May 05.

Ian, A. Frame and Liz, Allen (2002). A Flexible Approach to Ph.D. Research Training, *Quality Assurance in Education*, Vol. 12(02) pp. 98-103.

Power, K.B. (2011). Restructuring Research Education and Post Doctoral Training, Pune: DPU Publication

Swamy, R.N. (2013). Overview of Research Capacity of India: Trends and Gaps, University News, New Delhi, Vol. 15(17), April 29-May 05

UGC (2009). Minimum Standard and Procedure for Awards of M Phil/ Ph D Regulation, The Gazette of India, New Delhi.

11

Role of 'Social Software Tools' and 'E-skills' for Quality Enhancement in Social Science Research: A Study

Mary George Varghese

Introduction

In a rapidly changing global environment, research and innovation plays a vital role towards the advancement of society. Research involves the mastery of skills needed to design and conduct a systematic, empirical, objective, public, and critical investigation of an identified problem or an issue. It is a complex assignment which requires a set of skills and competencies as prerequisites like comprehensive theoretical knowledge and in depth understanding, framing a research question, the ability to design an instrument for collecting data, document related competencies, data analysis related competencies etc.

An examination of quality issues in the area of educational research reveals three perspectives 'achieving quality', 'controlling quality' and 'preserving quality' and it is an ongoing process. Hence, any effort to bring quality enhancement should reflect upon all these three domains. Research is also a part of the social advancement and the research culture is very much influenced by social changes. The 'digital metamorphism' demands a new set of research skills and culture among social science researchers.

Social software tools include software or Web service that allows people to communicate and collaborate while using the application. E-mail, blogs, and even instant messaging are all examples of social software. Social software enables people to rendezvous, connect and/or collaborate through computer-mediated communication. It enhances all communication that occurs via computer-mediated formats (i.e., instant messages, e-mails, and chat rooms) between two or more individual's weblogs, Skype, msn messenger etc.

The e-skills contemporary skills—the ability to use today's computer applications, enabling people to apply information technology effectively. The e-skills provide a store of practical experience on which to build new competence. In general it includes those skills needed to make use of Information and Communication Technologies (ICT) as well as those required to apply and develop them.

The researcher should be versed with the data analysis software and e-search techniques to scan the latest developments in his/her area of interest. The net-generation researcher should be a good e-net worker and should have a skill for being the part of collaborative or group researches throughout the world. The e-skills comprise the intellectual *capabilities*—include the ability to apply information technology in complex situations, encapsulating higher-level thinking in the context of IT. These capabilities empower people to manipulate the medium to their advantage and to handle unintended and unexpected problems when they arise. Intellectual capabilities foster more abstract thinking about information and its manipulation.

For a researcher the essential e-skills can be categorized as

- **ICT practitioner skills** are the capabilities required for researching, developing, designing, strategic planning, managing, ICT systems.
- **ICT user skills** are the capabilities required for the effective application of ICT systems and devices by the individual. ICT users apply systems as tools in support of their own work. User skills cover the use of common software tools and of specialized tools.
- **e-Business skills** correspond to the capabilities needed to exploit opportunities provided by ICT, notably the

internet; to ensure more efficient and effective performance and to explore possibilities for new ways of conducting and disseminating research and its outcomes.

Theoretical Foundations

Mainstream learning theories that underpin the development of educational material include behaviourism, cognitive and constructivism (Mason and Rennie, 2008). Behaviourism, which regards observable behaviour as more important than any attempt to understand internal activities (the mind is treated as a black box) was challenged in educational psychology theory by cognitivism, which emphasizes the importance to the educator of attempting to understand the mental process of learning, so that the process can be improved. Both these schools of thought consider the learning process to involve a largely passive internalization of knowledge about an objective external reality as a result of experiencing that reality. Constructivism on the other hand emphasizes the 'active involvement of the student in the search for knowledge' hence the use of social software tools is in line with constructivist theory.

Social Software Tools and Researcher

A critical analysis of the various researches conducted in the area of ICT and other document analysis shows the social software tools are of great help to the researchers. To list a few are:

- Engages users in 'learning to learn' and developing the practical research skills needed to make best use of online information networks.
- 'The power of many' exposes an individual to far more research, resources and ideas than they could possibly generate on their own.
- It matches well with modern thinking about educational practice.
- It promises learners of new opportunities to be independent in their study and research.
- Social software tools encourage a wider range of expressive capability.

- It facilitates more collaborative ways of working and to furnish a setting for learner achievements to attract an authentic audience.
- Developing the skills of problem solving, research and collaborative working equips students well for the world of work.
- 'The ability of learners to project themselves socially and affectively into a community of inquiry' and finds that social presence is correlated with student satisfaction and higher scores on learning outcomes.

Web 1.0 allows knowledge to be disseminated electronically and accessed widely. However, the interactive nature of social software allows students to participate in collaborative work, for example, creating a group report where the quality of the whole may well exceed the sum of its parts. In addition to higher quality learning outcomes, participants in the process benefit from both peer recognition and peer review, both excellent preparation for more modern collaborative teamwork (Crook *et al.*, 2008). Social software methods and tools actively engage learners both individually and in groups whilst still providing opportunities for differentiation since the individual contributions may be identified and tracked.

Barriers and Challenges

The use of social software methods and tools constitutes change and change has to be managed to minimize a fear of the unknown that throws up a combination of resistance and inertia. Such fears include invasion of privacy, exposure to ridicule, cyber-bullying, production of inappropriate material as well as the fear that some learners will be penalized by lack of prerequisite computer skills (Crook *et al.*, 2008). Armstrong and Franklin (2008) discuss some of the barriers:

- Institutional and network restrictions
- Lack of money to invest in technical infrastructure
- Lack of knowledge of some senior managers
- Inadequate ICT strategy
- using different social tools can involve endlessly logging

on to a multiplicity of accounts and the consequent difficulty of remembering and managing passwords
- some mature academic staff are resistant to having to learn new Web 2.0 tools, and fear losing control to the students.

However Crook *et al.* (2008) point out that even with increased "learner centreedness", there will still be significant demands on teachers to provide structure and facilitate the learning. It could also be argued that Web 2.0 places mature students (or "digital immigrants") at a disadvantage but a counter argument is that everyone needs to be computer literate and able to work collaboratively in the workplace. Therefore being exposed to the latest technology as a researcher is an excellent preparation for work and provides an opportunity to acquire additional skills.

References

ICT for Higher Education: Case Studies from Asia and the Pacific. Bangkok, Thailand: UNESCO, 2011 (http://unesdoc.unesco.org/images/0021/002141/214143e.pdf)

Anderson, S.E. and Gansneder, B.M. (1995) 'Using Electronic Mail Surveys and Computer Monitored Data for Studying Computer Mediated Communication Systems', *Social Science Computer Review*, 13, 1, pp. 33-46.

Babbie, E. (1992). *The Practice of Social Research* (6th ed.) Belmont, California: Wadsworth.

Boshier, R. (1990). 'Socio-psychological Factors in Electronic Networking' International *Journal of Lifelong Education*, 9, 1, pp. 49-64.

Berge, Z.L. and Collins, M. (1995). 'Computer Mediated Scholarly Discussion Groups', *Computers and Education*, 24, 3, pp. 183-189.

Coomber, R. (1997). 'Using the Internet for Survey Research' *Sociological Research Online*, 2.

12

Identification and Selection of a Research Problem

Ekta Priyadarshini

Introduction

Research in common parlance refers to a search for knowledge. One can also define research as a scientific and systematic search for pertinent information on a particular topic. In fact, research is an art of scientific investigation. According to Clifford Woody (as cited in Kothari, 1989) research comprises defining and redefining problems, formulating hypothesis or suggested solutions; collecting, organizing and evaluating data; making deductions and reaching conclusions; and at last carefully testing the conclusions to determine whether they fit the formulating hypothesis.

Research is a gateway to new knowledge that obviously depends on how meaningfully the problem has been identified and research questions have been answered. Finding and analyzing a problem is the first and crucial step in research. Identifying the exact nature and dimension of a problem is of major importance in research. It is the most thoughtful effort; even a little carelessness on the part of the researcher spoils the spirit of research. It is a systematic attempt to obtain answers to meaningful questions about a phenomenon through the applications of scientific procedures. The identification of research problem requires a great deal of patience and logical thinking on the part of the researcher. A beginning researcher finds the task of identifying a research problem a difficult one. This may be due to his/her limited knowledge of the research process and his/her unpreparedness for identifying the problem. He/she may also be unfamiliar with the areas in which research is needed and the procedure he/she needs to follow for selecting a suitable field of research. Therefore, an investigator must learn how to recognize and define a problem. How does one locate problems? What conditions give rise to them etc.?

Common Mistakes Made by Students When they Search for a Research Problem

According to VanDalen (1973) some common mistakes which students commit when they search for a problem for their research are as follows:

- They procrastinate for months rather than make a systematic search of the literature to locate several problem possibilities.
- They select a research procedure before they select a problem rather a clear formulation of the problem must be made before an appropriate method of resolving it can be selected.
- They select a problem according to the ease of data collection.

They present a generalized description of their problem rather than the exact dimensions and a clear definition of the terms.

How to Identify a Research Problem?

Clear and concise identification of the problem is not an easy matter. Some research studies are pursued in such a way that it is difficult to determine what the investigator is trying to investigate. A most challenging situation for a researcher occurs when she/he feels bewildered and suffers with diffused perceptions of the situations amenable to research. Identification of a research situation is an important phase of the entire research process. It demands a great deal of thinking, searching and speculation on the part of researcher. It consumes a lot of energy, time and effort.

A beginning researcher finds it very difficult as to how to locate the problem situation. This may happen because s/he has the limited knowledge of the research process. S/he may be unfamiliar with the areas in which research is needed and the procedures that s/he has to follow to identify a suitable area of research. Novice investigators have an unrealistic, glamorized conception of research problem.

In education field there are many broad areas such as teaching learning process, teacher education, guidance and counselling, curriculum, textbooks, information and communication technology, science education, value education, peace education, inclusive education etc. The researcher should first identify a general area in which she/he wishes to do research and then immediately set about reviewing the knowledge available in that area. Therefore, the researcher must first decide the area of his/her interest and the purpose of his research endeavours. It must be the area of research where the researcher is capable of demonstrating necessary initiative, insight, critical analysis and judgmental capacities. Thus the identification of a problem situation follows the following procedural efforts on the part of a researcher.

- A problem situation of research may emerge from the researcher's curiosity about something shared, seen, felt or wondered about or through the natural interest of a researcher.
- Life situations, relationships established by related researchers and implications advanced by technological advancements constitute the problem situation.
- New knowledge in the field of researcher's interest coming through the new arrivals of books, journals and researches extend a situation for research.
- The understanding of the known theories, facts and ideas in the field of researcher's interest structures his/her problem solving domain. The research focus is sharpened by what he/she already knows, what researches in the field have been conducted and what needs to be discovered.

A survey of suggestions for further research given at the end of research reports and reviews of research projects, the gaps which are there in a particular field of educational research are helpful in keeping the researcher informed about what researches are going on in the field in which he/she has the competence and deeper understanding.

Sources for Selecting a Research Problem

After the broad area of research interest has been identified, the researcher will proceed towards narrowing it down to a highly specified and focused problem. At this juncture, it is not possible to list all the educational problems that are needed to be researched. The problems do not germinate in barren brains but rather in minds enriched by variety of experiences and fertile layers of knowledge. Reading educational publications extensively will help to prepare an intellectual soil in which problem ideas are likely to sprout. There are various sources which are available to researcher and which help him to identify and specify the meaningful problem of research. Some of the main sources of selecting a research problem are as follows:

- Theory
- Experience
- Discussions
- Dissatisfaction
- Literature

Theory

Scientific conceptions of the nature of things involve theories. The researcher should have some understanding of the nature of theory and should avoid trying to build theories that are too sophisticated. Theory is a set of generalization arrived at by carefully analyzed and studied phenomena. The inferences that are drawn from psychological and educational theories when known to a researcher helps in identifying the research area. The applications of principles that are derived from theories extend an authentic ground to locate the problem. Research and theory go together. If research is conducted without consulting a theory, it means that many essential aspects of theory that could guide and control the researcher's efforts are ignored. Thus, the theory helps the researcher in following ways:

1. Explains the phenomena under research proposed,
2. Permits the prediction of the occurrence of the phenomena,
3. Enables the investigator to postulate and eventually to discover hitherto unknown and unobserved phenomena,
4. Explains the relationship among various components, facts and principles,
5. Pinpoints the crucial aspects to be investigated and crucial questions to be answered,
6. Helps the researcher to structure and restructure the domain of understanding and,
7. Helps to stimulate and control research.

Experience

The best single way for a researcher to find a good research problem is to attach him/her to a dynamic research environment, which increases the opportunities for finding and solving problems. Spirited intellectual discourses, in which ideas are presented, explained, analyzed and challenged is a rich source of inspiration. Attending seminars in which papers are read and discussed, conferences with stimulating professors, lectures by eminent educationists, discussions with fellow research workers, part time job in research worthy of investigation provide clues needed for the solution of problems. Professors and research experts who have had experience in tackling a particular type of problem can help in telling the novice what can and what cannot be successfully accomplished. Examining the everyday experiences gives and inspires the problem. Personal experience that the researcher gain is a potential source of research problems to be identified and formulated and it helps the researcher in following ways:

1. Develops insight into sharpening the focus of research,
2. Experiences the relative usefulness of various issues that emerge in his/her mind for research,
3. Explores the context for innovative researches,
4. Formulate the research problem more meaningfully and practically, and

5. Equips the researcher with such understanding that s/he is able to identify the problematic situations, behaviours and issues for which solutions are not available and which need to be researched.

Discussion

Discussion works as a brainstorming exercise. It helps in setting a problem. While discussing with researchers, professors and other intellectual persons, the shrinkages of mind are opened and then there is germination of a seed of a new problem. These discussions give chances to the researcher to get into close contact with crucial problems and issues concerning education. The researcher finds a group of individuals working enthusiastically on some enterprise and some of their enthusiasm will rub off on him/her. Sometimes researchers have problems in their mind but they are not able to verbalize and give proper shape to the problem. It is discussion with his/her fellows and other senior professors that help him/her to evolve a manageable research problem from the one which was very vague and complex. Discussion is a very useful resource of research problem identification. The following are some of the advantages which the researcher gets out of discussion:

1. Contemporary research areas capture the mind of the researcher,
2. Certain ambiguities that the researcher initially has get clarified,
3. The researcher is helped with new academic inputs to reflect upon problem situations and to come out with a suitable research problem identification,
4. Many unknown hazards that the researcher may experience while identifying a problem situation become known to him/her,
5. The meaningfulness of the research problem in the mind is further judged, e.g. whether this research problem will make a significant contribution to the existing knowledge or not,
6. The researcher may be able to make a clear classification as to how to classify his/her, problem.
7. Whether it will be fundamental, applied or action research.

Dissatisfaction

When a researcher attempts the identification of problem, s/he has to go through various situations, some satisfying and some dissatisfying. Research is a felt need of a researcher. Need itself leads to inadequacy and this inadequacy activates the researcher to design a course of action through which that need is fulfilled. The inadequacies and incompatibilities create dissatisfaction within the researcher for which s/he tries to identify the problem, which clearly shows the direction to the solution of the problem. After the researcher perceives the problem, for its proper identification and formulation s/he reviews the literature, discusses with people consults recent books and journals and traces some flaws, gaps and inadequacies in his/her thinking. S/he may find it difficult to give it a proper shape to his thinking and it becomes a gigantic task for him to formulate research questions. The dissatisfaction thus created, becomes a rich source of inspiration.

While working in the institutions, reading good books related to the problem area, the researcher is confronted with many dissatisfying situations that makes him/her problem sensitive, he/she then thinks about a problem, and comes out with a proper identification and formulation of the research problem. These days information and communication technology has revolutionized almost every aspect of human life, and so it has deeply entered into the orbit of an educational system, consequently posing new challenges and input for thinking. The researcher experiences dissatisfaction in him/her when s/he comes out with such problem situations as, impact of these technologies on mechanization of learning, impact on the source literature, etc.

The Literature

The review and the survey of literature may help the researcher to expand his knowledge, background, examine new findings in his field, identify gaps in knowledge, and discover contradictions in findings and the need for fresh studies and their direction. Through various readings the researcher comes to know about the various methods and techniques of research used by other researchers, learn about facts, phenomena, concepts, theories related to his field of research which may be useful to him/her in the formulation, description and conduct of his/her study. The source literature consists of surveys, periodicals and journals, foreign and Indian books, encyclopaedia, dictionaries, handbooks and year books, bibliographical literature and other references. Some specialized sources are Survey of Research in Education brought out by NCERT, Dissertation Abstracts International, and Handbook of Research on Teaching, Encyclopedia of Educational Research, Psychological Abstracts, and Educational Technology Abstracts etc.

Analyzing a Research Problem

After brainstorming various sources the researcher identifies the broad area where s/he want to conduct the research. But simply identifying the broad area of interest does not solve the problem. It is simply the first step of the problem identification. The next step is the analysis of the problem. Problem analysis helps the researcher to analyze all the aspects of the problems. Its pros and cons, the situations that lead to the problem, the feasibility factor in taking up that problem etc. Problem analysis in research may be quite complex. Thus, a researcher needs to employ inductive and deductive procedure to identify the factors that give rise to a problem. An investigator should follow the following major tasks in analyzing a problematic situation (VanDalen, 1973).

- Accumulating the facts that might be related to the problem.
- Setting by observation whether the facts are relevant.
- Tracing any relationship between facts that might reveal the key difficulty.
- Proposing various explanations for the cause of the difficulty.
- Ascertaining through observation and analysis whether these explanations are relevant to the problem.
- Tracing the relationship between explanations that may give an insight into the problem solution.
- Tracing the relationship between facts and explanations, and
- Questioning assumptions underlying the analysis of the problem.

Conclusion

The selection of suitable and relevant research problem is a systematic process. It requires a lot of determination, dedication, hard work, insight and interest of the researcher. While identifying the problem the existing literature is to be reviewed and the various sources, i.e. theory, experience, discussions, dissatisfaction and literature have to be relevantly used. While identifying a research problem the researcher should neither be in a hurry nor procrastinate for months. A detailed analysis of the research problem also needs to be done in order to get a clear cut idea about the research problem. Hence, the identification and analysis of a problem is the most important and difficult step in the research process. It is a most thoughtful effort; even a little carelessness on the part of the researcher spoils the spirit of the research. It is a systematic attempt to obtain answers to meaningful questions about a phenomenon through the application of scientific procedures.

References

Indira Gandhi National Open University. (2007). *Block 3 Research Design*. New Delhi: Author.

Johnson, B., and Christensen, L. (2008). California: Sage Publications, Inc.

Kothari, C.R. (1989). *Research Methodology Methods and Techniques*. New Delhi: Wiley Eastern Limited.

VanDalen, D.B. (1973). *Understanding Educational Research*. New York: McGraw-Hill Book Company.

13

Research Problem

Identification and Formulation

Mohd Shoket

Introduction

Research comprises creative work undertaken on a systematic basis in order to increase the stock of knowledge, including knowledge of man, culture and society, and the use of this stock of knowledge to devise new applications. Research problems are questions that indicate gaps in the scope or the certainty of our knowledge. They point either to problematic phenomena, observed events that are puzzling in terms of our currently accepted ideas, or to problematic theories, current ideas that are challenged by new hypotheses.

What is a Research Problem?

- It is the topic we would like to address, investigate, or study, whether descriptively or experimentally.
- It is the focus or reason for engaging in our research.
- It is typically a topic, phenomenon, or challenge that we are interested in and applications with which we are at least somewhat familiar.

Problem Formulation

Problem formulation is the logical first step toward this goal.

As Northrop (1966) writes, "Inquiry starts only when something is unsatisfactory, when traditional beliefs are inadequate or in question, when the facts necessary to resolve one's uncertainties are not known, when the likely relevant hypotheses are not even imagined. What one has at the beginning of inquiry is merely the problem" (p. 17).

The formulation of research problems also has an important social function. As Merton, Broom, and Cottrell (1959) suggest, researchers must justify the demands for attention and other scarce resources that research makes: "In conferring upon the scientist the right to claim that a question deserves the concerted attention of others as well as himself, the social institution of science exacts the obligation that he justify the claim" (p. xix).

Achieving significant research results is perhaps the most powerful justification for such claims, but this type of justification can be offered only after the fact, and only in the event that the research is successful. A compelling research problem, by contrast, **must marshal support in advance of research** and, if it is **sufficiently compelling**, can even sustain that support through the sometimes fruitless periods that researchers experience. However, despite research problems' logical priority on inquiry, and their importance as *a priori* justifications, a problem's formulation, as John Dewey stresses, is in fact a "progressive" matter.

The Role of Theory in Problem Formulation

Theory plays a dual role in research.

1. On the one hand, new theories solve research problems by accounting for unexplained phenomena and by superseding questionable older theories.
2. On the other hand, existing theory guides researchers in formulating research problems. In determining whether and in what respects a phenomenon or a theory is problematic, researchers consider the context of accumulated theoretical as well as empirical knowledge.

Sources of Research Problem

- Classroom

- School
- Community
- Own teaching experiences
- Classroom lectures
- Class discussions
- Seminars/workshops/paper presentations
- Internet
- Out-of-class exchange of ideas with fellow students and professors
- Reading assignment
  - Textbook
  - Special programme
  - Research reports
  - Term papers
- Consultation with
  - Course instructor
  - Advisor
  - Faculty member

How is a Research Problem Formulated?

We often think we understand problems when we don't. For example, when students encounter difficulties with word problems in math, teachers may initially think that students have not mastered the basic skills that would allow them to carry out the needed computations. However, the difficulty may actually lie in poor reading skills, which prevent the students from identifying the words in math problems.

As another example, when students do not hand in homework assignments or participate in class, some might be inclined to think that the students are not motivated. While there may be motivational issues, motivation may not be the only factor. A high school student may have an evening job that demands considerable time and energy. A younger student may be trying desperately to camouflage poor or non-existent skills. In some cases, the chosen instructional strategy may not be well matched to the student's cognitive or attention level. Therefore, it is crucial that researchers accurately identify the problem they want to study.

Formulating the Problem

The selection of one appropriate researchable problem out of the identified problems requires evaluation of those alternatives against certain criteria, which may be grouped into:

Internal Criteria

Internal Criteria consists of:

1. **Researcher's interest:** The problem should interest the researcher and be a challenge to him. Without interest and curiosity, he may not develop sustained perseverance. Interest in a problem depends upon the researcher's educational background, experience, outlook and sensitivity.
2. **Researcher's own resource:** In the case of a research to be done by a researcher on his own, consideration of his own financial resource is pertinent. If it is beyond his means, he will not be able to complete the work, unless he gets some external financial support. Time resource is more important than finance. Research is a time-consuming process; hence it should be properly utilized.
3. **Researcher's competence:** A mere interest in a problem will not do. The researcher must be competent to plan and carry out a study of the problem. He must possess adequate knowledge of the subject-matter, relevant methodology and statistical procedures.

External Criteria

1. **Research-ability of the problem:** The problem should be researchable, i.e., amendable for finding answers to the questions involved in it through scientific method.
2. **Novelty of the problem:** The problem must have novelty. There is no use of wasting one's time and energy on a problem already studied thoroughly by others.
3. **Importance and urgency:** Problems requiring investigation are unlimited, but available research efforts are very much limited. Therefore, in selecting problems, importance and urgency of the problem should be considered.

4. **Facilities:** Research requires certain facilities such as well-equipped library facility, suitable and competent guidance, data analysis facility, etc. Hence, the availability of the facilities relevant to the problem must be considered. Problems for research, their relative importance and significance should be considered.
5. **Feasibility:** A problem may be a new one and also important, but if research on it is not feasible, it cannot be selected.
6. **Usefulness and social relevance:** Above all, the study of the problem should make significant contribution to the concerned body of knowledge or to the solution of some significant practical problem. It should be socially relevant.
7. **Research personnel:** Research undertaken by professors and by research organizations require the services of investigators and research officers. But in India and other developing countries, research has not yet become a prospective profession. Hence, talented persons are not attracted to research projects.

Each identified problem must be evaluated in terms of the above internal and external criteria and the most appropriate one may be selected by a research scholar.

Guidelines for Selecting Problem

1. The problem should be such in which researcher may be deeply interested,
2. The problem should be related with the chain of thinking because a stray problem can mislead the whole research project,
3. The problem selected should not necessarily be a new one, it may be old problem or one on which work has already been done,
4. The problem should be within meaningful limits i.e. it should not be too comprehensive.

Considerations in Selecting a Research Problem

These help to ensure that your study will remain manageable and that you will remain motivated.

1. **Interest**: A research endeavour is usually time consuming, and involves hard work and possibly unforeseen problems. One should select a topic of great interest to sustain the required motivation.
2. **Magnitude:** It is extremely important to select a topic that you can manage within the time and resources at your disposal. Narrow the topic down to something manageable, specific and clear.
3. **Measurement of concepts**: Make sure that you are clear about the indicators and measurement of concepts (if used) in your study.
4. **Level of expertise**: Make sure that you have an adequate level of expertise for the task you are proposing since you need to do the work yourself.
5. **Relevance**: Ensure that your study adds to the existing body of knowledge, bridges current gaps and is useful in policy formulation. This will help you to sustain interest in the study.
6. **Availability of data**: Before finalizing the topic, make sure that data are available.
7. **Ethical issues**: How ethical issues can affect the study population and how ethical problems can be overcome should be thoroughly examined at the problem formulating stage.

Principle Components in the Formulation of a Problem

- The originating questions (what one wants to know?)
- The rational-theoretical or practical (why one wants to have the questions answered?)
- The specifying questions (possible answers to the originating) in term of that satisfy the rationale.

The Originating Questions

- Represent the beginning of certain difficulties or challenges.
- Are formulated specifically to indicate where exactly the answers to them can be searched for.
- Constitute the initial phase in the process of problem formulation.

- May be formulated in terms of broadly delimited categories of social variable but do not indicate specifically which particular variables in each class might be germane to the issues.
- Usually derive from a general theoretical orientation rather than a definite theory.

Rationale of Questions

- Is the statement of reasons why a particular question is worth putting across.
- States what will happen to other parts of knowledge or practice if the question posed is answered, i.e., how the answer to the question will contribute to theory and/or practice.
- Helps to effect discrimination between scientifically good and scientifically trivial questions.

Specifying Questions

- Culminate the process of formulating a research problem
- Involve the breaking down of originating question into several specifying questions related to particular aspects and their consequences.

Necessary Conditions for Formulating a Research Problem

We may now list some of the conditions that experience has proved to be conducive to formulation of significant research problems.

- Systematic immersion in the subject matter through first hand observation
- Study of relevant literature on the subject.
- Discussions with persons having rich practical experience in the field of study.

Sources of Research Problem

The research problem may be selected from the following sources:

- theory of one's own interest
- daily problems
- technological changes
- unexplored areas
- discussions with other people

Criteria of a Good Research Problem

The following are detailed list of criteria for the choice of research problem.

Novelty-It should be sufficiently original so that it does not involve objectionable duplication.

Interesting-The problem should be interesting for the investigator himself.

Importance-If it is not worthwhile, if adds to neither knowledge nor lead to any improvements in the current practices.

Immediate Application-The investigator should ask himself question, will my research help in solving an urgent problem

Feasibility or Amenability-Feasibility issue of research includes the following:

- Availability of data
- Availability of cooperation
- Availability of guidance
- Availability of other facilities
- Experience and creativity
- Coverage and confidence

Common Errors in Formulating Research Problem

Naming a Broad Field

- To choose the broad area of study instead of specific problem makes no justification.
- Narrowing or localizing a topic
- The problem should not be narrowed to such an extent that it becomes too small and insignificant from a research point of view.

Conclusion

In concluding lines I want to say that research is a creative work and this chapter gives the researcher an outline about the identification and formulation of research problem. Best selected problems serve, this purpose and provide solutions to many identified and unidentified problems.

References

Ali, A. (1990). Approaches to Educational Research: Analysis, criticisms and relevance. Perspectives in Educational Research and National Development (Vol. 1) Onitsha, Summer Educational Publishers Limited.

American Psychological Association (2001). *Publication Manual of the American Psychological Association* (5th ed.). Washington, D.C.: Author.

American Psychological Association (2009). *Publication Manual of the American Psychological Association* (6th ed.). Washington, D.C.: Author.

Bem, D. (1987) Writing the empirical journal article. In Zanna, M.P., & Darley, J.M. (Eds.), *The Complete Academic: A practical guide for the beginning social scientist* (pp. 171-204). Mahweh, N.J.: Lawrence Earlbaum Associates, Inc.

Best, J.W. (1970). *Research in Education.* New Jersey: Prentice-Hall Inc.

Gall, M.D., Gall, J.P., and Borg, W.R. (2006). *Educational Research: An Introduction* (8th ed.). Boston: Allyn & Bacon.

Kothari, C.R. (2006). *Research Methodology: Methods and Techniques.* India: New Age International Publishers.

Koul, L. (1992). *Methodology of Educational Research.* India: Vikas Publishing House Pvt Ltd.

Nwana, O.C. (1982). *Introduction to Education Research.* Ibadan: Heinemann.

14

Research Report and its Fundamentals

Sudershan Kumar Pathania

Research an Introduction

Research is all about addressing an issue or asking and answering a question or solving a problem. In every research area or subject, our knowledge is incomplete and problems are waiting to be solved. Research is a systematic process of collecting and analyzing information to increase our knowledge and understanding. Research is an attempt or an intentional act to discover the facts, revise the laws and theories or is a practical application of all these and research report is the key aspect of any research.

The Purpose of Research is to..........

- Review or synthesize existing knowledge
- Investigate existing situations or problems
- Provide solutions to problems
- Explore and analyze more general issues
- Construct or create new procedures or systems
- Explain new phenomenon
- Generate new knowledge

...or a combination of any of the above! (Collis & Hussey, 2003).

Fundamentals/Bases of Research are:

1. Problem Formulation; and
2. Reporting.

1. Problem Formulation

A research problem is an issue, topic, or question that motivates a study. Such problems may be theoretical, practical, or a combination thereof. A researchable question is an uncertainty about a problem that can be challenged, examined, and analyzed to provide useful information. A successful research project depends upon how well an investigator formulates the research question based on the problems faced in day-to-day research activities and clinical practice. The underlying questions of a research project provide important information to decide whether the topic is relevant, researchable, and significant. A well-formulated research question needs extreme specificity and preciseness which guides the implementation of the project keeping in mind the identification of variables and population of interest.

The Research Process

- Step 1: Identify knowledge gap
- Step 2: Formulate the research question
- Step 3: Search for existing information
- Step 4: Focus the research question
- Step 5: Design the study
- Step 6: Refine the specific aims and objectives of the study

The problem formulation should concentrate to find the answer of the following as:

- What was the research problem, topic, issue, or question?
- Why is this problem important?
- What rationale for the conceptual, methodological, and theoretical choices is made in addressing the problem?
- How the study contributes to knowledge or understanding about the problem?

- How does the project fit into the context of other research?
- How a problem is understood?
- What generalizations can be made?
- What are the extents to which a work can contribute to addressing significant issues?
- Why the results of the problem would be of interest to the research community?
- How an investigation is linked to prior knowledge and research?
- What can be addressed and the extent?
- How did you investigate the research problem?
- What are your findings?
- What do these findings tell you?
- What do you conclude?

2. Reporting

Reporting is a comprehensive picture of what the problem is about and how it has been approached.

It should address the question as:

- What was the research problem?
- Why is this problem important?
- How does the project fit into the context of other research?
- What do these findings tell you?
- What do you conclude?
- How did you investigate the research problem?
- What are your findings?

Sections of a Research Report

1. Title page

- Title of report
- Student name
- Course/subject
- Date

2. Executive Summary or Abstract

- Gives a summary of the whole report
- Outlines -purpose
- Research method
- Findings
- Main conclusions
- Recommendations

3. Body: It includes Introduction and Research Design

(a) Introduction
- Title Page
- Statement of the problem
- Description of the major constructs involve
- Review of the related literature
- Objective of the study
- Hypothesis

(b) Research Design
- Sample
- Variables
- Methodology
- Tool and Techniques

4. Analyses and Interpretation

Hypothesis is verified by using appropriate statistics and interpretation.

5. Results/Findings

Outcomes of the research are given.

6. Conclusion

It includes the general problem areas described in introduction followed by the suggestions for possible future research. It gives a summary statement of main findings and their significance.

7. References

It include the list of resources use in research

8. Table and Figures

Theoe are typed on separate sheet and placed in between reference and appendices

9. Appendix

Supporting document and tool used are placed here which are not included in research body

Conclusion

This chapter highlighted the formulation, reporting research, it's importance, nature of research, and its benefits for personal development. It also highlights some points to be followed for doing quality research. The ability to produce high quality written work will give anyone an advantage in the competitive job market. Finally, it illustrated some tips for the selection of a research problem and organization of research.

References

Ali, A. (1990). Approaches to Educational Research: Analysis, criticisms and relevance. *Perspectives in Educational Research and National Development* (Vol. 1) Onitsha, Summer Educational Publishers Limited.

American Psychological Association (2001). *Publication Manual of the American Psychological Association* (5th ed.). Washington, D.C.: Author.

American Psychological Association (2009). *Publication Manual of the American Psychological Association* (6th ed.). Washington, D.C.: Author.

Bem, D. (1987), Writing the empirical journal article. In Zanna, M.P., and Darley, J.M. (Eds.), The Complete Academic: A practical guide for the beginning social scientist (171-204). Mahweh, N.J.: Lawrence Earlbaum Associates, Inc.

Best, J.W. (1970). Research in Education. New Jersey: Prentice-Hall Inc.

Gall, M.D., Gall, J.P., and Borg, W.R. (2006). Educational Research: An Introduction (8th ed.). Boston: Allyn & Bacon.

Kothari, C.R. (2006). Research Methodology: Methods and Techniques. India: New Age International Publishers.

Koul, L. (1992). Methodology of Educational Research. India: Vikas Publishing House Pvt Ltd.

Nwana, O.C. (1982). Introduction to Education Research. Ibadan: Heinemann.

SECTION TWO
Planning of Educational Research

15

Researching Pioneer Competency

An Interdisciplinary Perspective

Chhaya Goel and *Devraj Goel*

Introduction

A researcher is one who is fully lost in quest of solutions to the problems round the clock through scientific, systemic, humanistic approach. A pioneer is noblest number one innovator, excellent explorer and creator, all alone in the crowd, twinkles unique in the sky, dives alone in the ocean to seek solutions to the problems of all, fully identifying with the universe and nature, always busy with what, how and why. A pioneer germinates, incubates, innovates, creates and constructs. Developmental challenges demand newness of the theme, as well as, methodology. A pioneer is round the clock lost in sensing, formulating and addressing problems through most innovative, creative, constructive and innovative approaches. The intent of the present paper is mapping the competencies of the pioneers and trying to emulate these to address day to day problems so as to recreate this sphere as a happy, healthy, peaceful residence for all, socially, synergetically. The focus is on addressing many challenges such as, dementia patients, heart and brain, entrainment problems, right to education problems, environmental education problems, and wholistic education problems. There is no space, no spot, no dot in the Universe which is *problem independent*, even, vacuum is an problem. But, with every problem simple or complex there is a solution.

The present chapter attempts to focus on pioneer competency in these areas with an interdisciplinary perspective.

A. Emerging Problem of Dementia in India

With the changed scenario of giant families to nuclear families in India the problem of dementia has emerged very widely. The elderly people of India are very commonly becoming victims of memory loss, that is, dementia. What is the answer? Which discipline does this problem belong to—Family and Community Studies, Social Work, Medicine, Education, Psychology, Sociology, Economics, Political Science, Architecture? It belongs to all these and many more. Below are presented the case studies of two Indian women.

A Woman of 75 Years

Here is a person, mother of 8 sons and daughters, all grown up well settled adults and aged. None is ready to live with her, except, one. She is suffering from a severe memory loss. For example, after washing, she very often forgets to close the tap. As, a result the over head water tanks become empty. She has not been in a position to attend to it despite daily reminders. As a result the family members have started shouting at her to close the tap. But, no results. Now the question is-Is shouting the solution? Answer is no. Instead, it is significantly damaging, both, the shouters and the shouted at. What is the diagnosis? What is the prognosis for its disposition? The answers of these questions could be:

1. Amelioration of dementia
2. Disconnection of tap
3. Support staff
4. Empathy of the family members
5. Dementia specific social architect
6. Separate abode for the dependent ("ANASHRIT ASHRAM")

A Dementia Patient of 67 Years

A young man, fed up, with the dementia state of his mother, not in a position to cope up with his stress, loads a gun to shoot his mother; controlled by the neighbours. Is that the solution?

The Government of India ought to have Dementia Patient Policy.

B. Falling Heart and Brain Entrainment Ratio in Many Indians

There is a falling heart and brain entrainment ratio in many Indians. It is a highly complex systemic problem. It could be attributed to many a factors, such as, eating habits, disregard of the cultural heritage of India, lack of convergence amongst legislative, executive, judiciary, education and society, lack of life skills. A large majority of us neither know our strength, nor do we know our weakness. Creative thinking and critical thinking, both, in one are rarely found. Neither we are in a position to cope up with stress fully, nor with emotions. Despite the ability we do not exercise choice in time. We are slow in decision making. Hence, we go on inviting problems. We do not enjoy life and living. The heart is always fine-tuning its dopamine/adrenaline balance. Both adrenaline and dopamine affect the heart. Every microsecond, in response to thoughts and to internal and external sensory perceptions, the heart is moving slightly more towards one nerve set and its neurotransmitter or towards the other. The degree and manner of heart wave resonance with thoughts and with internal and external sensory perception determines the moment to moment balance between adrenaline and dopamine. If the heart is more resonant, the neurotransmitter balance shifts more towards dopamine. If the heart is less resonant or emotionally shut down, the neurotransmitter blend shifts more towards adrenaline.

The ratio of adrenaline to dopamine at any given second determines how the brain will interpret the incoming sensory information at that moment, and the manner in which the brain will respond. Up until now, we have only mentioned dopamine as a paired neurotransmitter with adrenaline. In fact, dopamine is not just the "opposite" of adrenaline. Dopamine is the main driver of the heart. If the brain perceives a reason to be fearful, the heart's dopamine triggers adrenaline and a tilt towards the sympathetic nervous system's connection to the brain. If the brain is not fearful, the heart's basic dopamine supply triggers more dopamine and a tilt towards the parasympathetic nervous system's connection to the brain. Dopamine is the primary activator of the heart. Dopamine levels in the heart determine the vigour of the neural signals to the brain. Dopamine levels in the heart are determined by the amount of joy and the amount of resonance that the heart is feeling. The sheer joy of being alive is the energy that allows the heart to resonate and initiate the primary dopamine release for the heart. Dopamine does not cause joy. Joy causes the release of dopamine. The greater the joy, the greater the level of primary dopamine in the heart. Whether a person is happy or sad, he can always resonate with the sheer joy of being alive. Whether a person is in the midst of battle or in solitude, the sheer joy of living can be present behind his fear or his tranquility. Joy and the heart's ability to resonate are very nearly the same. The former is more purely energetic, the other is the more physical manifestation of the joy energy.

Just like light, which has a wave pattern and a photon, human joy has a purely vibratory component and a more tangible component. Just as the astral form of light does not require a photon, the vibratory component of joy exists whether the body exists or not. For example, light has two components: the light "wave" and the photon. The wave and the photon are considered to be equal and simultaneous, in terms of energy, but the photon is the denser, more tangible, more "crude" half of the combo. Like light's relatively more tangible half, the photon, the electromagnetic wave of the resonating heart is the denser, more crude, more tangible component of joy. When the heart is resonating with the joy of being alive, it releases dopamine to itself. That dopamine then energizes the other heart responses. This underlying source of dopamine is what powers the heart's balancing act between the dopamine and adrenaline that flows to the brain. The core dopamine in the heart drives the dopamine and adrenaline systems in the rest of the body. The dopamine stashes in the head, in the substantial area and other parts of the brain, are merely satellite supplies of dopamine. They are activated and dopamine is released into various parts of the brain, when the heart instructs the brain to respond to sensory events with joy. The core level of dopamine prepares a person, in body and brain, to be a feeling, sentient being.

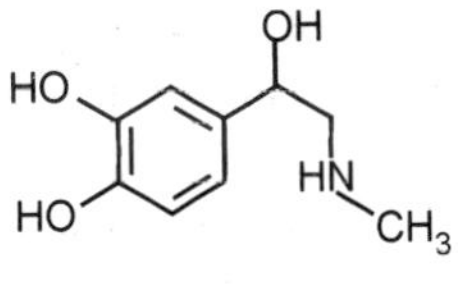

Adrenaline

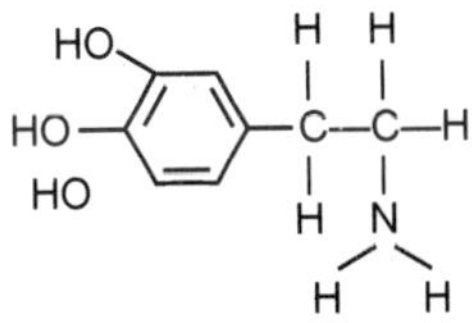

Dopamine

We should be in a position to sustain the equation of adrenalin and dopamine. There is a need to train thinking.

C. Right to Education

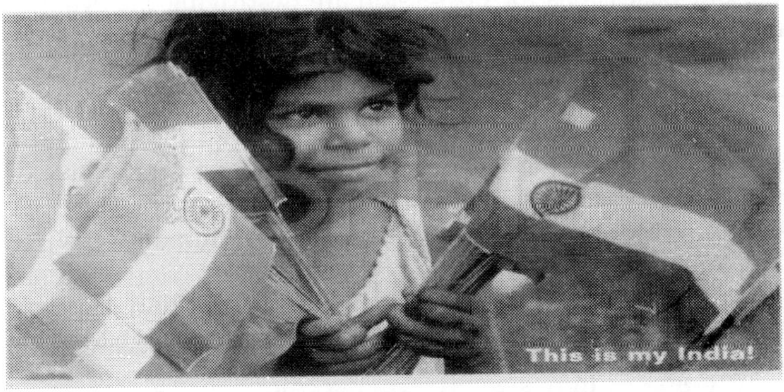

Fig. 15.1

Here is a daughter-the pride of India selling Indian flags. Where is Her Home? Who are Her Parents? Which School does She Study? From where she brings these Flags of India? For what purpose did she bring these Flags? Why is she holding these Flags? What flows through these Flags? How is she holding these Flags? How do we read the configuration of Her Face-Her Eyes, Her Hair, Her Ear Rings, Her Smile, Her Vision?

How about the UNO Convention on the Rights of Children? How about the Indian Constitutional Right to Education (RTE)? How about the KANYA KELVANI of Gujarat? How about the Maharaja Sayajirao Vision of Girl's Education? What is the Perceptions of Parents of their Girl Child? How about the Corporate Social Responsibility? How about the role of the Entire Universe?

Have the Legislative, Executive, Judiciary, Society, Polity, Education sincerely thought about why the state of many a girls is so miserable in India? Why are girls perceived as objects, rather than embodiments of all the values and virtues and the soul for the genesis of human life? For realizing civilization and humanization, we ought to understand the bipolarity—Positive and Negative, High and Low, Hills and Valleys, PURUSH and PRAKRTI. How to make the masses understand the bipolarity of Nature? Bipolarity is essentially the basis for genesis of life and living in this universe and sustainable development. It is not difficult to research the misperceptions of the beauties of nature. Beauties of nature need to be respected and appreciated. But, our obsessions for possession are destroying the beauties and bliss of the nature. Could we realize detached love for the nature through unconditional love for all the entities? Instead we have started treating the nature as a resource rather than adoring Thee as Source. Resource is endowed by the nature. Usage of resource has been presumed to be the prerogative of man. Man likes to be treated as a Source than Resource. The Apex Administrator of India is the Ministry of Human Resource Development.

Let, each one of us, determine to own a Girl Child. Here are some of the Proposed Actions by Young Indians, through Massive Action Research.

- I will adapt her as my daughter.
- I will purchase all the flags she is holding.
- I will make her realize the vision of human life.
- I will find some suitable children's home for her.
- I will support her economically, as much, as I can.
- I will seek help from NGOs for her.
- I will open educational classes for such children, free of cost.
- I will seek admission for her in a school and support her education.
- I will make her energetic, full of momentum, with vision and action.
- I will make her self-supportive.
- I will make her realize her childhood.
- I will educate the State to Revise Policies for Children.

Let us understand Bipolarity. Let us own our children Daughter or Son, Son or Daughter. Let us adore the Mother Nature as Source and abstain from exploiting Her, abusing Her, as Resource. Let us Learn to Respect the Preamble of the Indian Constitution:

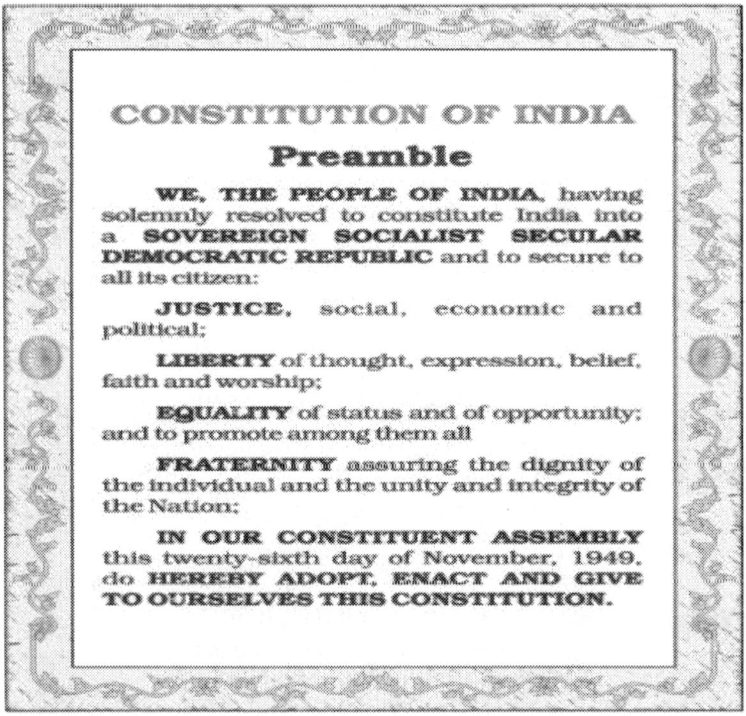

CONSTITUTION OF INDIA

Preamble

WE, THE PEOPLE OF INDIA, having solemnly resolved to constitute India into a **SOVEREIGN SOCIALIST SECULAR DEMOCRATIC REPUBLIC** and to secure to all its citizen:

JUSTICE, social, economic and political;

LIBERTY of thought, expression, belief, faith and worship;

EQUALITY of status and of opportunity; and to promote among them all

FRATERNITY assuring the dignity of the individual and the unity and integrity of the Nation;

IN OUR CONSTITUENT ASSEMBLY this twenty-sixth day of November, 1949, do **HEREBY ADOPT, ENACT AND GIVE TO OURSELVES THIS CONSTITUTION.**

Fig 15.2

D. Environmental Education

We have been found to be wanting in the areas of environmental awareness. A large majority of us are not in a position to respond correctly, whether landfills are designed to help biodegradable waste decompose quickly, whether 'green' washing powder is an alternative to conventional power, whether expanded poly styrene and poly propylene are recyclable, whether more than 50 million of Bangladeshis are exposed to excessive arsenic in their drinking water, which are the green house gases, whether it takes more than 1 million years for a plastic plate to decompose, whether acid rain causes most problems in Australia and California, which is the most beautiful, cleanest, greenest planned city in India and which one is the most polluted, how once common sparrows are now harder to see, how honey bees are disappearing the world over, how fast food contributes to ill health, which are the endangered species, which substances are more eco friendly, what is global warming due to. It seems inspite of environmental education as a special area in Teacher Education, it has neither led to the development of environmental awareness, nor environmental ethics. Even in the 21st century post graduate students with science background do not know the structures of many a polymers, such as, expanded polystyrene, polypropylene, poly-ethylene, poly vinayl chloride.

a. Expanded Polystyrene

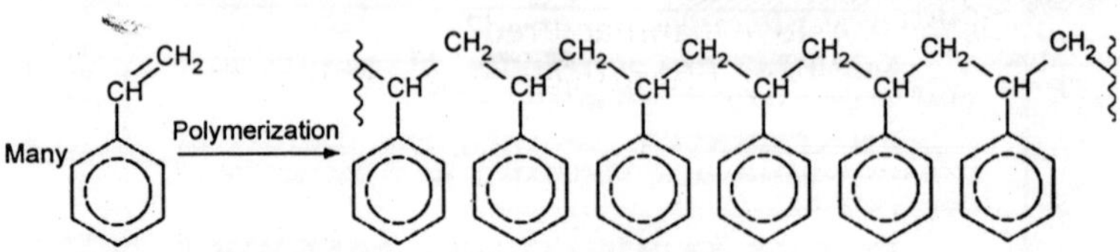

b. Polypropylene

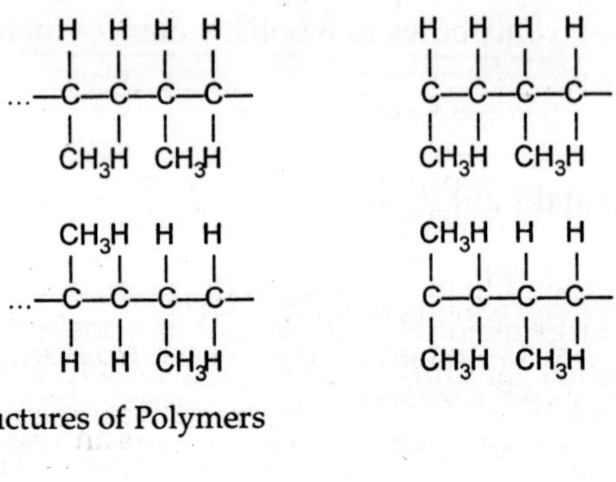

Fig. 15.3: Structures of Polymers

E. Wholistic Education

Wholistic approach demands development of a complete human being where ideas spring, feelings flow, motor creates, spirit reins, and the self resonates with the self and the environment.

For example:

a. Tea Preparation

Why do we prepare tea and how do we prepare tea?
Where are the tea gardens?
Where has the tea originated from?
Is it native or non-native?
If non-native, who introduced tea to India?
What is the chemical composition of tea leaves?
Which pan do we make use of while preparing tea?
What is the origin of the LPG which we make use of for tea preparation?
How is the gas stove manufactured?
Why is water very often used as a medium for tea preparation?
Why do we add milk and sugar?
Why do we add basil, black pepper and ginger?
What is final composition of the prepared tea?
How long should we extract tea leaves?
How should we serve tea?
How much and how frequently should we take tea?
How does tea contributes to wholistic development?

b. Production and Lighting of Crackers

Let us take up an example of production and cracking of a Diwali cracker, namely, the multi-colour fountain (ANAR):

What are the ingredients of an ANAR?
Where are these ingredients are procured from and how?
What is the ANAR container?
What are the determinants of multi-colours and height of the fountain?
Which chemical reactions take place when we light the ANAR?

After the ANAR is lighted how do the evolving gases interact with the environment?
What are the probable effects of lighting an ANAR?
What are the chemistry, physics, mathematics, economics, environmental science and sociology of ANAR?
Is it joyful, harmful, or joyfully harmful?
What is the status of child labourers who work in factory of crackers?

Concluding Remarks

Developmental challenges demand pioneers with interdisciplinary competencies. How long will we compromise with the fragmented research? Should not it be wholistic related to the ground realities, which are, very often, rather always, multi-parametric?

Should not the research be collective and collaborative: Formal-Informal-Non-Formal?

Why have scientists not come out of their laboratories? Is not there a need to conduct naturalistic situational research through deep observation, reflection and intuition and construct grass root theories, addressing our problems, through our tools, through our sources and resources, to better our quality of life and living?

16

Planning Researcher Competency

Mapping and Management in Education

R.S. Mani

Introduction

Educational research in India in the modern sense of the term started in the year 1954-1955. The Second National Seminar on Teacher Education held in The M.S. University of Baroda, Vadodara helped the broader envisioning of education from 'training' to 'education'. There is a big corpus of the research in education created in the past sixty years. The number of doctoral theses submitted with degree awarded has crossed ten thousand. This in quantitative terms is a growth that needs to be properly analyzed for its benefits for the development of education in terms of quality. There are six national surveys in education produced by CASE (first and second), NCERT, New Delhi that enlists the research at doctoral level and project level in the country. The graphic description and analysis of the trends of research is a direction that education is taking for growth. The number of research studies in philosophy of education, history of education, economics of education are very few in comparison to other areas of knowledge. This trend has developed due to the lack of appropriate environment and encouragement for philosophical work. INTEL along with Goel, D.R. *et al.* have developed a web site that provides the details of research at doctoral and project level in e-form. All the surveys have focused on the abstracts of the studies and trend analysis. They have also earnestly asked relevant questions for the researchers in education and policy makers to make the educational research more relevant and appropriate to school and college teaching. The innovations carried out in research in education has been in a way work in simulation with less practice or testing conditions. There are fewer studies that have focused on implementation of their strategies in the school or college and testing for its effectiveness for continuing as a sustained innovation in practice. Many a research study is satisfied with development and trying out of the strategy and testing in the school or college for the period of study.

The replications of the studies were found between the years 1960 to 1980 at CASE in teacher education in large number. This trend of research well established an innovation such as micro teaching, Flanders interaction analysis in teacher training colleges in India. The behaviour modification techniques were applied for behaviour correction, studying teacher behaviour patterns, feedback and evaluation. CASE, The M. S. University of Baroda, Vadodara developed four monographs in select areas of research such as Educational Technology, Teacher Education, Innovative practices and Motivation and Educational Administration (1960 to 1980).

CASE, The Department of Education, Faculty of Education and Psychology, The M. S. University of Baroda, Vadodara diversified its PhD study areas since 1980's to 2000 A.D. in areas such as teacher education, educational technology, environmental education, educational psychology, educational administration, etc,. However, the thrust areas that sustained research in the institution in this period and another decade (i.e., 2010) was teacher education and educational technology (computer education), language education, science education, education for disabilities was identified as a new area to be more inclusive in approach. The efforts to integrate the science and technology or the research in education with the technology has been more observed as a separate unit of knowledge than a integral knowledge that leads to interdisciplinary areas, questions and methodology. The research in terms of quantitative outcome has increased over years in education. But, the quality in educational research from the point of relevance to the regular classroom practice or improving some quality component in the school is less found. The two major areas of national concern in research have been elementary education and higher education. It could be observed that elementary education has shown more progress in terms of quantitative growth. There is significant enrolment (around 80% by the year 2008-2009) and further it shows a growth of one per cent per year. Retention has also shown some progress. The transition rate from primary level to upper primary, upper primary to high school, high school to higher secondary school and higher secondary school to higher education has shown a steady increase resulting in around seventy per cent students continuing studies up to higher secondary and further in the higher education. This trend has set a standard that makes the teachers concerned about the quality of teachers needed at different levels of school education and higher education.

Capacities of Research Scholars and the Needed Induction Programme

Research scholars in education have been filling positions at all levels based on their background and interest. Research scholars are also identified for teaching at teacher education institutions at the higher secondary/diploma level, college or higher education level. The basic question is that researchers are supposed to fulfil the requisite qualification at the appropriate level with certain experience that may be desirable (school teaching experience, working in the science laboratory, research programmes (projects), computer education). Due to the expansion that is taking place at all levels there is a need to provide the necessary inputs for quality at each of the levels of entry. Induction programmes will improve the status of research scholars and programmes are better than the general approach of fitting to the scale and scheme.

Identification of Research Talent at the Early Stage

The identification of the research talent at the early stage will facilitate better cadre development in research and improve quality. The total pool of researchers possible at the current stage of development is around 1.8 per cent of the population. In this, there is a need to identify scholars through testing such as National Talent Search Examination, Kishore Vigyan Protsahan Yojana, UGC

NET examination, lecturership examination etc. IGNOU, New Delhi in the year 1987 tried to select lecturers to their organization through a written test. But, it was found that this measure may not help.

Network for Research Scholars

A network for research scholars at present is non-existent. There is an attempt to start one for science scholars at http://www.ernet.com. It is being constructed for IIT, IISc, social media networking needs to be exploited for research purposes. Research scholars are not given adequate training in these aspects. Scholars are not aware as to how to use the net in a more meaningful and sustained way for message delivery and projection of estimates in a more scientific way. Some attempts have been made to create a research forum in a research institution. Research scholars at CASE had a network as a research forum for around five years (1996-2001). A project member created it and successfully tried it with researchers and later that member had to leave for Canada for gainful employment. Two years back a research scholar at CASE tried to upload all the seminar presentations at the M.Ed level in the Google network. All the M.Ed students could co-operate in this adventure and it was a successful presentation in e-mode.

CASE developed an e-journal with the name Spectrum to highlight the developments in research at CASE with the help of the UGC SAP funding. This feature encouraged the scholars to observe the progress in a wholistic way. There are a few research journals in print available in India such as:

- Edusearch
- Indian Educational Review (available in e-form and print), NCERT, New Delhi
- Resonance-Journal of Science Education (available in e-form and print), Bengaluru.

There is a need for a database for research scholars such as disciplinary-domain specific, interdisciplinary domains, multidisciplinary domains and frontier areas of knowledge in education and other disciplines. For example, an association of scholars teaching and learning English, Indian languages. A language survey being completed by Devi and *et al.*, Volume I Vadodara, 2014, has made an effort to map territory with language and culture related to language and scholars of language. The area of coverage has helped systematically to plan for language education, research and training.

Facility for Teleconferencing for Scholars

Scholars in various areas such as medicine, surgery, architecture, Structural Engineering, Educational Technology, Management, Economic Planning (Economists), Technologists etc. could meaningfully utilize teleconferencing facility with m-technology and VVIOP technology of BSNL available at Vadodara.

Similar attempts could be made in different regions of the country with the help of the EDUSAT.IGNOU, New Delhi will be a great beneficiary of this technology since it needs to plan for the future to cover hilly areas, remote areas, tribal belts and inaccessible places such as Ladakh. Scholars need to be trained for organizing and participating in teleconferencing. BISAG, Ahmedabad has already tried in the local area network to teach certain subjects such as Economics. A few higher secondary teachers are trained to deliver lectures in different subjects for example, Vadodara. (G.E.B. School, Vadodara). The interactive teleteaching-learning experiment inaugurated by the past President Dr. A.P.J. Abdul Kalam in Kerala is a success in interactive learning. An experiment conducted in Madhya Pradesh to telecast programmes from the EDUSAT and find its correlation to the achievement of students at primary level was also a success. Interactive teleteaching and learning could extend to many places through the existing smart class facilities in schools. Many of the teachers and research scholars are not trained to use smart classroom facility. There is a need for a structured programme for training of research scholars in teaching and learning in smart classrooms. Further, there is a need to research effects and variables that determine success of the smart classroom. Schools have become more optimistic and experiment oriented.

Research Scholars from SC/ST Background Need to be Protected and Promoted

UGC, New Delhi and other funding agencies are providing some scholarships to SC/ST students. They need to support further their various educational and social needs through a corpus developed by them. A certain contribution could be drawn from their community to fund such important work. It is research that determines the quality of higher education and quality of life.

Higher Education: The Search for Stability and Sustenance

There are nearly 634 university level institutions with around 36,000 colleges in India. This accounts for a good quantitative expansion. However, it accounts for 19 per cent of the student population of the age group that needs higher education. The expansion is 20 fold in university level institutions and 46 fold increase in colleges since the time of independence. It is interesting to note that the transition of students from higher secondary to higher education level is going up to almost 68 per cent in 2009 from 62 per cent in 2007 (Bora, A. 2014).

The RUSA (Rashtriya Uchcahtar Siksha Abhiyan) has become real and state universities are observing higher admissions and retention. A reasonably good percentage of students in various areas show migration to other countries in areas such as pharmacy, electronics, electrical engineering, molecular biology, medicine, management and other professional service areas. Most of these students go for post-graduate studies or doctoral studies in their respective areas. The reason for the migration is sighted as the opportunity to work in a better work environment and institutions with better facilities. The ranking of the universities in India has gone down in the world order. National Association of Software and Services Companies (NASSCOM) and McKinsey (2005) revealed that not more than 15 per cent of general graduates and 25-30 per cent of technical graduates in the country were at all worth employing (Mishra, *et al.* 2008). Liberalization, Privatization and Globalization (LPG) has opened the door for entrepreneurship, advanced studies and working with industries in the network for value addition.

Research in Educationally Backward Districts

The Educationally Backward Districts (EBDs) numbered 374 out of about 650 districts in the country with various major disparities. There are a few districts not having a single college (for example, Narmada district). Some of the districts have a few colleges in semi-urban and urban areas. Metropolitan areas have nearly 100 institutions in one district. A wide disparity exists in terms of geographical regions, gender, socio-economic and socio-religious groups among others. "In almost half of the districts in the country, higher education enrolments are abysmally low, almost two-third of our universities and 90 per cent of our colleges are rated as below average on quality parameters (Prime Minister Manmohan Singh, 2013)". This calls for a quality paradigm at the national level for the improvement of research. U.G.C., New Delhi may have a policy of promotion of the establishment of colleges on priority basis in the educationally backward districts. Research scholars coming from educationally backward districts may be placed in good institutions of higher learning to bring the fruits of development and modernization to the educationally backward districts. Research on the educationally backward districts needs to be encouraged. Educationally backward districts are mostly in the rural areas. These identified rural areas need to be developed with facilitative planning, progressive measures of inputs, continuous monitoring and evaluation to sustain development. The skill development programmes in these areas need to be placed and promoted on a priority basis.

Research and Open and Distance Education as an Alternative

It includes correspondence, online and study centres and at present have more than 4.2 million students on their rolls (FICCI, 2012) compared to 22 million in the conventional system. The ICT has to be protected and promoted in the conventional and distance learning institutions. There is a need to utilize the ICT providers available around the institution. There are around 160 internet service providers. Total broadband connection subscriber base in the country had increased to 15.01 million by January 2013 (Frontline, 2013). The encouraging trend is the transition of students from higher secondary to higher education level going up to almost 68 per cent in 2009 from 62 per cent in 2007. This favourable trend may create a research group as a thinly spread population in the country.

National Initiatives

MHRD, New Delhi launched the National Mission on Education through ICT (NME-ICT) for providing enhanced connectivity, content and access devices to higher education institutions. Under this initiative, about 400 universities and more than 18,000 colleges were provided with broad band connectivity. Selected high schools are provided with internet connectivity and technical education in Assam and most of the engineering colleges are also connected for providing engineering education, in-service education, and communication for faster development. Vishveshvaraiya Technology University, Belgaum has started an E-learning centre at an engineering college in Mysore to connect almost all the engineering colleges in Karnataka. The Government of Karnataka has been supporting this initiative. The EDUSAT satellite is supporting this initiative. Engineering students and educational technology researchers need to be properly nurtured from the beginning for this venture.

Virtual Reality Laboratories Need to be Promoted for Research

Government of Gujarat, Gandhinagar has started e-content development under an e-knowledge consortium. This has helped teachers and researchers in universities to use internet tools and develop e-courses for the improvement of higher education. Government of India, New Delhi has started the Inter-university Consortium for Teacher Education. This will provide more channeis for communication for teacher education and development of education.

There are efforts made to develop and launch e-courses, for example, massively online open courses (MOOC). Adult education programmes have also taken up the initiatives in offering short term technology courses that leads to awareness creation.

The big problem in the country has been that there is a craze for starting academic programmes scholars with fewer available with interdisciplinary knowledge and adequate skills in technology to create, develop, design, teach and provide facilities for interaction, evaluate and monitor programmes. There is a need to selectively create a group of scholars to take up policy issues and development in areas of technology in general and application of technology in social sciences.

Centres capable of growth could be identified and promoted on selective basis for upgradation of skills in technology so that websites being created, around 200 in numbers by IGNOU, New Delhi may be managed properly. The NCERT, New Delhi has already created around 103 websites throughout the country. These need to be properly managed by scholars from NCERT, appropriately trained for the purpose. The programmes have become almost functional.

The EDUSAT is going to cover major hospitals and research centres in medicine in India. Medical practitioners and researchers need to be properly trained for this purpose. The interdisciplinary research personnel available for example, from the Faculty of Social work, Department of Psychology, Department of Education, Faculty of Technology, Faculty of Home Science etc., need to be augmented for the training and research for the proper maintenance of the websites and service programmes in the related areas in the selected geographical areas. National University for Educational Planning and Administration, New Delhi, Delhi University, Jawaharlal Nehru University, NCERT, New Delhi need to be involved in the EDUSAT operations to observe more effectiveness. National research institutions need to be properly equipped with facilities for EDUSAT programmers' large cadre of technology literate, trained personnel and some specialized personnel with research knowledge and experience are needed for managing a huge national service of EDUSAT throughout the country.

Management of Research at Ph.D. and Project Level

U.G.C., New Delhi has made efforts to streamline the procedures for becoming research guides at post-graduate level. It has given clear guidelines for the purpose. It has been generally followed in the post graduate departments in the universities in India. The problem may lie in the post graduate guides in the colleges. The post-graduate centres need to be strengthened after proper evaluation. The research guides need to be properly strengthened for more productive purposes of research. Research funding agencies have fixed definite criteria for research.

One area in which many of the research guides in social sciences need proper training is computer education and its application in research for statistical purposes. There is need for use of internet for communication, data transfer, high speed data usage, downloading from the satellite and uploading to satellite.

Management of Research

There are certain strategies and measures that will help the management of research in India. Some of the strategies and measures are suggested to strengthen the research base in India:

- There is a network needed for the research scholars to communicate, correspond and interact on a continuing basis for raising questions, answering relevant questions of development, and discussing issues of development in contemporary terms.
- Quality Cells: These need to be created in each university that promises research. The institutions that show the interest and ability to perform research need to be protected, promoted and nurtured for further focused development of education.
- There is a need to facilitate women research scholars, for flexible entry and due promotion for their development.
- There is a need for the development of database of research scholars and research guides in education and other areas of knowledge for easy access, more interaction and better approach to research.
- Research scholars need to be familiarized with the web portal in education. Department of Education, Government of Gujarat, Gandhinagar has developed a web portal in education (higher education). It is developing a database for school education.
- There is a need for better peer-reviewed journals in education that could be accepted on the national and international levels. The existing journals are not sufficient

to take the load of work—editing, printing, publishing, reviewing.

- The Erasmus Mundus programmes in universities have helped the scholars to move abroad and learn a few skills better and gain some more knowledge in their interest area. However, the personal cost of the researcher has gradually increased. There is a need for some subsidy from government or university for better sustenance.
- The Senior scholars need to be sent abroad for a short term programme to visit laboratories, undergo some skill training, participate in conferences to gain more experience (the duration may be six to nine months). They may be allowed to work in a foreign university for one year to gain a feel of the new environment. It may have better impact on the Indian academic environment.

Some Experiments

- Research scholars in science, engineering, education need to be given some industrial exposure of up to six to nine months. They could be placed with a mentor in the industry. Scholars will be able to learn some application of skills and knowledge and understand the limitations of theoretical understanding in university studies. The Birla Institute is already providing such training and it is called inhouse school training for management and engineering students. A few management and engineering graduates were employed in industries in Gwalior for their induction training. It was observed that they imbibed better skills and gained knowledge in their areas.
- There need to be some place allocated in the university or college for experimenting with new knowledge and skills. Similar to the experience of Cambridge University and London.
- The Department of Educational Technology, Smt. S.N.D.T. Women's University, Mumbai started a M.Sc. programme of two years duration integrating education at master's level with software engineering with inhouse practicing experience in industries for six monthes. The NCTE (WRC), Bhopal did not approve of it. However, the

students who had undergone those courses were gainfully employed in India and abroad. In this sense, the students were more successful. The M.Sc programme was more useful.

- Research scholars at CASE have as a regular programme a research methodology course and they are evaluated. The presentation by the scholar on review of related studies and the conceptual scheme is evaluated by a committee of staff including the research guide.
- Research scholars are oriented to the new technologies in computer science as applied to education. For example, workshops are held for the application of SPSS package to education in Centre for Social Studies, Surat (ICSSR, New Delhi funded), workshops are held for scholars to discuss and acquaint the methodology of research report writing, reviewing and discussing and debating educational issues and problems (funded by NCERT, New Delhi in collaboration with CASE organized the programme).
- National Research Meets are organized every year or some-times alternate year to meet the research scholars to analyze the research problem, discuss the methodology allow for sharing, provide the guidance and counseling, and think of better methodology for the research problem. CASE has already organized two national researchers meets and it has been appreciated among scholars.
- Research scholars gain knowledge and experience in organizing the national seminars at CASE every year by helping in organization, participating by presenting papers, discussing, and publishing in books or journals for dissemination. This experience has helped them to understand the current issues and problems in research. The research guides have helped the scholars by becoming the second author, editing the paper and facilitating the publication of the paper in journals or books.
- Research scholars at CASE are getting the opportunity sometimes to work in a research project other than their doctoral work and gain more experience in the field. This has helped them to come out of their finer specialization for example, a research scholar in the area of special

education gains knowledge by working in another project on the curriculum development in schools.

- The M.Ed. Programme at CASE, has modified the M.Ed. programme (in the year 2014) including more features of research into the programme, to prepare for them for research and train them in thinking such as review of research studies, Internship in school, analyzing the trend report of studies, writing a research proposal and presenting it systematically in the seminar for better participation.
- Most of the M.Ed students have been helping the organization in organizing the national seminars at CASE, some participate in presentation, discussion and write the report as reporteurs of seminar. This has become a regular feature of the institution. Students have gained more knowledge and experience in the process to build confidence in them, consult research and guidance and develop relationships of academic nature.

Some Needed Initiatives

- Research scholars need to be given some teaching experience in the classroom on an experimental basis. One period per week in their area of research for one semester. This experience would give them the ability to perceive the needs of students and their area in a more focused way.
- Research scholars could teach a period a week with a senior teacher in an area other than their research work for a month to gain an insight into the classroom and its problems and issues of concern.
- Research scholars could organize themselves into a small group and provide some service on demand on call basis for a nominal charge for example, computer education scholars could attend to the computer hardware problems along with a professional personnel or problems of software, printer. Setting up a laboratory, planning a laboratory session, etc,. This experience would give them the needed practical experience, novice ideas of others and planning specific programmes for objective oriented solutions.

- Research students in computer education need to be exposed to the movie maker in the WORD 2010, other new software such as 2013 or 2014 software. The PowerPoint developed could be converted into video clips. A few scholars have already obtained experience in these aspects. It has been appreciated by scholars for creating more visualization.
- Research scholars could be trained in script writing for organizing a debate or discussion on important issues of development, for example, women's problems, protection of human rights, problem of enrolment in elementary level, retention, drop out and environmental problems, programmes of the state and central governments for the promotion of education among the students and teachers and public, prevention of diseases such as AIDS, Dengue, Rota virus etc.
- Some technology areas of concern such as stage setting, studio making, programme editing, programming, video shooting, editing, interactive methodologies of teaching and learning are to be learnt by research scholars and this experience would help them to participate in the national missions on education and development.
- Some scholars could be provided some short-term training in emergency care in health. It helps them to rise to the occasion in the case of an emergency. Scholars from population science, science, health science, biological science, home science, social work, psychology, etc., could be involved in the care of the psychological treatment and care on a voluntary basis. They may be involved in rehabilitation of these people.
- Some research scholars with medical or psychology background may be provided specific training in hypnotherapy to support the activities concerning the hypnotherapy. Majority of the scholars do not know about the administering of drugs for getting the patient into a hypnotic state.
- Preparation of psychological tests, standardising the test, are some of the activities that may be preferentially promoted.
- Online learning, distance education course production,

testing, and discussion may be the other areas that need more exploration. Personal resources in terms of mobile technology, internet, or the societal facilities such as kisoks may be hired or contracted for use for education for example, http://www.science@mobile.com uses SMS for sending concepts, asking questions and spreading science education in mobility and in the station.

Management of research is a difficult task. The multifarious tasks and time schedules makes multi-tasking more difficult. However, strategic planning and guided decentralization may be able to give results in increasing the efficiency and effectiveness. Online monitoring may be another solution to the management of the scholars.

References

Bora, A. Higher education in India: In search of a solution to issues of equity, inclusive education, quality, globalization, sustainable educational services, University News, 52(08), Feb24-March 02, 2014, 23-24.

Federation of Indian Chamber of Commerce and Industry (FICCI) Higher Education Summit, 2012 Report, Higher Education in India: Twelfth Five Year Plan (2012-2017) and beyond.

Mishra, J.K., Abidi, N and Sharma, R. (2008) Indian Higher Education: global challenges and local isssues, JBS working paper series No. JIITU/JBS/2008/01.

NUEPA (2010) National report on status of education in India, Delhi: NUEPA.

Pathania, K.S. and Pathak, A., Reforms in Ph.D. research work: The new dimensions in higher education, University News, 52(08), Feb 24-March 02, 2014, 7-11.

Rashtryiya Uchchatar Shiksha Abhiyan (RUSA): National Higher Education Mission I, University News, Special Issues, 51(28), July 15-21, 2013.

17

Researcher Competency: A View on Mapping and Management

L.B. Patted and *Nataraj B. Patted*

Introduction

Research is a systematic attempt to provide answers to questions. Such answers may be abstract and general as is often the case in basic research or they may be highly concrete and specific as is often the case in demonstration or applied research. In both kinds of research, the researcher uncovers the facts and then formulates a generalization based on the interpretation of those facts.

Educational research refers to a process wherein activity(ies) is/are carried out systematically to find a solution of the problem related to any aspect of education. Educational research should be planned so that it will be more effective and enables the researcher to go in-depth and find solutions. This necessarily require developing research attitudes among young researchers

Strategies for the Development of Research Attitudes

- Electrify our research capacity.
- Formulating professional learning communities.
- Establish the nature of research and innovation leadership ethics and integrity.
- Establish Research Development Centre at higher education institutes and universities.

- Create an environment for the flourishing and blooming of new ideas.
- Reward for published work.
- Train and mentor a new cohort of young researchers.
- Provide funding for publication of research papers.
- Assure our long term comprehensiveness with other countries.
- Increase innovation consciousness and alertness.
- Acknówledge and manage our research talent.
- Reach to un-reached.
- Produce ground breaking research across all colleges.
- Disseminate research and inform policy.
- Address the needs and aspirations of researchers.

The researcher must be acquainted with different dimensions of the research, so as to complete the research work successfully.

The Dimensions of Research

Selecting a Problem and Constructing of Hypotheses

Selecting a problem is one of the most important steps for a researcher in the research process, it is unfortunately one for which the least guidance is given. The researcher has to select a problem relevant to his/her areas of study and of particular interest in it. Researcher can identify a research topic by going to many sources, such as theories.

- A theory is an organized body of concept, generalizations and principle that may be investigated. For example, theories of learning and behaviour can provide the inspiration for many problems. Jean Piaget's three stages of children's thinking and development (The Sensory-motor stage, Pre-operational stage, Concrete operational stage and Formal operational stage). A researcher may explore factors that may affect the length of time children take to pass from one stage to next.
- The personal experiences such as daily classroom life and effects of teaching practices on students outcomes-the starting place for action research.

- The source of research topic is previously published studies many of which can be replicated. A replication is a repetition of a study using different subjects to re-test its hypothesis.
- Another commonly cited source for research topic is library research.
- Electronic mail lists: Through these lists, we can expect to receive announcements related to our area of interest.
- The modern (21st century) sources of research topics are digital research tools such as Face Book, Twitter, Blogs etc

The researcher can state his/her problem of study clearly and unambiguously, usually in question form. For example, is there a relationship between racial background and drop-out rate?

Formulating Hypotheses

A hypotheses is a suggested answer to the problem, to be stated clearly and unambiguously in the form of declarative sentence. For example, I.Q. and achievement are positively related. The drop-out rate is higher for black students than for white students.

The hypotheses may be inductive, deductive, non-directional, directional and null based on our design of study. Hypotheses are closely related to the objectives of the study also.

Reviewing Literature

The purpose of review is to expand upon the context and background of the study, to help further define the problem to provide an empirical basis for the subsequent development of hypotheses. The review of literature is seen as a necessary evil to be completed as fast as possible, so that one can get on with the real research. This is an important component of the process.

The review of literature involves systematic identification, location and analysis of a research problem. The reviews include articles, abstracts, monographs dissertations, books, and other research papers and media effort.

The purpose of review

- The major purpose of reviewing literature is to determine

what has already been done that relates to our topic. It gives understanding and insight into the study.

- Researcher needs to place his/her topic within logical framework.
- Previous studies which can provide the rational for our research hypothesis and indications of what needs to be done which can help us to justify the significance of our study.
- The review of literature helps the researcher to discover research strategies and specific data collection approaches that have or have not been productive in investigation of topics similar to our study. This information will help the researcher to avoid mistakes and profit from their experience.
- It may suggest to the researcher approaches and procedures that the researcher previously had not considered.
- The acquaintance of previous research also facilitates in the interpretation of researcher results. The result of the study can be discussed in term of to what extent they agree with the previous findings. Researcher can describe the difference between his study and others, providing rational for the discrepancy.

The Review for Research are:

- International encyclopedia of education.
- Encyclopedia of curriculum study.
- Handbook of Research on Teacher Education.
- Handbook of Research on the Education of young children.
- Handbook of Research practices and outcomes on E-learning: issues and trends.
- Handbook of Research on the Education of school leaders.
- Handbook of Education Policy Research.
- Handbook of Education Finance and Policy.
- Handbook of Research on School, Schooling and Human Development.
- Handbook of Research and new media literacy.
- International Dissertation Abstracts etc.

The primary sources of reviews contains original documents. For example: research reports, dissertations, experiments, surveys, conference proceedings, letters and interviews etc.

A secondary resources of reviews are educational encyclopedia, hand books etc.

Design of the Study/Research

This part is the most important part of study for the researchers. The researcher gives a detailed plan of a study proposed to investigate a given/taken problem. In this research design, the researcher includes the methodology, sampling procedure and sample, tools of the study, variable of the study, operational terms, the procedure of data collection and statistical techniques to be used for the analyses of collected data. The researcher has to submit the research proposal to a funding agency for approval before actual execution of the research plan. Some researchers have to present it through technological media before the funding agency in an effective manner for approval of undertaking the research work with financial assistance.

Table 17.1: Components of the quantitative research

1. Introduction	2. Method	3. Data Analysis
(a) Need of the study, statement of problem/topic	(a) Participants	4. Time budgeting
(b) Statement of research questions	(b) Instruments	5. Financial budget
(c) Review of related questions	(c) Design	
(d) Statement of hypotheses	(d) Procedure	

A researcher designs the proposal of the research after going through the review of related literature. Investigators formulate the hypothesis, topic statement, questions, operational definitions based on observable criteria and the rest of the research work. In quantitative research, the hypothesis will be the basis for determination of the participant group, measurement instrument, design and statistical technique/tests to be used in the study. In qualitative research, researcher questions will be the basis for gaining entrance to the research context, identifying research participants, spending time in the field, determining how to gather data and interpretation and narration of those data.

Components of the Qualitative Research Plan

A qualitative research plan is a less structured document than a quantitative research plan. The qualitative research is an intimate and open-ended endeavour that must be responsive to the context and setting under study, the plan probably flexible.

Table 17.2: Components of the Qualitative Research Plan

1. **Title of the study**
2. **Introduction to the study**
   (a) The purpose of the study
   (b) Framing the study (theoretical, policy are practical problem)
   (c) Statement of research questions
   (d) Review of related literature
3. **Research procedure**
   (a) Overall approach and rationale for the study
   (b) Site and sample selection
   (c) The researcher's role (entry to the research site, reciprocity and ethics)
   (d) Data collection and method
   (e) Data management strategies
   (f) Data analysis strategies
   (g) Trustworthiness
   (h) Ethical considerations
4. Potential contributions of the research
5. Limitations of the study
   (a) Timeline of the research
   (b) Proposed table of contents of the study
   (c) Content forms, IRB approval
   (d) Samples of structured surveyor questionnaire

Revising and Improving the Research

The adequacy of the research plan can involve both informal and formal assessment. A research plan should be reviewed by at least one skilled researcher and at least one in the areas of investigation.

For the formal assessment of the study, researcher can do the pilot study, a small-scale trial of a study conducted before the full scale study. A research design can be modified as per the results of the pilot study.

The Analysis of Data Results

The data analyses section describes the statistical design that was used and the statistical analyses that were undertaken (statistical tests such as analysis variance, t-test, chi-square analysis, correlation etc). The hypotheses of the study will be tested by statistical tests. Computers are used for the analyses of data.

The results of the study are to be explained with the help of tables, figures and graphs. The best way to structure the results section is in terms of the hypotheses which the study has set out to test.

The discussion section ties the results of the study to both theory and application by putting together the theoretical background, literature reviews, potential significance for application and results of the study. The researcher should be tactful enough to do all these research activities successfully.

Retrospect and Prospect of the Study

In this part of the research, a researcher gives the whole procedure of the study beginning with introduction, need of the study, statement of the problem/topic, objectives of the study, limitations, design of the study, analyses of data, results and discussions, educational implications, conclusion and suggestions for the further studies. The whole gist of the study would have been revealed by this part of the study. The researcher should be competent enough to structure this aspect beautifully and in a meaningful, understandable manner. The competence of presenting the researcher is in a concise, elaborated research work in a beautiful manner.

References and Appendices

The researcher should be grateful to the authors of various books, journals, survey reports, thesis reports, dissertations, dissertation abstracts, web sources etc., which he/she used in relation to the his/her study. The researcher has to list the all the references which have been used in the study. The references are cited in the text by author's surname, year of publication, name of the reference, publication and page number etc., in alphabetical order according to the senior author's surname. This should include all the sources that were cited in the report.

The researcher should list the sample, tools of the study, raw data analysis at the end of the research report of the study.

Preparing the Research Report

The researcher report should be written in a clear, simple, straight forward style that reflects the scholarship of the researcher. Obviously, the report should contain correct spelling, grammatical construction and punctuation. Computer probably has a spelling and grammar checker. It is also a good idea to have some one to review the manuscript and indicate errors.

Format and Style

Format refers to the general pattern of the organization and arrangement of the report. Research reports generally follow a format that parallels the steps involved in conducting a study although formats may vary in terms of which sections are included and how they are titled.

Style refers to the rules of grammar, spelling capitalization and punctuation followed in preparing the report.

The Main Body

The main body report contains an introduction to the topic that also includes the review of related literature and hypotheses, a method of procedure section describing the participants, the instruments and the procedures, a section presenting the results and discussion of the findings. The researcher may also suggest next step studies design to investigate another dimension of the problem. The report should end with reference and appendices.

Conclusion

In conclusion I would like to state that no doubt research is a struggle or endeavour to the researcher to undertake research work and complete it successfully. Each step of the research is a challenging task for the researcher. The researcher must have enough patience to cross each step successfully. The researcher obtains enough knowledge and good experience of conducting the research by undertaking the research work.

References

Gay, L.R., Mills, Geoffrey, E. and Airasian, Peter (2012) 'Educational Research: Competencies for Analyses and Applications', Pearson, pp. 61-64, 71, 79, 82, 111-121.

Sharma, Manoj Kumar (2014), 'Citation—Quality Benchmark for Research Journals', in University News, Vol. 52 (3), January 22-26, p. 57.

Tuckman, Bruce. W. (1972) 'Conducting Educational Research', Harcourt Brace Jovanovich, Inc, New York, pp. 1, 20, 285-295.

Talawar, M.S., Pradeep Kumar, T. and Ponnambaleswari, M. (2011) 'Planning for Effective Educational Research: What should go in to the briefs?' in University News, Vol. 49 (17), April, 25 – May, 01, p. 23.

18

Qualitative Assessment of Research Competency Through Portfolio

Sanjivani R. Mahale and *Minakshi Barve*

Introduction

Yashwantrao Chavan Maharashtra Open University (YCMOU), Nashik is a mega Open University in India. The University has eight schools. Each school has different programmes like Academic, Professional, Vocational and different level of programmes from Certificate to Doctoral degrees. School of Education (SOE) also has different level programmes like SHG, ECCE, B.Ed, M.Ed etc. According to the UGC guidelines the SOE started Masters in Philosophy (M. Phil) programme in Education and Physical Education in the year 2007.

Table 18.1: Structure of the Master in Philosophy (M. Phil) Programme in Education

Sl. No.	*Course Name*	*Assessment*	*Marks*
1.	Research Methodology	External	100
2.	Instructional and Training System Design	External	100
3.	Advance in Education (a course work related to research)	Internal	100
4.	Optional paper (any one) 4.1 Communication modes in Education OR 4.2 Assessment and Evaluation	External External	100
5.	Seminars and Assignment	Internal	100
6.	Research Dissertation and *viva-voce*	External	100

For research component, the University decided to give 100 marks for Advance in Education (a course work related to the research), and 200 marks for Research Dissertation and *viva-voce*. The programme has 40 per cent weightage for research work.

The University identifies 14 study centres throughout Maharashtra recognized as a research centre. The centre having at least four recognized guides having Ph.D degree and approval for post-graduate teaching experience.

The university conducts a three day Counselor and Guide training programme for academic purposes and a Director Coordinator meeting for administrative purposes. The Director and Coordinator have the role of counselor as well as guide. In the Counselor training programme some sessions are given for understanding and guidance of research activity and expectation of the University from students, guides and study centres.

The course "Advance in Education (a course work related to research)" was a new concept for all the guides. Therefore, two-hour session was conducted for understanding and activity for the course.

Uniqueness of Advance in Education (A Course Work Related to Research)

- This course is compulsory to all students. But the syllabus of the course differs according to the research topic of each students.
- The syllabus of the course was developed jointly by the students and respective guide.
- Research topic was related to the guide specialization area or related to the students' interest area.
- The evaluation of the course is totally internal, therefore the guide is having a judgement of his/her research students for deeper understanding of the course.

Expectation from Advance in Education (a Course Work Related to Research)

- To develop the student capacity to compare the syllabus of the same course in different universities at the M.Phil level.
- To develop the student's capacity for using the various recourses of his/her specialized area.

- To develop self-directed learning competency in the students.

Steps for Development of the Syllabus for Advance in Education (A Course Work Related to Research)

- Finalization of research area of the students.
- Collection of syllabi for the same course from the different universities in Maharashtra.
- Develop 8-9 chapters of the course with the help of encyclopedia, journals reference books and internet.
- Students should collect the related reference material from respective places.
- Students have to develop point and sub-point of each chapter by studying the reference material and get it approved by the guide.
- This syllabi was sent to the university in a described format for approval.
- Expert Committee approved the syllabi developed by each student.

For this work student and guide get 3-4 months.

Observation of the Experts About Syllabi

SOE got the syllabi of each student from the study centre. It was given to the expert for approval.

The expert having following observation

- Most of the syllabi did not have latest knowledge.
- Syllabi are at B.Ed. and M.Ed. level.
- Primary references and secondary sources are not shown in the reference list.
- Most of the students and few of the guides don't know how to frame the Syllabi.

Conclusion—There is Need of a Different Strategy for Development of Syllabi

SOE decided to give some input to the guide and students. The member of the committee identified the research area by taking reference "Surveys of Educational Research". They study all research proposal submitted to the university. They classify the research topic into 17 areas.

These areas are as follows: according to these 17 areas the university select experts from all over Maharashtra and conduct three days workshops for development of syllabi. This latest Syllabus was sent to the guide and students with the help of a study centre. If the research topic was related to more than one area then from this syllabus the guide and students have to revise their syllabi according to the guideline.

The guide has to develop two term paper questions and two short assignments questions and give it to the students. The students are expected to complete these activities. One term paper has be to presented in the next workshop, and other is evaluated internally by the guide. From this activity the SOE expected the impact of this work on the thesis of the students.

19

Developing Researcher Competency for Quality Research in Education

Hemlata Talesra

Introduction

Research is a well-knitted, well debated, well researched, highly academic and data based quality work. In some cases this definition is only on paper. A large number of researchers are not very serious about their research work. The Central and State Universities have strict rules and regulations and their researchers are also serious about their research work. They participate regularly in research seminars organized by the department, but in some universities researchers have full freedom to do their research work and finish their own way. This will create a problem indicating negatively on the morale of the researcher. A recent study on the competency of research students shows that 30 per cent of Ph.D. students, 40 per cent of the M.Ed. and 90 per cent of M.A. (Distance Education) students have not submitted their own work and in the *viva-voce* they do not answer the basic questions of their dissertation work. They copied the research work completed earlier and want to only get a degree. Even they do not remember the title of their dissertation. Recently, some universities started distance course in M.A. education and Ph.D. courses for irregular students and arrange one meeting with the Ph.D. scholars before submitting and presenting the synopsis. The scholars prepare the synopsis or copy the synopsis from earlier research and present it their own way. They do not answer any question at the time of presentation. Many times the researcher gives the money and purchases a completed typed dissertation or thesis and submits it to the university for getting a degree. The universities also award Ph. D. or M.A (Education) degree on the basis of completing research work, but not have any programme to develop competence among the researchers.

This is very serious problem and puts a question mark on the competence of the researcher. Therefore, there is an urgent need to find out the competence of the researchers and orient them for different aspects of quality research. The chapter is based on a research study based on the development of research competency among researchers.

Objectives

Following are the main objectives of this study:

1. To find out the competency of researchers (by pre-test)
2. To analyze the strong and week points of researchers
3. To develop and organize a competence-based orientation programme to orient the researchers.
4. To organize a follow-up workshop to see the effect of orientation programme on the competency of the researchers.

Theoretical Framework

Knowledge of different components of quality research is very important for the researcher who is undertaking research at any level. Without deep knowledge and insight about the concept, objectives, sampling, methodology, using tools, techniques, analysis and report writing the researcher cannot complete quality research work successfully. With the result of this, the researcher depends on the other persons to complete his/her research work or copying the earlier researches. To avoid this situation orientation for the researchers on quality research is very important and useful for developing insight among them about different components of quality research. Some universities and institutions are regularly organizing orientation programmes and providing knowledge and understanding about the different components of research. In this regard workshops on quality research are also important to assess the result of orientation programme.

Key Questions

The chapter has given an answer to the following questions on the point of view of researchers:

1. How much competency the researchers have?
2. Why are the researchers not competent in their research work?
3. What are the strong and weak points of researchers?
4. Is the orientation programme helpful to develop competency among the researchers?

Methods, Technique and Mode of Inquiry

For this study 40 Researchers (30 M.Ed. and 10 Ph.D. scholars) have been purposely selected from Gujarat State. All the M.Ed. students were admitted in the academic session 2012-13 in one college of north Gujarat and Ph.D. scholars were registered in the same session. Experimental (pre- test, post-test design) method was adopted and interview and observation schedule were the main tools for data collection.

Results and Discussion

On the basis of collected data the following results and conclusions have been found:

1. Researcher Competency before Orientation Programme

To find out the inherent research competency a list of questions were asked to the researchers and the results are given in Table 19.1

Table 19.1: Researcher Competency before Orientation

Research Components	*Ph.D. Scholars Out of 10*	*M.Ed. Trainees Out of 30*
Knowledge about quality research	05	08
Knowledge about importance of quality research	06	11
Knowledge about how quality research is conducted?	03	07
Knowledge about writing research report	04	09
State the research problem clearly	07	13
Explain and justify the research approach	04	11
Locate the investigation with in a current body of knowledge	02	01
Can plainly portray the context which the research is set	02	01
Report and justify the research design, methodology, instruments and means of analysis?	03	04
State the limitations	07	15
Acknowledge the amount and kind of research involvement	04	21
Show and handle the ethical considerations	01	05
Possess an overview of research paradigm of theory and practice in research and of research methods and methodologies	04	10
Use an effective writing style and appropriate language	05	09
Provide effective statistical analysis, tabulation, findings, recommendations and suggestions for possible future researches	04	11

Table 19.1 shows that very few researchers have proper knowledge of research components. During interviews most of the respondents told us that they do not received much exposure about the components of research and also they do not have much time to collect research knowledge from different sources. The weak point of the researchers was lack of self-confidence and appropriate guidance.

Their strong point was still that they want some orientation programmes for their research competence development.

Table 19.2 shows a high difference from Table 19.1. It means that the orientation programme was certainly useful for the researchers to gain the knowledge of research components. Most of the Ph.D. and M.Ed. researchers responded that they got knowledge during the five days orientation programme about quality research components and expressed their willingness for

Table 19.2: Researcher Competence after Orientation

Research Components	*Ph.D. Scholars Out of 10*	*M.Ed. Trainees Out of 30*
Knowledge about quality research	10	17
Importance of quality Research	09	21
How quality research is conducted?	07	23
Knowledge about writing research report	10	19
State the research problem clearly	10	23
Explain and justify the research approach	08	22
locate the investigation with in a current body of knowledge	07	20
can plainly portray the context which the research is set	05	14
Report and justify the research design, methodology, instruments and means of analysis?	08	21
State the limitations	10	29
Acknowledge the amount and kind of research involvement	09	28
Show and handled the ethical considerations	07	26
Posses and overview of research paradigm of theory and practice in research and of research methods and methodologies	09	27
Use an effective writing style and appropriate language	08	21
can provide effective statistical analysis, tabulation, findings, recommendations and suggestions for possible future researches	07	23

more orientation programmes. In the workshop organized after the orientation programme the researchers prepared a quality research design and included all the components of quality research. When the research designs were assessed 100 per cent Ph.D. scholars and 80 per cent M.Ed. trainees perfectly analyzed all the research components.

The observations also show researcher competence. Before the orientation programme most of the researchers were sitting silently and not taking an interest in answering questions about their research work but after the orientation programme most of them were showing their interest and asked questions related to their research problems and progress.

The researchers suggested that the follow up programmes on quality research is a necessity for all researchers of any level and it should be organized continuously at the time of research work and after.

References

Best, J.W. (1982) *Research in Education* (4th edition), New Delhi: Prentice Hall of India Pvt. Ltd.

Buch, M.B., All six volumes of *Researches in Education.*

Creswell, J.W. (2003). *Research design: Qualitative, quantitative, and mixed method approaches.* Thousand Oaks, CA: Sage Publications.

Denzin, N.K., and Lincoln, Y.S. (2000). *Handbook of qualitative research (2nd ed.).* Thousand Oaks, CA: Sage Publications.

Denzin, N.K., and Lincoln, Y.S. (2011). *The SAGE Handbook of qualitative research (4th ed.).* Los Angeles: Sage Publications.

DeWalt, K.M. and DeWalt, B.R. (2002). *Participant observation.* Walnut Creek, CA: AltaMira Press.

Fischer, C.T. (Ed.) (2005). *Qualitative research methods for psychologists: Introduction through empirical studies.* Academic Press.

Franklin, M.I. (2012), "Understanding Research: Coping with the Quantitative-Qualitative Divide". London/New York. Routledge

Fox, David (1969), *The Research Process in Education,* New York: Holtb Rinchart and Winston.

Holliday, A. R. (2007). *Doing and Writing Qualitative Research, 2nd Edition.* London: Sage Publications.

Mitzal, H.E. (1982), Encyclopaedia of Educational Research, New York, Free Press.

Patton, M.Q. (2002). *Qualitative research and evaluation methods* (3rd ed.). Thousand Oaks, CA: Sage Publications.

Taylor, Steven J., Bogdan, Robert (1998), *Introduction to Qualitative Research Methods,* Wiley.

Travers, Robert, M.W. (1958), *An Introduction to Educational Research,* New York, Macmillan.

Turney, B.L. and George Robb (1971). *Research in Education,* Peplinois, Dryden.

Vockell, E.W. and Asher, J.W. (1995), *Educational Research,* New Jersey, Merril.

Witney, Frederick, I. (1950), *The Elements of Research,* New York, Prentice Hall Inc.

20

Quality Research

A Dream in the Present Scenario

Harishankar Singh and *Aradhana Sethi*

Introduction

In the modern scenario, the world is transforming at a faster pace. No doubt the credit of its transformation goes to education and especially higher education. Higher education occupies a very pertinent place in the development of the nation because its aim is to serve the human and society. Because of the power of transformation of knowledge in society, it has to advance knowledge, create new knowledge and solve the problems of society for the sustainable development of human beings. Research can play a major role in this major task. In fact, research is the corner stone of higher education and key to national development and has a prominent place in developmental issues. The quest for knowledge has increased in today's knowledge society. Research has to involve itself in different and challenging problems plaguing the country today. Research and national development go hand in hand. In such a scenario, it is important to maintain the quality of research. It is widely recognised that a nation's transformation to a Knowledge and Skills Economy is critically dependent on original research and development taking place within the country. If India is to make the transition to a Knowledge economy, it is therefore vital that research and development within the country be dramatically improved.

Quality of Ph.D. in India

In India the quality of Ph.D is deplorable and pathetic. Gone are the days when Ph.D was considered as a mean to nurture five P's, i.e., Passion, Patience, Perseverance, Perspective, and Purpose. In the modern scenario, a very large number of Ph.D scholars, supervisors, and academic institutions are increasingly approaching it with a mindset focussed on three D's, i.e., Degree, Designation, and Dough (money). They are not at all bothered about the quality of research. They have forgotten that the aim of research is to prepare intellectual leaders who will do the groundwork to create new paradigms and products for tomorrow. During the past few years, it has become the tendency of some universities to increase their Ph.D production without necessarily being sufficiently ambitious about the quality benchmarks. The reason for unproductive research in education in India is the easy going tendency of most of the researchers. Their sole aim is to obtain a Ph.D degree by fair means or foul. They normally follow the maxim of cut, copy, paste of the earlier done researches. How can one expect originality with such researchers? In the present time, U.G.C. Ministry of human Recourse Development (MHRD), National Assessment and Accreditation Council (NAAC) and other government agencies, responsible for funding and monitoring higher education are giving much importance to the research work in the academic performance of teachers, but it is observed that original works are not done at universities. Today the main purpose of doing research in the universities and colleges are to get a degree or other benefits for career advancement, not for the sake of research. Teachers are interested in taking more and more students as career advancement, number of Ph.Ds guided are one of the contributing factor. Many of the students join Ph.D because at the time of joining they have no other option. As soon as they get other work, they leave it or are not so devoted in their work. Some do Ph.D because of getting the tag of 'highly qualified'. Such people only want degree and are not at all bothered with quality work. Some take it because of a academic compulsion. They have to take a senior position for which Ph.D is a must. So, one of the most important factors that determine quality research is the aim and attitude of the students to pursue research work.

New UGC Rules for Quality Ph.D.s

In order to overcome the above mentioned lacunae, U.G.C. formulated minimum standards and procedures for award of M.Phil/Ph.D Degree, Regulations 2009 which has made an entrance examination, known as RET (Research Eligibility Test) mandatory for admission to Ph.D and M.Phil Programme, followed by interviews in which doctoral candidates are expected to discuss their research area. Only the predetermined number of students may be admitted to M.Phil/Ph.D programme. After admission to Ph.D., students will have to do course work for at least six months which will be considered as Pre-Ph.D preparation. After the completion of pre Ph.D course, the candidate is required to quality for the exams of Pre-Ph.D course work. The Ph.D registration will be granted through submission of synopsis similar to the earlier rules. The major purpose of the UGC expert committee in formulating the above stated rules for the awards of Ph.D is to improve the quality of research which for a long time has been a neglected issue. As far as the allocation of Supervisor/Research Guide for selected students shall be decided by the department in a formal manner, on the basis of the available specialization among faculty supervisors and the research interest of the student as indicated during interview by the student. UGC regulations also made it clear that allocation of a supervisor shall not be left to the individual student or teacher.

Now the question arises whether these rules are being followed seriously or for name sake, things are going on. As far as the course work of pre-Ph.D for the duration of six months is concerned, its aim is to make pre-preparation for Ph.D i.e. to develop expertise of research methodology so that the students may produce quality research. But in how many universities does this pre-Ph.D programme go on seriously? Normally during pre-Ph.D course work, students are asked to take classes of B.Ed and M.Ed in order to reduce their own work load. So how can it be a guarantee of a quality Ph.D. Moreover replication and repetitive research is going on. Knowledge advances not by repeating the known facts, but by refuting false dogmas. Most of the research done in universities are replicate and repetitive and also not relevant either on the global or local level. Students choose topics either of the choices of the supervisor or such through which they can easily complete their research work. Sometimes the researcher manipulates the result with the fear that his data is not in congruence with the previous studies. They should keep in mind that in the social sciences, the purpose of the research is to create new knowledge which has implications in the changing society. Another important threat to the quality of Ph.Ds is that all the students enrolled for the course, get awarded. Though the procedure has been made tough and lengthier it does not guarantee quality research.

Reasons for Low Quality Research in India

1. *Directionless Attitude of the Youth*

The attitude of the most of the research scholars is directionless in many ways. They only want a degree (as any other) for their increment. Ninety-nine per cent of Ph.D. registered students are totally dependent on faculty members (guides). They even don't have their own idea that what exactly they want to do in research. What can you hope even from premier institute's students if students are even not self-motivated?

2. *Plight of Awarding Ph.D Degrees*

There is a big deficiency in the Indian system for awarding Ph.D degrees. It is indeed pathetic. In the Indian scenario, everything is governed by the law, and we Indians have developed the habit of manipulating the law to our benefit. The deficient quality of Ph.D production in India is an outcome of laxity in Ph.D Ordinances of the Indian Universities. When an Indian University bounds to acquire Ph.D within 5 years, then definitely the student will try to manipulate by publishing his papers in some low quality Journals/ conference, when the time is at the verge of expiring. What quality can be expected from the research which has been done in the verge of expiring its duration?

3. *Doctoral Degrees as Means of Material Gain*

In the modern scenario, doctoral degrees serve as a means for material gain rather than improving analytical capabilities and opening up the thinking process and problem solving skills.

Absence of a proper metric and some arbitrary bench mark like two or three papers in National/International Journals/Conferences and published work of good standing is more misuse rather than an improvement of the quality. Nowadays, publications in so called National/International Journals is easy and is done after payment of subscription charges or publication charges charged on page basis making the system a mockery. Impact Factors and Citation Indexes may to some extent check the quality. Basic domain knowledge, intense interest and a minimum maturity is required for pursuing research leading to award of Doctoral degree, but combination of the above three is hard to find in the modern scenario.

4. Commercialisation and Privatisation

In the last few years, there has been the flood of Ph.Ds in private universities. Some of the private universities have made it a practice literally sell hundred Ph.Ds every two years. Some universities are providing Ph.D degrees to the students without their attending course work. The height of immortality is that they don't have to write their Ph.D thesis themselves. They are just required to pay heavy amount of fee for which they get even back dated Ph.D degrees (that is enrolment before 2009). The miserable plight of the courses is that they are affiliated to UGC.

5. Lack of Scientific Training

There is a lack of scientific training in research i.e. how research is to be conducted and which methodology is to be used for a particular topic. Many researchers undertake research work without having actual knowledge of research methods. They just look for similar studies and copy the methodologies listed in it. Even the research guides do not have a thorough knowledge of the various methodologies. This scenario warrants the need for some sort of short-term training to be imparted to researchers prior to undertaking, research activities, a daunting task.

8. Improper Library Management

There is found to be a lack of good libraries in the colleges and universities. These libraries are not managed systematically. Much of the precious time of the researchers is spent in looking for books, reports, newspapers, etc. rather than searching relevant information from them. Some universities and colleges do not have basic facilities for research with limited number of computers and no internet facilities. Such inadequate research facilities discourage researchers.

9. High Cost of Publishing

According to the recent guidelines of UGC, a Ph.D. degree should be supported by the published research papers. Once their research is completed, the researchers have to look for a means to publish it. Publishing in international journals is highly expensive. As a result they keep their research unpublished. Very little research is being published in peer reviewed journals, having a ISSN number of national and international repute. Such problems discourage most of the researchers from taking up research work.

10. Lack of Practical Applicability of Research

Most of the research undertaken by research scholars do not have any practical applicability. Most of the theses remain in the library racks to show for counting of Ph.D thesis completed in the university. Such theses do not have any quality concern. The sole aim of undertaking such research is to just obtain a Ph.D degree.

Reforms Needed to Improve the Quality of Ph.Ds in India

1. Need to Emphasise on Originality and Creativity

To improve the standard of the Ph.D programme, one of the most essential elements is that the topic allotted to a research scholar should be original and there should not be duplication or any repetition of any research work being done presently or at other Indian Universities. However, the problem arises when simultaneously same topic is registered at two or more universities at the same time, whether knowingly or unknowingly. Unfortunately, there is no Central Registration Agency which can provide data before registration of a particular topic whether the same topic or variables taken in a modified form, is being pursued at some other University or not. In order to improve the quality of research work for a Ph.D programme, UGC should create a cell where information from all the Indian Universities regarding registrations of topics in a particular subject for Ph.D is available at the initial stage of research. As soon as P.G. Board of Studies of a University clears a topic, it should be sent to UGC and only after clearance from UGC, should students finally be registered for Ph.D.

2. *Need to Improve Evaluation System of Ph.D Thesis*

The Evaluation System of a Ph.D. thesis is the root cause of poor quality research. Unfortunately, many research scholars acquire the degree because the theses are sent to their supervisor's friend/colleague/contemporary for evaluation. In most of the Universities, the supervisors themselves suggest the names of Ph.D examiners. As a result of this (mal) practice, the supervisor has a casual approach and does not take much interest in scrutinizing the thesis of his student because he knows that irrespective of the quality of the Ph.D thesis, the student will get the work approved as it is going to be evaluated by his friend. Something serious has to be done with the evaluation system if we really want to improve our standard. Firstly, the supervisor should not be involved at any stage, in selecting the panel of the examiners. Secondly, there should be a centralized system of evaluation. The UGC can play a major role in this direction. It should build a data bank of all specialized serious and good workers in the country who can act as examiners of a Ph.D. thesis. The Universities should send the Ph.D. thesis to the UGC, from where it will be mailed to at least two examiners by masking the names of student, supervisor and their affiliations. Alternatively, universities can have its own data bank and pool of examiners from where the Vice-Chancellor can pick names of any two examiners in a particular subject without bringing it to the knowledge of the Chairperson or Supervisor. The evaluation should be strictly on merit. At times rejection of a Ph.D. thesis would serve the purpose because either the supervisors will start taking things seriously or they will stop guiding any Ph.D. student. It is better to produce only a few good quality theses than to have a number of feeble theses.

3. Professionally Dedicated Faculty and Research Guides

There is no shortcut for successful research. Successful research requires dedication, focus and hand work on the part of both researcher and research guide. At present we find that there is the paucity of supervisors and resources. The number of students aspiring for Ph.D is increasing but the number of guides to assist them does not increase in the same proportion, so timely promotions and dedication and perseverance is must on the part of research guide which can help a great deal in this major task as the quality of research depends upon the quality of research scholar and supervisor.

4. Uniformity in the Ph.D Course Work

There is a dire need to have uniformity in the course work, duration, syllabus, time of entrance examination, time for RDCs etc. No doubt, UGC has provided guidance in this direction. But simply guidance is not going to serve the worth of degree. Some strict rules and laws need to be framed and efforts need to be initiated in this direction on prompt basis.

5. Organisation of Research Methodology Workshop for Research Scholars

There is a need to organise research methodology workshops exclusively for research scholars. It should be mandatory for research scholars to attend a research methodology workshop of 40 days, so that they develop expertise in the same. Besides this, UGC Academic staff colleges should be revamped to provide training in laboratory methods in different emerging areas. Every year, there must be at least 200 training courses, of 3-4 weeks duration, at research institutes and university departments.

6. Focus on Quality Research

There should be focus on quality research. There is a need to have well defined criteria to differentiate quality and poor research work. Research is considered to be higher level of intellectual growth of a person, so there is a need to evolve a research quality indicator. For this a national independent authority should be established. All research work should be registered with this authority.

7. Video Recording of Viva-Voce of Ph.D. Candidates

In order to improve the quality of Ph.D and higher research, there must be a procedure to have the video recording of *viva-voce* of Ph.D candidates. If the *viva-voce* of a Ph.D candidate is excellent, then the video recording of such a *viva-voce* will help future candidates for Ph.D to learn and to improve their own performance. In some cases, where the research scholar in connivance with their supervisor and external examiner has indulged in malpractice then video recording of *viva-voce* will act as deterrent.

8. Strictly Full Time Ph.D Course with Good Amount of Fellowship

Although UGC has made certain guidelines for full time Ph.D yet these are not followed everywhere. While framing the regulations, UGC was aware of the fact that a Research degree cannot be pursued on a part-time basis without sacrificing the quality. Even a reasonable compromise on quality requires intense effort both by the candidate and by the guide which is not forthcoming from either. One cannot ride two horses at the same time. It should be made strictly compulsory for the research scholar to be a full time scholar and every research scholar should be entitled to get a fellowship.

9. High Tech and Enriched Libraries

It has been noticed that the conditions of libraries in universities is not at all good. Indian universities should concentrate more on providing quality education and excellent library facilities with broad band internet connection. Libraries should be equipped with the latest books, journals and periodicals. These libraries should be conducive for serious study. The scholars should be provided the facility of e-text books, e-research papers, e-reference books in the library.

10. Need to Improve Publication System

In order to improve the quality of research, there is a need to evolve a publication system at national level for humanities, social sciences, management and languages. To improve thc quality of research work and research papers, peer review papers should be strict and all the papers should be carefully assessed before acceptance for publication.

Conclusion

Thus it can be concluded that research is a long journey. One needs perseverance and endurance throughout the journey. Creating a conducive environment is needed for growth and utilization of research. If we actually want to take this journey towards excellence, we have to make certain amendments in the existing system. There is a dire need to develop research competency among our research scholars as it has been rightly said that "A good teacher may not be a good researcher but a good researcher is always a good teacher".

References

Aggarwal, A. and Aggarwal, R. (2013). Concerns for Quality Research in Higher Education, University News, September 23-29, Vol. 51, No. 38.

Goel, D.R. and Goyal, C. (2012). Educational Research thrust in India, Nov-26-Dec 02, University News, Vol. 50, No. 48.

Joshi, J. and Raviya, H.D. (2011). UGC Regulations 2010 with Illustration, Aadi Publications, Jaipur, ISBN No. 978-93-80902-53-1.

Pathania, K.S. and Pathak, A. (2014). Reforms in Ph.D Research Work: The New Dimensions in Higher Education, University News, Vol. 52, No. 8.

Rao, M.S. (2013). Sage Advise for Students and Educators: Stay Inspired, Encourage Research among Students, Book Enclave, Jaipur, ISBN No-978-81-8152-312-9.

Singh, J.D. (2013). Research Excellence in Higher Education: Major Challanges and Possible Enablers, Univrsity News, Vol. 51, No. 32.

Standards for high quality research, retrived from http://www.rand.org/standards.html

What are the standards for quality research, retrived from http://www.ktdrr.org/ktlibrary/articles_pubs/ncddrwork/focus/focus9/Focus9.pdf

How to improve quality of research of Ph.D programme, retrived from www.indiaeducationreview.com/.../how-improve-quality-research-phd-p.

SECTION THREE
Administration of Educational Research

21

Researchers' Competency: Reflections on the Bhagavad Gita

Harsha Patadia and *Pramila Gururajan*

Introduction

(Wikipedia, 2014) Research comprises "creative work undertaken on a systematic basis in order to increase the stock of knowledge, including knowledge of man, culture and society, and the use of this stock of knowledge to devise new applications." It is used to establish or confirm facts, reaffirm the results of previous work, solve new or existing problems, support theorems, or develop new theories. The person undertaking research is called a researcher. In order to be a good researcher he/she should possess certain characteristics that will be discussed latter in this paper. All these qualities are possessed by Arjuna and certain qualities are explained by Lord Krishna in *Bhagavad Gita*. Only Chapter 2 'Transcendental Knowledge' is considered for this paper. Arjuna learns this 'Transcendental Knowledge' in proper sequence. The sequence can be taken in this manner -in the beginning of Chapter 2 Arjuna continues his reasoning against the war, teachings of the Gita begin with the true knowledge of spirit and the physical body, The spirit is eternal, body is transitory, Death and transmigration of soul, Lord Krishna reminds Arjuna of his duty as a warrior, Importance of KarmaYog, the selfless service, The Vedas deal with both material and spiritual aspects of life, Theory and practice of KarmaYog, Marks of a Self-realized person, Dangers of unrestrained senses, Attainment of peace and happiness through sense control and Self-knowledge. Ultimately Arjuna understands about Sankhya Yoga—the Eternal Reality of the Soul's Immortality. Arjuna possessed patience and perseverance throughout the chapter and finally he gains knowledge. A researcher should possess these qualities in order to undertake research. A researcher follows the scientific method in order to solve the problem he is encountering and finally arrives at a certain conclusion. To be a successful researcher one should possess good qualities. Even in our life to be a successful person one should possess the competency and attitude of a good researcher. We can see this from Vedic period till today. To be or not to be is arrived through scientific guided discoveries. To be successful in business, politics, teaching, in fact in all professions, a person should be a competent researcher. Even in our day to-day life like buying rice from a shop it is applicable.

Qualities of a Good Researcher

A researcher should have interest, motivation, inquisitiveness, commitment, sacrifice, excellence, knowledge, recognition, scholarly approach, and integration. (Qualities of a Good Researcher?, 2014) The first key attribute of any successful researcher is organization; a second desirable quality is open mindedness. Finally, a good researcher is an honest researcher. (Good Qualities of a Researcher: A Note to Beginners, 2010). The basic qualities of a researcher are intelligence, honesty, curiosity and initiative, enough knowledge, and competence in oral and written communication. Research requires critical analysis, logical reasoning, and common sense, curiousity and initiative. It is more interesting to note the good qualities needed by a researcher in the dynamic parts of doing research. We can call these qualities the good qualities in the process. They are as follows: diligence, patience and persistence, creativeness and innovativeness, objectiveness, open mindedness, orderliness and cleanliness, cautions, accuracy and precision, quickness and responsiveness, keenness, systematic and reasonable, and cooperative and a leader.

Qualities of a Good Researcher (Regoniel, 2012)

1. A good researcher manifests thirst for new information.
2. A good researcher has a keen sense of things around him.
3. A good researcher likes to reflect or think about the things he encounters.
4. A good researcher must be intelligent enough to express his ideas.
5. A good researcher applies a systematic approach in assessing situations.

Basically, to get research success, following research competencies are prerequisites (Genesis Framework, 2014):

1. Critical review of the literature and comprehensive theoretical knowledge and in depth understanding. Employees/Students or any other person, who is going to conduct Research, must demonstrate the ability to synthesize and critically review a body of literature that is more comprehensive than what is expected for a standard.
2. Framing a research question. The success of the research mainly will depend on the research questions. Therefore, this ability/competency is vital for research. All the research conductors must demonstrate the ability to correctly identify a researchable question.
3. Capability of developing instruments for effective research. The person who wish to conduct research must demonstrate the ability to design an instrument for collecting data. This competency includes the identification of existing instruments, the ability to adapt existing instruments for new modalities and to create a new instrument etc.
4. Data collection related competencies. Students/employees/ scientists must have document related competencies with primary data collection including activities relating to data coding and data entry.
5. Data analysis related competencies. It's needed to have document related experience with scientific and systematic experience with analyzing either primary data they have collected as part of a supervised research project.

Above are the basic competencies required to get effective research done and those competencies can be developed in many ways. Continuous training and learning, effective coaching and counseling, will help everyone to master their research competency level.

How to Write a Good Research Paper (Binghamton University, 2014): Finding a good and feasible topic constitutes one of the most essential parts of writing a research paper.

Fig. 21.1: Google Image Good Researcher referred on 10.3.14

(Library, 2014) ASK: The first step in the research process is to ASK a research question. Research is a process. It begins with your question, and ends with your answer. How do you come up with a good research question?

- Analyse the assignment
- Develop your research question/thesis

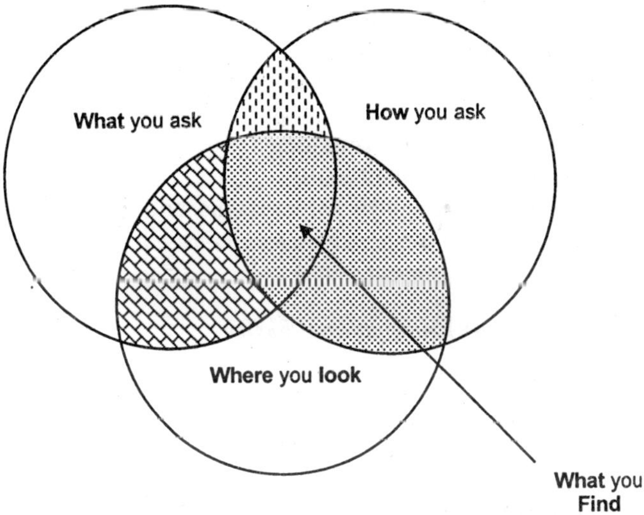

Fig. 21.2: Google Image Good Researcher referred on 10.3.14

Key Competencies Required for the Future Researcher

(APEC, 2010) In the eight studied countries (France, Germany, Finland, Netherlands, the United Kingdom, Switzerland, Japan and the United States) the competencies required by the researcher who should possess scientific competencies, project and team management skills and personal aptitudes/interpersonal skills are elaborated as follows (Source: APEC/DELOITTE Study 2010).

Scientific Competencies

1. Scientific knowledge
2. Ability to learn and adapt
3. Ability to formulate a research issue
4. Capacity for analysis and grasp of sophisticated IT tools
5. Ability to work in an interdisciplinary environment
6. Ability to incorporate existing knowledge

Project and Team Management Skills

1. Ability to work in a team,
2. Ability to develop a network,
3. Communication skills,
4. Ability to assess,
5. Language skills,
6. Business culture and management skills,
7. Project management skills,
8. Ability to manage and steer teams, and
9. Awareness of the pertinence of the research and its impact on the environment.

Personal Aptitudes/Interpersonal Skills

1. Creativity,
2. Open-minded approach,
3. Motivation/Involvement,
4. Adaptability, and
5. Ability to self-assess.

The following are the researchers' competencies as described by Faculty of General Dental Practice (UK) The Royal College of Surgeons England. (Research Competencies Framework, 2007) The competencies have been grouped into five domains. They are:

- Practical skills,
- Problem-solving, thinking and communication skills,
- Personal attitudes and professional ethics,
- Dissemination, and
- Roles and functions.

A researcher should possess cultural competencies because every culture has its own specialities and should consider the diversities of the populations (Centre, 2010).

Definition of Cultural Competence in Research

Cultural competence in research is the ability of researchers and research staff to provide high quality research that takes into account the culture and diversity of a population when developing research ideas, conducting research, and exploring applicability of research findings. Cultural competence in research plays a critical role in study design and implementation processes, including the development of research questions and hypotheses, outreach and recruitment strategies, consent activities, data collection protocols, analysing and interpreting research findings, drawing conclusions and presenting the results. Altogether, cultural congruence in these research processes helps to ensure the research is applicable to diverse populations and if necessary can be adapted to meet the target population's social, cultural and linguistic needs. Depending on the type of research, cultural competence can be crucial to successfully recruiting and retaining diverse individuals as study subjects.

Steps in Attainment of Transcendental Knowledge

Arjuna attained the transcendental knowledge in the following steps:

Step 1: Arjuna, continues his reasoning against the war
Step 2: Teachings of the *Gita* begin with the true knowledge of spirit and the physical body
Step 3: The spirit is eternal, body is transitory
Step 4: Death and transmigration of soul
Step 5: Lord Krishna reminds Arjun of his duty as a warrior
Step 6: Importance of *KarmaYog*, the selfless service
Step 7: The Vedas deal with both material and spiritual aspects of life
Step 8: Theory and practice of *KarmaYog*
Step 9: Marks of a Self-realized person
Step 10: Dangers of unrestrained senses
Step 11: Attainment of peace and happiness through sense control and Self-knowledge

Arjuna as a Competent Researcher

Arjuna as a good researcher possesses the following qualities which are explained in bullets. He gains transcendental knowledge in ten steps which is explained in the following paragraph.

- A good researcher manifests thirst for new information.

Step 1: Arjuna continues his reasoning against the war (*Bhagavad Gita* Chapter 2, 2006).

> Arjuna said: How shall I strike my grandfather, my guru, and all other relatives, who are worthy of my respect, with arrows in battle, O Krishna?
>
> अर्जुन उवाच
>
> कथं भीष्ममहं संख्ये द्रोणं च मधुसूदन।
>
> इषुभिः प्रतियोत्स्यामि पूजार्हावरिसूदन ॥२-४॥
>
> My senses are overcome by the weakness of pity, and my mind is confused about duty (Dharma). Please tell me what is better for me. I am your disciple, and I take refuge in You.
>
> कार्पण्यदोषोपहतस्वभावः
>
> पृच्छामि त्वां धर्मसम्मूढचेताः।
>
> यच्छ्रेयः स्यान्निश्चितं ब्रूहि तन्मे
>
> शिष्यस्तेऽहं शाधि मां त्वां प्रपन्नम् ॥२-७॥

- **Confused in Begining**
  Sanjaya said: O King, after speaking like this to Lord Krishna, the mighty Arjuna said to Krishna: I shall not fight, and became silent.
  संजय उवाच
  एवमुक्त्वा हृषीकेशं गुडाकेशः परन्तप।
  नयोत्स्य इति गोविन्दमुक्त्वा तूष्णीं बभूव ह ॥२-९॥
  O King, Lord Krishna, as if smiling, spoke these words to the distressed Arjuna in the midst of the two armies.
  तमुवाच हृषीकेशः प्रहसन्निव भारत।
  सेनयोरुभयोर्मध्ये विषीदन्तमिदं वचः ॥२-१०॥
- A good researcher possesses inquisitiveness, motivation and involvement.

Step 2: Teachings of the *Gita* begin with the true knowledge of spirit and the physical body (*Bhagavad Gita* Chapter 2, 2006)

> There was never a time when these monarchs, you, or I did not exist; nor shall we ever cease to exist in the future.

न त्वेवाहं जातु नासं न त्वं नेमे जनाधिपाः।
न चैव न भविष्यामः सर्वे वयमतः परम् ॥२-१२॥

Just as the soul acquires a childhood body, a youth body, and an old age body during this life; similarly, the soul acquires another body after death. This should not delude the wise.

देहिनोऽस्मिन्यथा देहे कौमारंयौवनं जरा।
तथा देहान्तरप्राप्तिधीरस्तत्र न मुह्यति ॥२-१३॥

- A good researcher possess creativity, open-minded approach, adaptability

Step 3: The spirit is eternal, body is transitory

(*Bhagavad Gita* Chapter 2, 2006) The Spirit is neither born nor does it die at any time. It does not come into being, or cease to exist. It is unborn, eternal, permanent, and primeval. The Spirit is not destroyed when the body is destroyed.

न जायते म्रियते वा कदाचि-न्नायं भूत्वा भविता वा न भूयः।
अजो नित्यः शाश्वतोऽयं पुराणो न हन्यते हन्यमाने शरीरे ॥२-२०॥

- A researcher should be curious, intelligent and should critically analyse things.

Step 4: Death and transmigration of soul

(*Bhagavad Gita* Chapter 2, 2006) Just as a person puts on new garments after discarding the old ones; similarly, the living entity or the individual soul acquires new bodies after casting away the old bodies.

वासांसि जीर्णानियथा विहाय नवानि गृह्णाति नरोऽपराणि।
तथा शरीराणि विहाय जीर्णा न्यन्यानि संयाति नवानि देही ॥२-२२॥

- A researcher should be diligent, have perseverance till the end of research and consider duty first.

Step 5: Lord Krishna reminds Arjuna of his duty as a warrior

(*Bhagavad Gita* Chapter 2, 2006) Treating pleasure and pain, gain and loss, and victory and defeat alike, engage yourself in your duty. By doing your duty this way you will not incur sin.

सुखदु:खे समे कृत्वा लाभालाभौ जयाजयौ।
ततोयुद्धाययुज्यस्व नैवं पापमवाप्स्यसि ॥२-३८॥

- A researcher should be balanced and unconcerned with the thought of acquisition

Step 6: Importance of KarmaYog, the selfless service

(*Bhagavad Gita* Chapter 2, 2006) No effort is ever lost in selfless service, and there is no adverse effect. Even a little practice of the discipline of selfless service protects one from the great fear of repeated birth and death.

नेहाभिक्रमनाशोऽस्ति प्रत्यवायो न विद्यते।
स्वल्पमप्यस्य धर्मस्य त्रायते महतो भयात् ॥२-४०॥

- A researcher should have scientific knowledge, ability to learn and adapt and ability to work in interdisciplinary environment

Step 7: The Vedas deal with both material and spiritual aspects of life

(*Bhagavad Gita* Chapter 2, 2006) A portion of the Vedas deals with three modes, goodness, passion, and ignorance of material Nature. Become free from pairs of opposites, be ever balanced and unconcerned with the thoughts of acquisition and preservation. Rise above these three modes, and be Self-conscious, O Arjuna.

त्रैगुण्यविषया वेदा निस्त्रैगुण्यो भवार्जुन।
निर्द्वन्द्वो नित्यसत्त्वस्थो नियीगक्षेम आत्मवान् ॥२-४५॥

- A researcher should be unattached with his research and subject

Step 8: Theory and practice of KarmaYog

(*Bhagavad Gita* Chapter 2, 2006) A Karma-yogi or the selfless person becomes free from both vice and virtue in this life itself. Therefore, strive for selfless service. Working to the best of one's abilities without becoming selfishly attached to the fruits of work is called Karma-yoga or Seva.

बुद्धियुक्तो जहातीह उभे सुकृतदुष्कृते।
तस्माद्योगाययुज्यस्वयोग: कर्मसु कौशलम् ॥

- A researcher should be curious, professional and self-realised (unattached and undisturbed by result).

Step 9: Marks of a Self-realized person

(*Bhagavad Gita* Chapter 2, 2006) Arjuna said: O Krishna, what are the marks of an enlightened person whose intellect is steady? What does a person of steady intellect think and talk about? How does such a person behave with others, and live in this world?

अर्जुन उवाच

स्थितप्रज्ञस्य का भाषा समाधिस्थस्य केशव।

स्थितधी: किं प्रभाषेत किमासीत व्रजेत किम् ।।२-५४।।

The mind and intellect of a person become steady who is not attached to anything, who is neither elated by getting desired results, nor perturbed by undesired results.

य: सर्वत्रानभिस्नेहस्तत्तत्प्राप्य शुभाशुभम्।

नाभिनन्दति न द्वेष्टि तस्य प्रज्ञा प्रतिष्ठिता ।।२-५७।।

- A researcher should be peaceful and free from bewilderment

Step 10: Dangers of unrestrained senses

(*Bhagavad Gita* Chapter 2, 2006)

Delusion or wild idea arises from anger. The mind is bewildered by delusion. Reasoning is destroyed when the mind is bewildered. One falls down from the right path when reasoning is destroyed.

क्रोधाद्भवति संमोह: संमोहात्स्मृतिविभ्रम:।

स्मृतिभ्रंशाद्बुद्धिनाशो बुद्धिनाशात्प्रणश्यति ।।२-६३।।

- A researcher should have sense control and should have self-knowledge

Step 11: Attainment of peace and happiness through sense control and Self-knowledge

(*Bhagavad Gita* Chapter 2, 2006)

Therefore, O Arjuna, one's intellect becomes steady whose senses are completely withdrawn from the sense objects.

तस्माद्यस्य महाबाहो निगृहीतानि सर्वशः।
इन्द्रियाणीन्द्रियार्थेभ्यस्तस्य प्रज्ञा प्रतिष्ठिता ॥२-६८॥

Conclusion

A researcher should possess certain competencies in order to conduct research. He/she should sustain it throughout the research. These competencies are not only related to researcher but needed by each and everybody to apply in day-to-day life. These competencies are needed for all professionals. Certain companies demand such competencies and their degree of demand is different for different countries. Today's world is moving towards an interdisciplinary approach therefore there will be more demands and more expectations from researchers. The dialogue between Krishna and Arjuna is not only important from the religious point of view but important in every aspect of our life.

References

APEC. (2010, November). *Skills and Competencies Needed in the Research Field Objectives 2020: Summary of the APEC—Deloitte Consulting Study*. Retrieved March 11, 2014, from Deloitte: http://www.deloitte.com/assets/Dcom-France/Local%20Assets/Documents/Votre%20Secteur/Secteur%20public/Synth%C3%A8se%20Etude%20APEC%20Deloitte/Synth%C3%A8se%20Etude%20Apec%20Deloitte%20Anglais.pdf

Bhagavad Gita Chapter 2. (2006, June 19). Retrieved March 10, 2014, from http://sanskrit-texts.blogspot.in/2006/06/bhagavad-gita-chapter-2.html

Binghamton University, S. U. (2014). *How to Write a Good Research Paper*. Retrieved March 10, 2014, from Binghamton University: http://www2.binghamton.edu/isss/getting-good-grades/goodrespaper.html

Cultural Competentce in Research. Retrieved March 11, 2014, from Harvard Catalyst Programme for Faculty Development and Diversity: http://www.mfdp.med.harvard.edu/catalyst/publications/cultural_competence_annotated_bibliography.pdf

Genesis Framework, (2014). *Research Competency*. Retrieved March 10, 2014, from My ESI: http://youremployment.biz/competency/research-competency/

Good Qualities of a Researcher: A Note to Beginners. (2010, July 24). Retrieved March 10, 2014, from Science 2.0 Join the revolution: http://

www.science20.com/flexi_chem_teacher/blog/good_qualities_researcher_note_beginners_camilo_tabinas-70065

Kennedy, R.E. (n.d.). *California Polytechnic State University*. Retrieved March 10, 2014, from http://lib.calpoly.edu/research/tutorials/101/ask.html

Qualities of a Good Researcher? (2014). Retrieved March 10, 2014, from Ask: http://www.ask.com/question/qualities-of-a-good-researcher

Regoniel, P. A. (2012, October 24). *5 Qualities of a Good Researcher*. Retrieved March 2014, 2014, from SimplyEdcuate.Me-Free online Education: http://simplyeducate.me/2012/10/24/5-qualities-of-a-good-researcher/

Research Competencies Framework. (2007, April 4). Retrieved March 11, 2014, from Faculty of General Dental Practice (U.K.) The Royal College of Surgeons England: http://www.fgdp.org.uk/_assets/pdf/research/research%20competencies.pdf

Wikipedia. (2014, March 1). *Research*. Retrieved March 10, 2014, from Wikipedia, The Free Encyclopedia: http://en.wikipedia.org/wiki/Research.

22

Researcher Competencies in Physical Education

The Need of the Hour

P.B. Thumar

Introduction

Research is actually an act of studying something carefully and extensively in order to attain deep knowledge in the same. For being successful, research should be systematic, arranged, summarized and recorded properly. Research is not only a process that is limited to the field of science. It can, as well, cater to people and scholars from artistic, historic or any other field where an individual is willing to do extensive study to get relevant information. Research can be creative, explorative or just reassuring in nature. Each one of us does some or the other research in our lifetime for sure. Research can affect a subject both positively and negatively and can be constructive or destructive in nature. Some people believe that research is mostly destructive in nature. However, you need to understand that it's not the results from a research that determine its use; it's the people who handle the results. In the following lines, we have just tried to emphasize the importance of research.

Significance of Research

To Gather Necessary Information: Research provides all necessary information in field of work, study or operation before one begins working on it. For example, an athletics coach wants to know how much time an athlete should spend on a particular exercise to develop strength. He will try to find out the different types of exercises and its effect on strength. This is how collected information will help him to do his work better.

To Make Changes: Sometimes, there are in-built problems in a process or a project that is hard to discover. Research helps us find the root cause and associated elements of a process. The end result of such a research invokes a demand for change and sometimes is successful in producing changes as well. For example, many U.N. research studies have paved the way for changes in environmental policies.

Improving Standard of Living: Only through research can new inventions and discoveries come into life. It was C.V. Raman's research that prompted invention of radio communication. Imagine how you would have communicated had Graham Bell not come out with the first ever practical telephone! Forget telephones, what would have happened if Martin Cooper did not present to the world the concept of mobile phones! Addicted as we are to mobile phones, we need to understand that all the luxuries and the amenities that are now available to us are the result of research done by someone. And with the world facing more and more crises each day, we need researchers to find new solutions to tackle them.

For A Safer Life: Research has made ground breaking discoveries and development in the field of health, nutrition, food technology and medicine. These things have improved the life expectancy and health conditions of the human race in all parts of the world and helped eradicate diseases like polio and smallpox completely. Diseases that were untreatable are now history, as new and new inventions and research in the field of medicine have led to the advent of drugs that not only treat the once incurable diseases, but also prevent them from recurring.

To Know the Truth: It has been proved time and again that many of established facts and known truths are just cover ups or blatant lies or rumours. Research is needed to investigate and expose these.

Competency

A competency is an underlying characteristic of a person which enables him/her to deliver superior performance in a given job, role or a situation. Competencies are seen mainly as inputs. They consist of clusters of knowledge, attitudes and skills that affect an individual's ability to perform.

Hayes (1979): Competencies are generic knowledge motive, trait, social role or a skill of a person linked to superior performance on the job.

Albanese (1989): Competencies are personal characteristics that contribute to effective managerial performance.

UNIDO (2002): A Competency is a set of skills, related knowledge and attributes that allow an individual to successfully perform a task or an activity within a specific function or job.

Common in the Definitions

- underlying characteristic of a person
- inputs.
- clusters of knowledge, attitudes and skills
- generic knowledge motive, trait, social role or a skill
- personal characteristics
- set of skills, related knowledge and attributes

Need for Research in Physical Education

Education without activities is always incomplete. A child may mug up the history textbook, but for how long? May be until the last bell of exams but if it gets a bit of interactive touch, then the same student may have such a memorization and understanding that he will not only just forget it ever in his life but also implement it in his life with an equal degree of effectiveness.

The importance of sports in the life of a young student is invaluable and goes much further than the basic answer that "it keeps kids off the streets." It does in fact keep kids off the streets, but it also instils lessons that are essential in the life of a student athlete. Sports play a pivotal role in the makeup of a young athlete, especially in the middle school to high school years where student athletes are much more mature and mentally developed. Where else can a young, impressionable youth learn values like discipline, responsibility, self confidence, sacrifice, and accountability? Television, which may be the most influential tool in the lives of young adults, does not show enough of these qualities, nor is it on the Internet, or radio. Rather it is up to the parents, teachers, sports teams, clubs, and after school programmes to help mold, develop, and instill these qualities into the lives of student athletes.

In the present situation, education is being increasingly linked with national development. Increased amount of quality research in various fields of education make progress possible. As we have already learnt that research in education not only follows scientific method but at the same time also plays a major role in inculcating scientific and inductive critical thinking. It promotes the development of logical habits of thinking and organization.

The role of research in several fields of education, whether related to psychology, technology, economics, planning, administration and supervision as a whole has greatly increased in modern times. The increasingly complex nature of teaching and learning has focused attention on the use of quality research in solving problems. In educational research, therefore, the first priority is given to the problems relating to the conceptualization of variables with regard to teaching and learning for the formal, non-formal and informal situations.

Research provides the basis for solving nearly all problems relating to teacher preparation, educational administration and supervision. The efficiency of teaching-learning programmes hinges mostly on expediency of educational administration and supervision. In nutshell, we can say that educational research is the fountain of knowledge for the sake of knowledge. It provides important guidelines for solving different educational problems. At the same time, it is a sort of formal training which enables the researcher to understand the new development in educational discipline in a better way.

Research Areas in Physical Education

The spectrum of research areas in which one can study and do research is varied. Supervisor and students decide together on course based on their specific area of research. There is also a scope of trans-disciplinary area of research.

- Active, healthy children
- Adapted physical activity
- Analysis of Human Movement

- Athlete Health
- Coach Education
- Exercise Physiology and Biochemistry
- Behavioural Medicine and Health Psychology
- Leadership and Instruction
- Recreation and Leisure Studies
- Socio-cultural Studies of Sport and Leisure
- Sport and Leisure Organisations
- Sports Nutrition
- Sports Psychology
- Sports Sociology
- Sports Medicine
- Sports Management
- Kinesiology
- Yoga and Meditation

We take a very broad-based approach to research. This multidisciplinary approach sparks collaborations between faculty members in a variety of areas, from biomechanics to neurophysiology, from leisure studies to sport management, among others. Our researchers collaborate with faculty members across campus, and at universities around the world, in diverse fields.

Need for Researcher Competencies

One of the major inputs towards enhancing the quality of teaching and learning in schools as well as the teacher education institutions would be the extent to which research outputs and the outcomes of innovations are utilized by the system. Research on teacher education has been and is being conducted in universities, national level institutions and other establishments but its utility for the teacher educator or the classroom teacher remains rather low. Majority of the research is undertaken to obtain a degree and hence the focus on its possible utility and relevance gets misplaced. The situation is compounded by non-availability of appropriate dissemination mechanisms, like journals, publication of findings in different forms and opportunities to the target group to get an access to these. Institutional capabilities and resources need to be augmented, enabling them to undertake relevant researches.

There is a definite requirement of bringing in research methods and methodologies in appropriate form in teacher education at pre-service and in-service programmes. The basis for the framework for the research competencies utilises an evolutionary model. An individual entering the Career Pathway will previously have acquired a range of competencies of varying levels, some of which have relevance to research. The initial phase is therefore to map the individual's existing competencies against those defined in the curriculum of competencies for research, and then identify those that may need to be developed.

Individuals will have acquired some competencies during their undergraduate studies. The framework is designed to help them identify, and where necessary achieve, a higher level of competence in some areas, and/or acquire new competencies in other areas.

Within the framework its five domains cover aspects relevant to research. Each domain is sub-divided into more specific areas of competence. A description is given of the training activities that can be undertaken to enable individuals to achieve each competency. At the end of the description, there are cross-references to the relevant research leaflets that the FGDP (UK) has produced, and to other materials.

In future, within health and healthcare, it is expected that one will identify the areas and levels of competency that any prospective one will require, to ensure that they can meet the requirements of the job/post concerned. In an era of evidence-informed practice, all those working in healthcare will require some of the competencies identified, which are:

A. Practical skills
B. Problem-solving, thinking and communication skills
C. Personal attitudes and professional ethics
D. Dissemination
E. Roles and functions

Researcher Competency Framework in Physical Education

The rationale for the selection of these topics is based on three concepts. The first is the logical process of the scientific method, namely the identification of a problem; the formation of a hypothesis; deductive reasoning, data collection and analysis; and the derivation of a conclusion. The second is the utilisation of a framework using the concepts of structure, process and outcome to complete the scientific method and the adoption of current good practice. The third is the importance of dissemination, and the skills required to write a research paper.

A. Practical Skills

Practical skills include:

- Find and use resources.
- Use library and information technology effectively.
- Recognise and know when to use primary and secondary resources.
- Observe and record behaviour.
- Demonstrate basic computer competency.

B. Problem Solving, Thinking and Communication Skills

Problem-solving, thinking, and communication skills include:

- Understand the difference between subjective and objective information.
- Recognise when information provided is sufficient.
- Evaluate when the basis for conclusions is laid out completely and clearly.
- Generate research questions by recognising gaps in knowledge.
- Use oral and written communication to express ideas effectively.

C. Personal Attitudes and Professional Ethics

Personal attitudes and professional ethics includes:

- Demonstrate an appreciation of the necessity and value of research for competent clinical practice.
- Demonstrate an awareness and adherence of ethical principles underpinning research, in particular those produced by the Department of Health.

- Design and implement research studies that evaluate clinical practice and service delivery.

D. Dissemination of Research Findings

Dissemination of research findings includes—

- Demonstrating the skills required for publication of research reports.
- Changing clinical practice based on outcome studies and other research.

E. Roles and Functions of a Researcher within a Care System

Roll and functions of a researcher within a care system includes:

- Engage in activities that contribute to the development of a body of knowledge relevant to health and oral healthcare.
- Design and implement a series of studies that address a significant issue.
- Write research funding applications to major funding bodies.
- Offer help and support to other researchers.
- Publish in major journals, both dental and non-dental.
- Contribute to theory within a particular area of study.

Conclusion

In a nutshell, a researcher doing research in the field of physical education must have scientific competencies i.e. scientific knowledge, ability to learn and adapt, ability to formulate a research issue, capacity for analysis and grasp of sophisticated IT tools, ability to work in an interdisciplinary environment. Moreover he must have the ability to work in a team, develop a network, communication skills, ability to assess, manage and steer teams, awareness of the pertinence of research and its impact on the environment. He must also possess creativity, open-minded approach, motivation, involvement, adaptability and ability to self-assess.

References

Andrew, C. Sparkes (1992), *Research in Physical Education and Sports: Exploring Alternative Vision*, The Falmer Press, London.

Kris, E. Berg and Richard, W. Latin (2008 Third Edition), *Essentials of Research Methods in Health, Physical Education, Exercise Science, and Recreation*, Loppincott Williams & Wilkins.

Lorraine, R. Gay *et. al.*, (2012), *Educational Research: Competencies for Analysis and Applications*, Addison Wesley Publishing Company.

Tahir, P. Hussain (2011), *Research Methodology in Physical Education*, Sports Publication, New Delhi.

23

Initiative by UGC for Developing Research Competency

Sheetal Helaiya

Introduction

"Necessity is the mother of invention." This indicates that the individual can discover any thing when he has need of it. The advancement in various fields is through the search for the solution to the problem. These advancements have affected individual life in many ways. Earlier there are major three disciplines such as science, social science and humanities, but today, within these broad categories of disciplines many branches have developed. These developments take place due to research in those fields. The research facilitiates requestioning what is already done and present practices. The purpose of research is not always to discover new thinking but to find out the knowledge that exists in the universe. Social science research is more challenging compared to other fields of research because the researcher has to search out knowledge from a field which is ever changing. Social science research is related with society. The purpose of this research is to bring change or correct things for the welfare of society. There are many types of research which are carried out at various times in the field of society. The research in the field of education is mostly to evaluate present education system and bring change in the education system for the betterment of the society. The research is one of the rigorous act which requires competent person to understand, analyse, interpret data and suggest action with future perspective.

In India, higher education training for research is provided at post graduate level through project work or research work. The students of postgraduation are trained during their course work study. In the field of education, at the masters level (M.Ed.) Dissertation work, is provided to prepare for carry out research in the field of education. One of the purposes of this course is to develop competencies required in the reseracher. In this paper, the author has made an attempt to present quality of research work in India.

World Wide Scenario of Research

Research is required in every part of the world. The government and educational institutions spend many on research and development in the country. There are various agencies that are also providing funds for carrying out research in various fields for the betterment of country or world. The research results facilitate policy decisions for further improvement. The research at the higher education level is also having an impact on policy making. Various types of research are carried out at the higher education level, a few of them are funded by the agencies in the form of projects and others are doctoral and dissertation works of higher education students. The doctoral degree is the highest degree in the field of higher education. In India, the doctoral degree is offered under various disciplines by universities and colleges. At the world level, research and development has received dual attention.

World-Wide Ph.D. Holders

The world-wide scenario of research with prospect to Ph.D. holders is presented as follows:

The Graph 23.1 shows that USA has the highest number of Ph.D. holders and India has the lowest. There is an increase in the number of Ph.D. holders in India. The number of Ph.D. holders, in India, in 2002 was 12,000 which has increased in 2007 and reached to 20,000. There is an increment of 8000 Ph.D. holders during this period (five years).

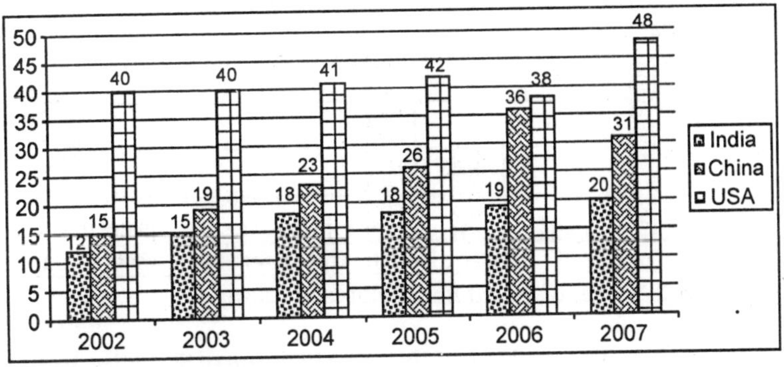

Source: RUSA report, 2013.

Graph 23.1: Number of Ph.D. holders in world (in 000s)

This indicates that India has more researchers compared to earlier. So, these researchers may contribute in their field for the welfare of the society.

Country-wise Contribution of Researchers

The role of a researcher is to contribute in a field of knowledge for the welfare of society. There is an increment in number of Ph.D. holders worldwide but the contribution of these researchers country-wise is not appreciable.

The share of world researcher is presented graphically as follows:

Table 23.1: Share of World Researchers (in %)

Country	*Year*	
	2002	*2007*
USA	23.02	20.20
UK	3.00	2.50
Japan	11.20	10.00
China	14.00	20.10
France	3.20	3.00
Germany	4.60	4.00
India	2.30	2.20

Table 23.1 and the graph shows that only the contribution of China's researchers has increased over a period. The contribution of USA's researchers has reduced during this period from 23.02 per cent to 20.02 per cent.

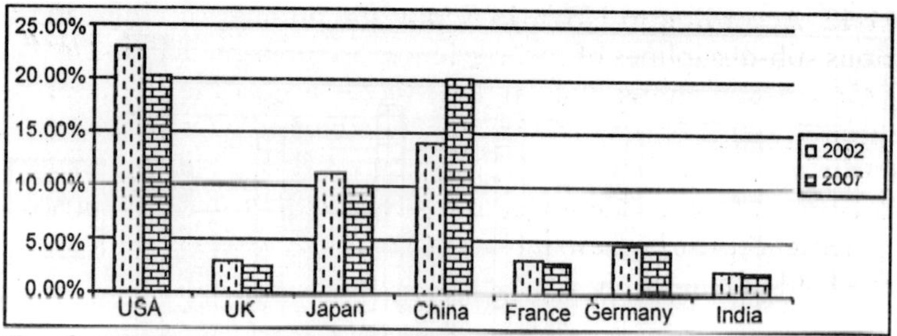

Graph 23.2: Shares of World Researchers

As per data compiled by UNESCO Institute of Statistics, India's contribution to world's research publications has increased from 26,000 in 2002 to 44,000 in 2007. The number of researchers has increased in India but their contribution has reduced by 0.10 per cent which raises questions about the quality of research in India.

Quality of Indian Research

Day-by-day, the quality of Indian research is declining. There are many reasons for the reduction in the quality of research. On one hand, the number of Ph.D. holders are increasing after the 2009 UGC guidelines, in which, UGC made the Ph.D. degree equal to NET. According to figures compiled by the University Grants Commission (UGC), the number of research degrees awarded increased by over 50 per cent from 10,781 in 2008-09 to 16,093 in

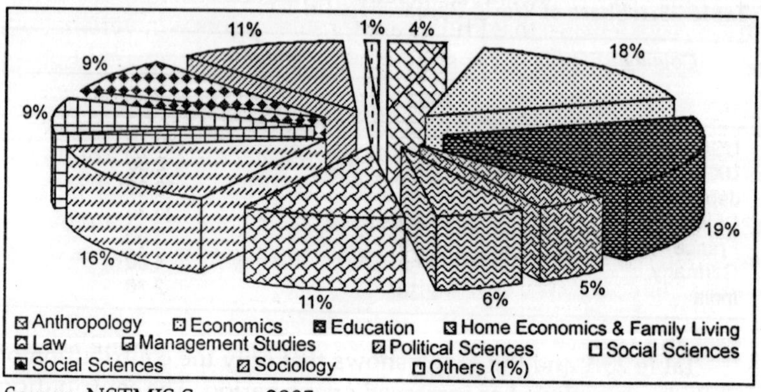

Source: NSTMIS Survey, 2005.

Graph 23.3: Distribution of Ph.D. in Sub-Disciplines of Social Sciences

2011-12. According to NSTMIS Repot, the number of Ph.Ds in various sub-disciplines of social sciences are presented as above.

Graph 23.3 shows that highest Ph.Ds are in the fields of Education and Economics and lowest number of Ph.Ds are in the field of Law and Anthropology. Ph.Ds in the fields of Management and Political Science are more compared to other disciplines of Social Science. The highest number of Ph.D awarded is 19 per cent in the field of education.

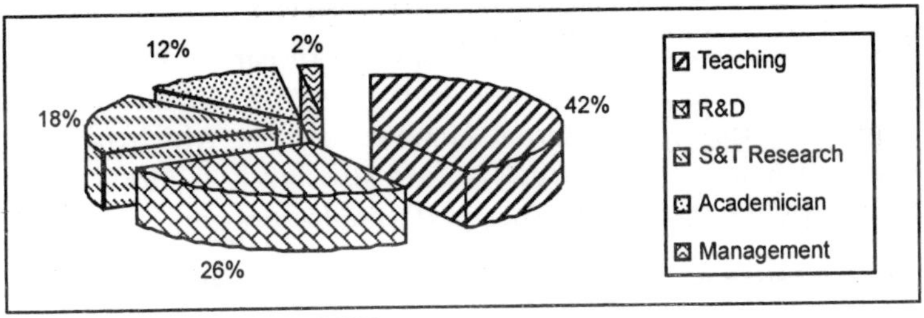

Source: NSTMIS Survey, 2005.

Graph 23.4: Sector wise Employments of Ph.D. holders in 2005

Graph 23.4 shows that the major field where Ph.D. holders hold present employment is Teaching, R&D and Academician. The majority of Ph.D. holders have selected teaching and academics as their field of work.

If they are to become academics or researchers it is an essential to give attention to their quality of work. As Prof. Rao Vemuri commented on this issue, "What bothers me most is the quality of Ph.D.'s being produced and especially the mad rush to get Ph.D.'s. I am appalled to learn that Ph.D.'s are for sale by some universities (and professors). This sorry state of affairs is the direct result of the apathy of guides (advisers) not doing their job. In India there is a growing need to put more emphasis on course work because many of the students and new Ph.D.'s that I encountered are ill-prepared to provide the intellectual leadership we expect of a Ph.D." "...A typical Ph.D student in India, it appears, is a part-time student who spends one hour a day and gets the degree in about 3 calendar years. You do the numbers."

- The Indian research is more degree oriented rather knowledge contributor.
- There is a less originality of work. More dupliction of work in various fields.

- Very less reach of research result to the field of knowledge.
- There is a weak network for sharing knowledge created and share knowledge created through reaserch.
- There are few researchers who take research after Ph.D.

These all are a few aspects which highlight the quality of research in India.

Reasons for Low Quality Research in India

There are many reasons for low quality research in India. This research can be classified into two categories as external and internal factors. The external factors are those which facilitate research work. The external factors also work as motivational factors for the researcher. These external factors are:

- **Finance:** Very few agencies provide financial support to carry out research. The funds allocation for research is a demotivating factor for the researcher.
- **Infrastructure facilities:** To do research work certain basic infrastructure facilities are required within a higher educational institution. The poor quality of library and laboratory facilities demotivates or restricts the researcher to do research work.
- **No network between researchers in same or different field:** The researcher requires certain information and guidance from the other researchers. In India, there is no such network existing which provide guidance to a new researcher in that field. Due to lack of guidance, sometimes, the researcher withdraws himself from the research or does faulty research which might lead to wastage of time, energy.
- **Unfurnished Library:** In many institutions very few journals are available. It is said that an average Indian University subscribes to less than 500 journals and an average American university subscribes to 500+ journals (Biswal, 2008).

The internal factors are basic qualities possessed by the researcher. Skills are also required by the researcher to do research work. The researcher is required to be competent enough. The researcher needs to have knowledge, skills and aptitude for research.

Meaning Research Competency

Research competency means the competency required by the researcher to carry out research. Research is a systematic process to discover knowledge. To discover knowledge the researcher requires certain skills and knowledge related to research. The core competencies required by the researcher are given as follows:

1. **Scientific competencies**
   - Scientific knowledge,
   - Ability to learn and adapt,
   - Ability to formulate a research issue,
   - Capacity for analysis and grasp of sophisticated IT tools,
   - Ability to work in an interdisciplinary environment, and
   - Ability to incorporate existing knowledge.
2. **Project and team management skills**
   - Ability to work in a team,
   - Ability to develop a network,
   - Communication skills,
   - Ability to assess,
   - Language skills,
   - Project management skills (organisation skill), and
   - Awareness of the pertinence of the research and impact on the environment.
3. **Personal aptitudes/interpersonal skills**
   - Creativity,
   - Open-minded approach,
   - Motivation/Involvement,
   - Adaptability, and
   - Ability to self-assess.

These competencies are required by the researcher to carry out quality research work. The UGC has initiated developing researcher competencies by modifying Ph.D. guidelines in the year 2009.

Anaysis of Ph.D. Guidelines with Reference to Core Research Competencies

The UGC has introduced various components in the Ph.D. course to improve the quality of Ph.D. research work. The UGC has tried to cover all research competencies. Here, the UGC Ph.D. guidelines are analysed with reference to research compentencies required by the researcher.

- **Entrance test:** The UGC has introduced a Ph.D. entrance examination to get Ph.Ds. enroll as scholars in any field of higher education. The purpose of the entrance test is to check the research aptitude of the candidate. The components covered as courses for entrance test relate to language skills, computer IT skills for research, knowledge related to research, analytical skill, etc.
- **Registration Procedure:** The UGC has changed the procedure for Ph.D. registration. The purpose of bringing about a change in procedure of registration is to guide the research scholar in planning of research work and monitoring research work in the field. The effort is to reduce the duplication of research work and do the required modification at the initial stage of the research work. By this UGC has tried to address the core competency of a researcher regarding the knowledge of research as a systematic procedure.
- **Course Work:** The UGC has introduced course work as mandatory component of Ph.D. course work, which every Ph.D. scholar has to complete. The course work is related to specific and general area of research. The general areas of research include knowledge related to research and application of computer/IT in research. The Ph.D. scholar has to complete course work related to the field in which he has planned to do research work. By completing this course work, researcher gains knowledge and skills required for the research work. These courses are known as University course work which is general course work and Department course work which is specific related to his area of research.
- **Publications:** As a part of a Ph.D. course, the Ph.D. scholar has to publish some of his Ph.D. work in referred journals. The purpose of such publication is to develop the writing skills of the researcher. The UGC has made it mandatory to publish before submitting a Ph.D. thesis. This initiative facilitates the researchers to organise and share their ideas

with others. It is also facilitates other researcheres who wish to work in such field.

- **Open Defense:** The work of researchers usually remain in the institution as there is no proper network for sharing the knowledge generated by the researcher. The UGC has provided a forum for the researcher to share his knowledge with others before getting Ph.D. degree. Now, it is compulsory for the Ph.D. scholars to share their Ph.D. work with others in open defense or open viva where all research scholars, academician and post graduate students remain present. Through this, the researcher develops presentation skills and sharing of knowledge opens doors for further research in that field.

The initiatives taken by the UGC to improve quality of research is really helping the researcher in many ways. The researcher requires certain skills to carry out his research work which he gains from his Ph.D. course work. This initiative does not only improve the quality of research at institutional level but globally. This also facilitates the researchers to share their knowledge at world level which improve status of Indian research at world level. Through this modification in the Ph.D. course work, the UGC has made an attempt not only to improve quality of research in the country but also develop research competency of the researcher which makes him lifelong researcher.

References

Biswal, G.C. (2008). *Quality Research: A Few Determinants.* New Delhi: Edutracks. Vol. 7(11), pp. 5-6.

Goel, S. (n.d.). *Is Today's Ph. D Education in Indias Aiming To Create Inspiring Intellectual Leaders of Tomorrow?* Retrieved on 3rd March, 2014. In www.indiaeducationreview.com

Kurup, A. and Arora, J. (2010). *Trends in Higher Education: Creation and Analysis of a Database of Ph.Ds.* Bangalore: National Institute of Advanced Studies.

MHRD, (2013). *Rashtriya Uchchatar Shiksha Abhiyan: National Higher Education Mission.*

24

Relative Focus on Various Types of Research in Education

Sandhya Milind Khedekar

Introduction

Research is the orderly investigation of a subject matter for the purpose of adding to knowledge. Research can mean 're-search' implying that the subject matter is already known but, for one reason or another, needs to be studied again. Alternatively, the expression can be used without a hyphen and in this case it typically means investigating a new problem or phenomenon.

Within the realm of educational planning, many things are always changing: the structure of the education system, curriculum and textbooks, modes of teaching, methods of teacher training, the amount and type of provisions to schools such as science laboratories, textbooks, furniture, classroom supplies, and so on. These changes may lead to an improvement, or a worsening, in the quality of an educational system. Sometimes they may result in no impact upon quality—in which case major government expenditures on such changes have been wasted. The educational planner working within this kind of environment must be able to undertake assessments of the effects of major changes and then provide policy advice that will consolidate and extend the post productive courses of action, and also intercept and terminate existing practices that are shown to be damaging and wasteful.

There are many types of educational research studies and there are also a number of ways in which they may be classified. Studies may be classified according to topic whereby the particular phenomena being investigated are used to group the studies. Some examples of educational research topics are: teaching methods, school administration, classroom environment, school finance, etc. Studies may also be classified according to whether they are exploratory or confirmatory.

An exploratory study is undertaken in situations where there is a lack of theoretical understanding about the phenomena being investigated so that key variables, their relationships, and their (potential) causal linkages, are the subject of conjecture. In contrast a confirmatory study is employed when the researcher has generated a theoretical model (based on theory, previous research findings, or detailed observation) that needs to be tested through the gathering and analysis of field data.

A more widely applied way of classifying educational research studies is to define the various types of research according to the kinds of information that they provide. Accordingly, educational research studies may be classified as follows:

1. Historical research generates descriptions, and sometimes attempted explanations, of conditions, situations, and events that have occurred in the past. For example, a study that documents the evolution of teacher training programmes since the turn of the century, with the aim of explaining the historical origins of the content and processes of current programmes.

2. Descriptive research provides information about conditions, situations, and events that occur in the present. For example, a survey of the physical condition of school buildings in order to establish a descriptive profile of the facilities that exist in a typical school.

3. Correlational research involves the search for relationships between variables through the use of various measures of statistical association. For example, an investigation of the relationship between teachers' satisfaction with their job and various factors describing the provision and quality of teacher housing, salaries, leave entitlements, and the availability of classroom supplies.

4. Causal research aims to suggest causal linkages between variables by observing existing phenomena and then searching back through available data in order to try to identify plausible causal relationships. For example, a study of factors related to student 'drop out' from secondary school using data obtained from school records over the past decade.

5. Experimental research is used in settings where variables defining one or more 'causes' can be manipulated in a systematic fashion in order to discern 'effects' on other variables. For example, an investigation of the effectiveness of two new textbooks using random assignment of teachers and students to three groups—two groups for each of the new textbooks, and one group as a 'control' group to use the existing textbook.

6. Case study research generally refers to two distinct research approaches. The first consists of an in-depth study of a particular student, classroom, or school with the aim of producing a nuanced description of the pervading cultural setting that affects education, and an account of the interactions that take place between students and other relevant persons. For example, an in-depth exploration of the patterns of friendship between students in a single class. The second approach to Case Study Research involves the application of quantitative research methods to non-probability samples—which provide results that are not necessarily designed to be generalizable to wider populations. For example, a survey of the reading achievements of the students in one rural region of a particular country.

7. Ethnographic research usually consists of a description of events that occur within the life of a group—with particular reference to the interaction of individuals in the context of the socio-cultural norms, rituals, and beliefs shared by the group. The researcher generally participates in some part of the normal life of the group and uses what he or she learns from this participation to understand the interactions between group members.

For example, a detailed account of the daily tasks and interactions encountered by a school principal using observations gathered by a researcher who is placed in the position of 'Principal's Assistant' in order to become fully involved in the daily life of the school.

8. Research and development research differs from the above types of research in that, rather than bringing new information to light, it focuses on the interaction between research and the production and evaluation of a new product. This type of research can be 'formative' (by collecting evaluative information about the product while it is being developed with the aim of using such information to modify and improve the development process). For example, an investigation of teachers' reactions to the various drafts and redrafts of a new mathematics teaching kit, with the information gathered at each stage being used to improve each stage of the drafting process. Alternatively, it can be 'summative' (by evaluating the worth of the final product, especially in comparison to some other competing product). For example, a comparison of the mathematics achievement of students exposed to a new mathematics teaching kit in comparison with students exposed to the established mathematics curriculum.

In research on issues concerned with educational planning, the main educational research questions can be subsumed under three categories: descriptive, correlational, and causal.

There are three types of research questions in educational planning.

Descriptive Questions

In the field of educational planning, the research carried out on descriptive questions is often focused on comparing the existing conditions of schooling with: (i) legislated benchmark standards, (ii) conditions operating in several other school systems, or (iii) conditions operating in several sectors of a single school system.

Some examples are:

- What is the physical state of school buildings in the country? Do some districts or regions have better or worse school buildings than others? (Behind these two questions are the implications that the Ministry of Education wishes to ensure that all schools have a minimum standard of school building while at the same time ensuring that there are not large differences among schools with respect to the state of their buildings.)
- Do the supplies and equipment in classrooms in the schools match the legislated standards set by the Ministry? (The supplies and equipment might be textbooks, exercise books, pencils, erasers, seats and desks. The Ministry may have norms that each student in a particular grade must have one mother tongue textbook, one math textbook, one science textbook and one social studies textbook, four

exercise books, three pencils and one eraser in a year, and that each student must have one seat and one writing place. The research required in this situation then consists of undertaking a count of the supplies and equipment in all schools, or in a scientific sample of schools that can be used to estimate the situation in all schools, and then matching every school or classroom against the Ministry's norms. The main aim of this kind of research study would be to examine whether there are particular districts or regions which are under-supplied or over-supplied.)

- Where systems of education have teacher housing, how adequate is the housing? (Some Ministries take the view that if the personal needs of teachers such as teacher housing do not satisfy the teachers then they will not be committed teachers. So, again, the research will consist of fact-finding about teacher housing and about teachers' satisfaction with these housing conditions.)
- What is the level of achievement in the core subject areas at a particular level of schooling? Does such achievement accord with the Ministry's view of what should have been learned by all students or particular sub-groups of students? A further question is often raised about student achievement—is it better, worse, or the same as last year's achievement for the particular grade group? And, again, are there differences between regions, or urban and rural children, and so on? (By the early 1990s there was a thrust from some systems of education—especially that of the United States of America—to have comparisons of achievement (at the same age level) of different national systems of education for countries at a similar level of economic development.)

Correlational Questions

Behind these kinds of questions, there is often an assumption that if an association is found between variables then it provides evidence of causation. However, care must be exercised when moving between the notions of association and causation. For example, an 'association' may be discovered between the incidence of classroom libraries and average class reading scores. However, the real 'cause' of higher reading scores may be that students from high socio-economic backgrounds, while they tend to be in classes with classroom libraries, read better than other students because their home environments (in terms of physical, emotional, and intellectual resources) facilitate the acquisition of reading skills.

Some examples are:

- Do students in poorer school buildings have lower achievement scores than those in better buildings?
- Do students in better equipped classrooms have better achievement scores than those in less well-equipped classrooms?
- Do students in schools where the teachers have better teacher housing have higher achievement than students in schools where teachers have poorer teacher housing?
- Do male students do better than female students in the scientific/technical subject areas?

Causal Questions

Causal questions are usually the most important to educational planners. For example, in some schools it is considered normal for children to have a desk at which to sit. In other schools the children sit on the ground and write on their laps. It is important to know if schools (with a particular socio-economic background of children) with a shortage of desks and seats achieve less well than schools (with a similar socio-economic background of children) with an adequate supply of desks and chairs. Or, to put the question in a different way, is it the desks and chairs, or something else, which really cause the better achievement? It may be a better supply of books or better qualified teachers or, or, or.... It is, therefore, important to disentangle the relative influence of each of the many input and process factors in schools on achievement.

As will be seen from another module in this series on 'Research Design' both survey and experimental designs can be used to assess the relative influence of many factors on educational achievement. It is unusual in education to find only one factor influencing student educational achievement. It is rather the case that several, or even many, factors from outside and inside the school influence how well or poorly students achieve in school.

Thus, causal questions take one of two forms. Some examples are:

- **All other factors being equal** do students with Textbook A achieve better than students with Textbook B?
- **What is the relative effect** on school achievement of the following factors:
  - the socio-economic level of students in the school;
  - the general parental help given to the children with their homework;
  - peer group pressure;
  - the condition of the school buildings;
  - the supplies and equipment in the classroom;
  - the curriculum; and
  - the quality of teaching, etc.

Given that many factors will affect student achievement, then it is those factors that have a large influence which must be of concern to educational planners. Once the important factors have been identified then the planners can decide on the action they wish to take. Let us assume that it is found that the existence of sufficient desks and chairs does have a major influence on achievement, then it is up to the Ministry of Education to ensure that sufficient desks and chairs are made available. But, once this has been accomplished it will be necessary to undertake further research to discover what now is the most important factor influencing achievement.

Identifying Research Issues for Educational Planning

The reason why all educational planners should be prepared to undertake research is that it is important to be sure of the facts before making suggestions for changes in educational policies and practices. The maxim must always be "when in doubt, find out".

The questions listed above are only examples and are very general in nature. It is up to each Ministry and educational planning office to pose its own questions in order to remove doubt. The formulation of research questions is, however, not an easy matter.

A wise educational researcher, educational planner, and ex-Minister of Education, Dr. C. E. Beeby from New Zealand, once wrote:

"I have suggested areas of research that seem to me to be of special importance. But not once have I asked a specific question to which I want an answer... I know enough about research to be aware that the formulation of the proper question may take as much skill and professional insight as the finding of an answer to it, and it may be a skill in which the administrator is not adept. So, the research workers must be involved in the asking of the questions, and must be prepared, in turn, to play a necessary, but secondary, part in devising the policies that may follow from the research, where their expertise is limited". (ACER Radford Memorial Lecture, Melbourne, Australia 1987).

The examples of questions given earlier are general questions. There is a lot of work involved in turning such general questions into research questions. How this is done is dealt with in another module in this series that is entitled: "Specification of Research Aims".

Before proceeding to a discussion of the sequential steps in the research process, some examples are given of issues on which research was undertaken by educational planners in the 1980s.

1. Indonesia national evaluation of grade nine achievement levels (Jiyono and Suryadi, 1992)

- A description of the achievement of the Grade nine students in Mathematics, Science, Social Studies, Moral Education, Mother Tongue, and English.
- The identification of the relative importance of the in– and out-of-school factors associated with achievement in each subject matter.
- A comparison of the achievement in 1981 with the achievement of the students in the same grade in 1976 (Jiyono and Suryadi, 1982).

2. Indonesia non formal learning behaviour (Mappa, 1982)

- To compare the 'booklet only' learning groups with 'booklet plus radio' learning groups in a distance education project on the achievement of learners in: literacy, general knowledge, and numeracy.
- To measure the attitudes of learners toward innovation,

health and nutrition, marriage, family planning and agriculture.

References

Brown, A. L. (1992). Design experiments: Theoretical and Methodological Challenges in Creating Complex Interventions. *Journal of the Learning Sciences, 2*, 141-178.

Chinn, C. (2006). The microgenetic method: Current work and extensions to classroom research. In J.L. Green, G.C. Mailli, and P.B. Elmore (Eds.), *Handbook of Complementary Methods in Education Research*, pp. 439-456. Mahwah, NJ: Erlbaum.

Cobb, P., Confrey, J., diSessa, A., Lehrer, R., and Schauble, L. (2003). Design Experiments in Educational Research. *Educational Researcher, 32*, 9-13.

Cook, T.D., and Campbell, D.T. (1979). *Quasi-experimentation: Design and Analysis Issues for Field Settings*. Boston: Houghton Mifflin.

Creswell, J.W. (2002). *Research Design: Qualitative, Quantitative, and Mixed Method Approaches*. Thousand Oaks: Sage Publications.

Ferrance, E. (2000). *Action Research*. Providence, RI: Northeast and Islands Regional Educational Laboratory at Brown University.

Fraenkel, J.R., and Wallen, N.E. (1996). *How to Design and Evaluate Research in Education* (3rd ed.). New York: McGraw-Hill.

Institute of Education Sciences. *Identifying and Implementing Educational Practices Supported by Rigorous Evidence: A User Friendly Guide*. Washington, DC: U.S. Department of Education.

McMillan, J.H. (2000). *Educational Research: Fundamentals for the Consumer* (3rd ed.). New York: Addison Wesley Longman.

National Research Council. (2002). *Scientific Research in Education*. Committee on Scientific Principles for Education Research. Shavelson, R.J., and Towne, L., Editors. Centre for Education. Division of Behavioural and Social Sciences and Education. Washington, DC: National Academy Press.

Pressley, M.; and Harris, J.R. (2006). Cognitive strategies instruction: From basic research to classroom instruction. In P.A. Alexander and P.H. Winne (Eds.), *Handbook of Educational Psychology* (2nd ed., pp. 265-286). Mahwah, NJ: Erlbaum.

Turner, J.C., Midgley, C., Meyer, D.K., Gheen, M., Anderman, E.M., Kang, Y., and Patrick, H. (2002). The classroom environment and students' reports of avoidance strategies in mathematics: A multimethod study. *Journal of Educational Psychology, 94*, 88-106.

25

Towards a More Authentic, Productive and Ethical Research

Sarla A. Santwani and *Dhirendra Patel*

Introduction

The community of the researchers is the intellectual capital for any country. Therefore, identifying this capital, nurturing it, multiplying it and enhancing its quality should be the major concerns for any country. According to S. Goel. 'One of the main objectives of postgraduate education, especially PhD education, is to prepare intellectual leaders who will do the groundwork to create new paradigms and products for tomorrow.' He therefore, suggests, 'Postgraduate education needs to provide deeper experience in the values, norms, and practices of the chosen profession while also developing the skills, tools, and habits of inquiry within a discipline.' However, the reality of the research being conducted in the Indian Universities is exactly opposite to this, especially in case of research in the discipline of Education. Most of the research carried out is meaningless, irrelevant, stereotyped, repetitive and unproductive. Research ends up being piled up in libraries, occasionally redeemed by the subsequent researchers who might use it for reference. It is rare to find any research making an intervention in the existing system of education or social/economic/political scenario at large. One wonders if research even brings in some real change in the researcher's own self, leading him/her to become a better academic professional, a more reflective intellectual and a better citizen concerned deeply with the welfare and progress of the nation. A time has actually arrived that research on the research process and researchers must be conducted, if we intend to direct our human and financial resources in the right direction.

We all talk about quality of research but parameters of quality are not clearly defined. Generally, while talking about quality, the aspects emphasized are research rigour, and sophisticated and ingenious methodology. 'More detailed and descriptive the statistics, better the quality of research is' seems to be the defining characteristic of the research. The other aspects of research such as relevance of the research in the context of actual issues and problems encountered in the discipline of education, academic profession or larger society, involvement of the researcher in research, transformation of the researcher during the research process and ultimately the outcome of research which is to solve the real problems in the field or intervention of some sort are neglected. Research ethics remains an alien term in the arena of educational research. According to Sanjay Goel (n.d.), instead of viewing Ph.D 'as a means to nurture five P's, i.e., Passion, Patience, Perseverance, Perspective, and Purpose, a very large number of Ph.D scholars, supervisors, and academic institutions are increasingly approaching it with a mindset focuses on three D's, i.e., Degree, Designation, and Dough (money).'

If we wish to seek a remedy for such a dismal scenario of educational research, we must begin right at the beginning:

- Identifying the human capital which has potential to become the intellectual capital is the first step in this direction. The best talent with a potential for carrying out innovative research needs to be first attracted to the University. How do we identify talent with such a potential? For mapping of research competence, we have introduced qualifying tests such as NET/SET/JRF etc. and Ph.D. entrance tests conducted by the universities. Have these entrance tests really helped us in mapping the competence of the researcher at the entry level? We still find researchers directionless as to what is expected of them. These entrance tests just test their content in their limited area of knowledge. They don't have provision to map the attitudes of the researchers, which are as crucial as the content knowledge. Through personal interviews, authentic references from their teachers/mentors/supervisors and through their performance in the discussions and research forums, this may be mapped.

- Identifying Research Problems: When the young researchers embark on their doctoral research, many of them don't have clarity about the specific topic or even the broad area on which they intend to do research because they have so far operated only within the narrow range of their specific disciplines and not developed the broader vision to view their own disciplines in the perspective of overall knowledge or in the context of national and global development. Most of them depend on their guides to provide them research topics. Researcher, here, generally goes by the criteria of what interests him/her and what is easy and manageable for him/her. It is not uncommon to find research topics imposed on the researchers by the guides for various reasons. The main concern of the researchers remains to sail through the entire research process anyhow until acquisition of Ph. D. degree. In such a situation, the researcher hardly feels involved in the research process because s/he doesn't own the research topic. It does not spring from his/her practice or observations. It is superimposed. These kind of fake attributes to research also raise questions about research ethics, the honesty issue. There is hardly scope of thinking about what is the need of the hour, what are the real issues which need attention. In such a situation, how can one hope for meaningful, relevant research which contributes to the national development. The high, noble goals like National Development or development of their own profession or even their own development is far from their minds. Expecting to spell out the broad research agendas from the apex bodies such as NCERT, ICSSR, UGC etc. is desirable but there are other mechanisms too. Creating a mechanism to find out the actual issues/problems faced by the schools/colleges/universities/students etc. and encouraging the researchers to conduct researches to work on these. Making experience eligibility criteria for research and encouraging researchers to work on the real issues they have faced as academic professionals can surely pave way for the authentic and productive research.

- The quality of research process is of great importance while talking about research management. Even if the researcher may not be able to produce excellent research as it is usually the first research, the process must impart training in conducting research, inculcate desirable attitudes through efficient research management and a researcher gradually should get integrated into the academic research community. One issue which is not a lot talked about in this regard is the relationship between the research guide and the research student. There are no standard guidelines about this hence, the dynamics of this relationship result in great complexity affecting the quality of research. It generally becomes a matter of 'essential tensions' as it entails aspects of exercising power on one hand and mutual dependence on the other hand. We find different types of guides ranging from over-protective guides who make their students totally dependent and in return of this total surrender even ensure better placement for their students if they happen to be in powerful positions, to the autocratic and over controlling types who deny any academic freedom to their students and even forbid their students from interacting with other scholars within or outside the institution to the exploitative and apathetic types. There is no consideration given to the comfort level of this relationship which can help the researcher to develop research skills and lead towards a more involved and meaningful research process. The policies regarding this vary from time-to-time and from one university to another and usually vacillate between 'allotments of the guide from the above' versus researcher choosing his/her guide. However, there is scope for more options in the mechanisms to determine this relationship. In some countries, a researcher initially starts not with one fixed guide but has free floating interactions with several guides, who are members of a research team and then gradually arrives at the final decision about the guiding supervisor. Sonneveld (2009) describes the procedure of pairing the researcher and the research guide most appropriately as an exercise in 'Social Engineering.' In case of interdisciplinary research, a researcher may have an additional co-guide from other discipline. If more consideration is given to the nature of research and types of expertise needed for guiding specific research rather than rigid bureaucratic criteria, it will lead to healthier researcher-guide relationship which can enhance the quality of research process.

- Another issue which is related to the research guide is their competence not only in terms of content mastery but ability to carry out the supervision of the research process more efficiently and fruitfully. The training of research guides needs to be recognized as an important aspect. The research guides need to be trained as to how to perform their supervisonary duties. Some other issues faced by them and demand attention are finding enough time for guidance, how to monitor the research process and at times how to make up for the lack of knowledge on part of the researcher in one or more aspects of research. There is possibility of forming research teams wherein new guides can learn from the senior and experienced guides. There is a need to clearly define the role of Ph.D. guides and state explicitly the desirable attributes. Workshops wherein they are trained accordingly can go a long way in this direction.
- Last but not the least an ethical dimension needs to be given its due place in the educational research. Apart from the plagiarism issue about which at least some deliberations have been made, there are other ethical issues such as authenticity and legitimacy of the research. Fake research on the issues not actually experienced or observed lead to unauthentic research. A researcher cannot feel deeply involved in such fake research, hence conducts it robotically. Research focusing more on the scientific methodology than on the nature and relevance of research should be discouraged. The issues of 'objectivity' and 'truth' in the context of research need to be deliberated. The philosophical and metaphysical dimension of 'objectivity' and 'truth' should not be overlooked. More

qualitative research seeking phenomenological truths also should be given its due place. Appropriate methodology for such research needs to be evolved. Our indigenous cultural heritage has much to offer in this regard but our obsession with the behaviouristic models and paradigms does not allow us to tap this resource.

- Kopatsy. S. (1999), a Hungarian economist, well known for his writings about the relationship of economic prosperity and social well being in society, states, "The Intellectual capital is the most Important" and argues that Intellectual Capital cannot be treated and measured like tangible properties. He proposed an equation: Intellectual Capital = Knowledge × Effort × Talent × Morality. Absence of any one of these four components makes Intellectual Capital ZERO. According to him with good effort and high academic morality, even mediocre knowledge and talent, can create good intellectual capital.
- In conclusion, I wish to draw attention to the different types of research being produced, from mediocre to excellent yet the value attached to all these researchers is the same. To put a researcher who has produced excellent research and someone who has produced a mediocre research in the same category is unethical too. Why not grade the research?

References

Goel, Sanjay *'Is Today's Ph.D. Education in India Aiming to Create Inspiring Intellectual Leaders of Tomorrow*? www.indianeducationreview.com

Sonneveld, Hans, (2009) 'Monitoring PhD Supervision Quality: The Dutch way.'

26
Research Competencies for Teacher Educator

R.L. Madhavi

Introduction

Research is the search for knowledge through systematic investigation, to establish new facts, solve existing problems, establish new ideas, or develop new theories, using a systematic approach. The primary objective of research is discovering, interpreting and developing methods and systems for the advancement of human knowledge on a wide variety of scientific matters. Research involves the mastery of different skills needed to design and conduct a systematic, objective, and critical inquiry of an identified problem or an issue. Research may be descriptive, developmental or experimental. The ability to conduct independent research and to make appropriate use of quantitative, qualitative, or mixed methods of analytical techniques decides the success of research undertaken. The success of research is to be disseminated through participation in conferences, seminars and publishing.

Basically, to get the research success, following research competencies are prerequisites.

1. Critical review of the literature and comprehensive theoretical knowledge and in-depth understanding. Employees/students or any other person, who is going to

conduct research, must demonstrate the ability to synthesize and critically review a body of literature that is more comprehensive than what is expected for a standard.

2. Framing a research question: The success of the research mainly will depend on the research questions. Therefore, this ability/competency is vital for research. All the research conductors must demonstrate the ability to correctly identify researchable questions.
3. Capability of developing instrument for effective research: The entire team of persons who wish to conduct research must demonstrate the ability to design an instrument for collecting data. This competency includes the identification of existing instruments, the ability to adapt existing instruments for new modalities and to create new instruments etc.
4. Data collection related competencies: Students/employees/scientists must have document related competencies with primary data collection including activities relating to data coding and data entry.
5. Data analysis related competency: It's needed to have document related experience with scientific and systematic experience with analyzing the primary data they have collected as part of a supervised research project.

Above are the basic competencies required to get effective research done and those competencies can be developing in many ways. Continuous training and learning, effective coaching and counseling, will help everyone to master their research competency level. (*Source: http://youremployment.biz/competency/research-competency/*)

The Competencies Needed in a Researcher By 2020

'Competence is a structured set of knowledge, skills and attitudes acquired through learning, which enable problem solving in new situations. Competencies are of different types and degrees of development and levels of specific products, differential learning. The concept of competencies is meaning of "organizing" against which are selected and organized learning content, training methods, assessment procedures. Competence is a "red thread" that crosses all school and all courses of instruction, from primary school to high education. The competence required from a subject in a "knowledge-based society", corresponds to his/her individual "potential" in terms of his/her being capable of combining elements and resources: from this perspective competence consists in the *"flexible assets of the individual, as acquired and developed through diversified, occasional and intentional experiences, which enable him/her to creatively operate in a wide range of activities"*.. Skills are competence being implemented (for instance, within the framework of specific processes) and are the result of competence.

As each skill is the result of a mix of elements/resources, the asset and self-reliance of a subject (and a worker, in particular) consist exactly in his/her being capable of producing a winning combination. The wider the baggage of resources an individual can count on, and his/her "excellence" in combining them, the higher his/her level of skills mastery would be, namely his/her knowing how to act in specific and new situations, in order to produce required/expected output.' (Doinita Ariton, 2009). The ideal experienced researcher is expected to possess the following twenty key competencies for today's and tomorrow's research needs.

Key Competences required for the Future Teacher Educators

Scientific competencies	*Personal aptitudes/ interpersonal skills*	*Project and team management skills*
• Scientific knowledge • Ability to learn and adapt • Ability to formulate a research issue • Capacity for analysis and grasp of sophisticated IT tools • Ability to work in an interdisciplinary environment • Ability to incorporate existing knowledge	• Creativity • Open-minded approach • Motivation/ Involvement • Adaptability • Ability to self-assess	• Ability to work in a team • Ability to develop a network • Communication skills • Ability to assess • Language skills • Business culture and management skills • Project management skills • Ability to manager and steer teams • Awareness of the pertinence of the research and its impact on the environment

* Based on the 8 countries (France, Germany, Finland, the Netherlands, the UK, Switzerland, Japan and the USA) study report.

Source: APEC/DELOITTE Study (2010).

These competencies will become decisive as future changes in the world of research become reality. The ability to take into account the pertinence of research and its impact on society is now the most important of all the competencies. Relationships with clientele and stakeholders are important in deciding the relevancy of research. Researchers must therefore be capable of understanding what the market demands, focusing on the research the market wants, and translating the commercial potential of the problems they study into practical solutions. This will minimise the time spent on research and maximise the efficiency of the research. This competency is thus a key factor for the efficiency of research in general. The more business-oriented the researcher is, the greater his awareness of the potential for applying the research is, and the greater his future career opportunities are. The researcher of tomorrow will need to retain all this scientific excellence while also being able to think in terms of market potential. Today's students want to know the benefits of a research subject to society. This concern has gained ground with the current economic crisis and is currently one of the main factors driving changes in university education. The majority of research managers, however, feel that this competency is not as yet sufficiently developed in the world of research. Competencies are very much dependent on the nature of the structure in which the researcher works. The more developed an organisation's research support structures are, the more its expectations regarding the competencies of its researchers which are precise and focused on specific areas of expertise. In large structures, support and back-up functions allow the researcher to focus on his/her core activity.

Principles Behind the Development of Competencies

The principles underpinning competency development are common to all areas of training. They are that:

- Competencies can be acquired through multiple means. Knowledge alone is unlikely to allow an individual to achieve competency. Other experiences that complement training should reinforce the acquisition of competencies.
- A single curriculum is unnecessary to define the acquisition of competencies. Individuals will have

experienced opportunities that are unique, and the programme to help them achieve competencies should be tailored to their specific needs.

- Those involved in the development of curricula should identify the target audience and level of competence to be achieved on completion of training. These should be specified in a training contract.
- The competencies for research will in part be common with other existing competencies developed for adoption within the career pathway.
- The competency framework should be monitored and updated as the science and practice of discipline evolves.

Source: Research Competencies Framework, Published 4 April 2007.

Competencies need to be identified and developed according to contextual needs. Experiences through intended opportunities provided for trainees will help in comprehending and developing competencies. The development process needs to be unique and the process needs to be specific need focused. The curriculum for competency development need to be target oriented. The competencies for research are not separate but mingled with other competencies necessary during training and also in future career pathway.

Teacher Education for the 21st Century

The rapidly changing aspects of the 21st century in terms of training, development and employment of aspirant teacher trainee made it necessary to think about new models of teacher education. One such model thought for 'thinking teachers' by Singapore National Institute of Education is presented here. To develop students competent to face challenges of 21st century, teachers also need new skills, ideas and knowledge bases.

TE21*: Towards a strong teaching force for the 21st century—Enhanced Partnership with MOE and Schools: commitment from all key stakeholders—NIE, MOE and schools is required in transforming teacher education to produce 21st century teachers.

*TE21 = Teacher Education

R1*: New Values3 (V) Learner Centre Values, Teacher identify and Service to the profession and community; Skills (S) Reflective skills and thinking dispositions, Pedagogical skills People management skills, Self-management skills, Administrative and Management skills, Communication skills, Facilitative skills, Technological skills, Innovation and Entrepreneurship skills, Social and Emotional intelligence; and Knowledge (K) Model—Self, Pupil, Community, Subject content, Pedagogy, Educational foundation and Policies, Curriculum, Multicultural literacy, Global awareness, Environment awareness;

R2: Graduate Teacher Competencies (GTC) Framework—Professional Practice, Leadership and Management, Personal Effectiveness;

R3: Strengthening the Theory-Practice Nexus-reflection (Theory)—Pedagogical tools that bring the classroom into the University -Experiential Learning (Practice)— School-based enquiry or research;

R4: Programme Refinements and an Extended Pedagogical Repertoire;

R5: Assessment Framework for 21st Century Teaching and Learning;

R6: Enhanced Pathways for Professional Development.

Transforming for the 21st century—*Walking the Talk through initiatives like,* Evidence-based, research-informed improvements to teaching and learning, Academic Quality Management, Faculty professional development, Infrastructure and systems to support learning.

Teacher Educator

Teacher educators are defined as people "who provide instruction or who give guidance and support to student teachers, and who thus render a substantial contribution to the development of students into competent teachers" (Koster *et. al.*, 2005, p. 157). They are the ones who are responsible for the quality of teachers, and, of education. Thus, it is of crucial importance to explore the factors that contribute towards the professional development of teacher

*R = Recommendations

educators and to set the quality requirements and specific competencies for them. The role of professional standards set by academic publications, professional organizations, institutional guidelines for promotion and tenure, and other relevant sources should be highlighted, as standards. These are the main criteria by which performance and professional development of teacher educators can be assessed. The National Professional Standards outline seven key elements for effective teacher educators (identified as "lead teachers"), which are summarized below:

Standard 1—Know the students and how they learn. Lead teachers are expected to select, develop, evaluate and revise teaching strategies "to improve student learning using knowledge of the physical, social and intellectual development and characteristics of students" in order to meet the needs of students from diverse cultural and economic backgrounds (AITSL, 2011).

Standard 2—Know the content and how to teach it. Lead teachers must be able to "lead initiatives [...] to evaluate and improve knowledge of content and teaching strategies," as well as to "monitor and evaluate the implementation of teaching strategies to expand learning opportunities and content knowledge for all students" (AITSL, 2011).

Standard 3—Plan for and implement effective teaching and learning. Qualified lead teachers should "demonstrate exemplary practice and high expectations [...] and lead colleagues to plan, implement and review the effectiveness of their learning and teaching programmes" (AITSL, 2011).

Standard 4—Create and maintain supportive and safe learning environments. Lead teachers are expected to be active in "the development of productive and inclusive learning environments," as well as to "lead and implement behaviour management initiatives" (AITSL, 2011) in order to ensure students' well-being.

Standard 5—Assess, provide feedback and report on student learning. Lead teachers are required to "evaluate school assessment policies and strategies" to diagnose learning needs and to "co-ordinate student performance and programme evaluation using internal and external student assessment data to improve teaching practice (AITSL, 2011).

Standard 6—Engage in professional learning. Lead teachers should "initiate collaborative relationships to expand professional learning opportunities, engage in research, and provide quality opportunities and placements for pre-service teachers" (AITSL, 2011).

Standard 7—Engage professionally with colleagues, parents/careers and the community. Lead teachers are expected to "model exemplary ethical behaviour and exercise informed judgements in all professional dealings with students, colleagues and the community," as well as taking a "leadership role in professional and community networks and supporting the involvement of colleagues in external learning opportunities" (AITSL, 2011). (Servet Celik, 2007)

Importance of Research for Teacher Educators

With above description of teacher educators and expected standards, it is clear that research to understand, develop and use data for carrying on duties effectively is the main focus for a teacher educator. A prosperous candidate has to establish himself/herself as an effective professional in developing and providing efficient teachers to all needs of society in order to claim a position in teacher educator category. For this they need to research for professional development aspects very carefully. Research occupies an important aspect of the development of self and institution for a teacher educator. Not only researching, disseminating information of the research is also the responsibility of the teacher educator. For this proper research aptitude is necessary in a teacher educator.

Research aptitude is the natural inclination of a person towards research. Particular to this context it is the ability to think in different ways to find solutions to educational problems. A general understanding about this concept includes a person's capacity to identify a problem and to find solutions suitable to the situation of that problem and possessing skills to express and explain a problem, defend questions raised logically, analytically and ability to present the findings before learned persons. Research is needed to improve upon the present situations so that a proper future context could be created. Research is a continuous process always aiming at achieving better results than the previous attempts. So this aspect of education needs to be included in the curriculum at graduation level itself, so that students will be able to develop proper aptitude, attitude and interest in the problems related to their respective field.

Particular to teacher education, research must be conducted in all aspects like, school situations and problems; policy and administrative issues; classroom issues like manage nent; evaluation procedures; examination reforms and future aspects. Proper research related to all the issues of education system will enhance the awareness of people and helps in finding different innovative practices to overcome the problems. So there is a need to inculcate the researching ability in students of teacher education at least from the master's level programme. There is a need to expose students towards practical aspects of conducting research using different research methods, techniques to develop proper awareness. If the natural inclination of students towards this aspect is measured from admission level itself, it could be honed to proper levels through practical exposure during the training programme (Madhavi, 2011)

Needed Research Competencies in Teacher Educators

Normal research capabilities to carry on a research process explained as identification of problem, reviewing, formulating question, data collection and data analysis etc., are important for any researcher. A teacher educator also needs to possess these qualities to research with a specific problem. But the added competencies are adopting and working with the new challenges and environments of work according to evolving trends. Accordingly the competencies need to focus on:

- Capacity for analysis and grasp of sophisticated IT tools. As explained in the framework improving social networking, web tools availability, social group formation, network establishment are providing easy access to discussion, tools and methods to carry on research effectively. Developing IT use related competencies is necessary now.
- Ability to work in an interdisciplinary environment. With globalization and internationalization now the focus is on interdisciplinary research. The alienation of one discipline with the other is gradually disappearing.

Developing competency to work in an interdisciplinary arena improves the professional development. It also helps in establishing proper networking with related institutions in the field.

- Ability to incorporate existing knowledge. A researcher is able to develop knowledge but not able to find the relevance of knowledge developed by other researchers. It is related to the problem and if it is properly used in the present research it will enhance the findings and evolve extended knowledge. How to incorporate existing knowledge for present problem solving is another competency needed in an teacher educator.
- Awareness of the pertinence of the research and its impact on the environment. Relevance of research to contextual needs is more important. In the present day of materialization of the education process, market needs occupy an important part of research process. Identifying this is important to bring profitability to the process of educational research, which is a dire need.
- Ability to self-assess. This is with reference to the growth of a teacher educator with relation to experience and time spent in a specific environment of working. All the time this process requires assessment of improvement from earlier times in the research process as a whole and also a note on things that are not achieved.
- Engage professionally with colleagues, parents/careers and the community. Networking is very important in the times of globalization and internationalization. To carry on interdisciplinary research this is more important. It will also help in providing ample varieties of solutions to research problems.
- Extension services and research are one of the important competencies needed. Dissemination of one's own research and fine-tuning research according to the context needs is possible only through this process.

Conclusion

Understanding students and their requirements of learning; create and maintain supportive and safe learning environments; assess, provide feedback and report on student learning are the important duties of a teacher educator just like other teachers teaching at different levels and subjects. But being a person responsible to develop teachers for different contextual needs through teaching, research and service it is the responsibility of a teacher educator to be competent enough to research and disseminate the research through establishing reciprocal relations with the context.

Reference

R.L. Madhavi, D.R. Goel, 2011, "Predictivity of Selected Variables for M. Ed. Admission in India," Germany: VDM Verlag.

Website Referred

http://www.fhcrc.org/en/education-training/ocd/core-competencies.html

http://ro.ecu.edu.au/cgi/viewcontent.cgi?article=1563&context=ajte

http://www.nie.edu.sg/files/spcs/TE21_Executive%20Summary_101109.pdf

https://www.sensepublishers.com/media/181-competence-oriented-teacher-training.pdf

http://www.deloitte.com/assets/Dcom-France/Local%20Assets/Documents/Votre%20Secteur/Secteur%20public/Synth%C3%A8se%20Etude%20APEC%20Deloitte/Synth%C3%A8se%20Etude%20Apec% 20Deloitte%20Anglais.pdf

http://www.fgdp.org.uk/_assets/pdf/research/research% 20competencies.pdf

http://youremployment.biz/competency/research-competency/

https://univ-danubius.academia.edu/AlinaBeatriceRaileanu,

http://www.vitae.ac.uk/CMS/files/upload/Vitae-Review-of-literature-relating-to-competency-frameworks-for-researchers-Oct-2009.pdf,

http://www.saskcropinsurance.com/Default.aspx?DN=7df3877c-5b34-4fe1-ba46-1e7186af8b12,

27

Research Competency

Mapping and Management

Harsha J. Patadia

Introduction

Research comprises "creative work undertaken on a systematic basis in order to increase the stock of knowledge, including knowledge of man, culture and society, and the use of this stock of knowledge to devise new applications." It is used to establish or confirm facts, reaffirm the results of previous work, solve new or existing problems, support theorems, or develop new theories. A research project may also be an expansion on past work in the field. To test the validity of instruments, procedures, or experiments, research may replicate elements of prior projects, or the project as a whole. The primary purposes of basic research (as opposed to applied research) are documentation, discovery, interpretation, or the research and development (R&D) of methods and systems for the advancement of human knowledge. Approaches to research depend on epistemologies, which vary considerably both within and between humanities and sciences. There are several forms of research: scientific, humanities, artistic, economic, social, business, marketing, practitioner research, etc.

This paper addresses a wide audience: PhD students, professors, researchers, research personnel, recruitment and career management professionals in every type of organization (laboratory, business, university department, etc.). Researchers will have to be able to "think globally" and be open to the rest of the world they deal with. They will need to be increasingly multicultural and able to engage in dialogue with teams in countries all over the world, reinforcing multidisciplinary and interdisciplinary approaches. Everywhere, the emphasis is on the need to innovate. Multidisciplinary approaches encourage research at the interfaces between disciplines, ideal breeding grounds for new ideas. The key factors applied consist of funding for multi- and interdisciplinary projects and a greater awareness of the expectations of civil society. The growing importance of issues of intellectual property, regulation and ethics feed into the conduct of research work, from initial training to the commercial exploitation of research work. Development of new tools influencing how research is done, breakthrough innovations in technology and in IT capacity (modeling and simulation tools, Web-based collaboration tools, open source software) are changing the face of research in almost all disciplines. The latest developments in technology have totally changed the way researchers investigate and the possibilities offered by simulation have expanded enormously. IT has made a big contribution to reducing testing in humans and replacing it with simulations. The impact on fundamental research is limited; the changes are much more apparent on the development level.

This changing scenario demands a rethink into research competency, its mapping and management.

The Mapping of Competency Needed in a Researcher Today and by 2020

Competencies are the measurable or observable knowledge, skills, abilities, and behaviours critical to successful job performance. They are broadly divided in three categories viz.

- Knowledge Competencies—practical or/and theoretical understanding of subjects.
- Skill and Ability Competencies—natural or learned capacities to perform acts.
- Behavioural Competencies—patterns of action or conduct.

These competencies needed in the modern era in a researcher

can be divided into two parts based on the requirements to work individually as well as in team for any research project. This further encompasses the personal and interpersonal skills along with ideal qualities and behaviour of the researcher to work independently as well in a team as mentioned below.

First of all the competencies required to work independently are mentioned as follows.

- Cognitive ability and scientific knowledge of the discipline/s within which research project is conducted
- Personal effectiveness and ability to learn and adapt
- Ability to formulate a research issue
- Capacity for analysis and grasp of sophisticated IT tools
- Ability to work in an interdisciplinary environment
- Ability to incorporate existing knowledge existents
- Creativity
- Interaction with open-minded approach
- Motivation/Involvement
- Adaptability
- Ability to self-assess

Along with these eleven competencies the researcher also requires project and team management skills which are required and of most important when a researcher is employed in an organization to enable the researcher to grow and develop individually as well as enrich the organization. These nine competencies are as follows:

- Occupational ability to work in a team
- Ability to develop a network
- Communication skills
- Ability to assess individuals and team
- Language skills
- Business culture and management skills
- Project management skills
- Ability to manage and steer teams
- Awareness of the pertinence of the research and its impact on the environment

Management of these Competencies

Management deals with the organization and coordination of the activities of a task in order to achieve defined objectives. So, management of competency also deals with organization and coordination of activities related to every dimension of that competency. Each competency has different dimensions which can be related to specific behaviours or activities for the management of that particular competency. Some of them are explained through the following tables with illustrations of dimensions and corresponding behaviour/activity.

Competency Dimensions	*Description of behaviour/activity*
Competency—Communication	
Listening	Understands and learns from what others say.
Reading Comprehension	Grasps the meaning of information written in languages such as English, vernacular, and applies it to work situations.
Speaking	Conveys ideas and facts orally using language the audience will best understand.
Writing	Conveys ideas and facts in writing using language the reader will best understand.
Competency—Cognition	
Analysis/Reasoning	Examines data to grasp issues, draw conclusions, and solve problems.
Creative and Innovative Thinking	Develops fresh ideas that provide solutions to all types of workplace challenges.
Decision Making and Judgement	Makes timely, informed decisions that take into account the facts, goals, constraints, and risks.
Mathematical Reasoning	Uses mathematical techniques to calculate data or solve practical problems.

(Contd.)

(*Contd.*)

Competency Dimensions	*Description of behaviour/activity*
Problem Solving	Resolves difficult or complicated challenges.
Researching Information	Identifies, collects, and organizes data for analysis and decision-making.
Competency—Personal Effectiveness	
Accountability and Dependability	Takes personal responsibility for the quality and timeliness of work, and achieves results with little oversight.
Adaptability and Flexibility	Adapts to changing business needs, conditions, and work responsibilities.
Attention to Detail	Diligently attends to details and pursues quality in accomplishing tasks.
Customer Focus	Builds and maintains customer satisfaction with the products and services offered by the organization.
Development and Continual Learning	Displays an ongoing commitment to learning and self-improvement.
Ethics and Integrity	Earns others' trust and respect through consistent honesty and professionalism in all interactions.
Results Focus and Initiative	Focuses on results and desired outcomes and how best to achieve them. Gets the job done.
Safety Focus	Adheres to all workplace and trade safety laws, regulations, standards, and practices.
Self Management	Manages own time, priorities, and resources to achieve goals.
Stress Tolerance	Maintains composure in highly stressful or adverse situations.
Tact	Diplomatically handles challenging or tense interpersonal situations.

(*Contd.*)

(*Contd.*)

Competency Dimensions	*Description of behaviour/activity*
Competency—Interaction with Others	
Influencing Others	Influences others to be excited and committed to furthering the organization's objectives.
Relationship Building	Builds constructive working relationships characterized by a high level of acceptance, cooperation, and mutual respect.
Teamwork	Promotes cooperation and commitment within a team to achieve goals and deliverables.
Valuing Diversity	Helps create a work environment that embraces and appreciates diversity.
Competency—Occupational	
Advocating Causes	Influences others to act in support of ideas, programmes, or causes.
Enforcing Laws, Rules, and Regulations	Enforces governmental laws, rules, and regulations, and initiates enforcement actions in a way that the public perceives as fair, objective, and reasonable.
Facilitating Groups	Enables cooperative and productive group interactions.
Gaining Voluntary Compliance	Convinces others to follow recommendations and advice to bring them into compliance with regulations, standards, or policies
Interviewing Others	Asks questions in ways that enhance the clarity, quality, and reliability of information.
Managing Projects or Programmes	Structures and directs others' work on projects or programmes.
Mediating Disputes	Helps others resolve complex or sensitive disagreements and conflicts.
Negotiating Agreements	Reaches deals or compromises.
Operating Equipment	Uses tools, machines, and vehicles to transport goods or people, or to create work products.

(*Contd.*)

(Contd.)

Competency Dimensions	*Description of behaviour/activity*
Providing Consultation	Partners with clients to identify and resolve complex or sensitive issues.
Training and Presenting Information	Formally delivers information to groups.
Competency—Management Qualities	
Competency Dimensions	Description of behaviour/activity
Business Alignment	Aligns the direction, products, services, and performance of a business line with the rest of the organization.
Coaching and Mentoring	Enables co-workers to grow and succeed through feedback, instruction, and encouragement.
Leadership	Promotes organizational mission and goals, and shows the way to achieve them.
Fiscal Accountability	Follows fiscal guidelines, regulations, principles, and standards when committing fiscal resources or processing financial transactions.
Organizational and Political Savvy	Uses knowledge of the organizational and political climate to solve problems and accomplish goals.
Planning and Organizing	Coordinates ideas and resources to achieve goals.
Staff Management	Manages staff in ways that improve their ability to succeed on the job.
Strategic Vision	Sees the big, long-range picture.

Conclusion

Looking to the modern era the above mentioned twenty competencies are needed in a multicultural globe to enhance the quality of research and its world-wide application. Hence universities should reframe the curriculum of research methodology courses which would help in developing and managing these competencies through appropriate and suitable instructional strategies among researchers.

References

http://en.wikipedia.org/wiki/Research

OECD (2002) Frascati Manual: proposed standard practice for surveys on research and experimental development, 6th edition. Retrieved 27 May 2012 fromwww.oecd.org/sti/frascatimanual

28
Educators Educate Thyself

Pranav Vyas

Teeming Discontent

Democratic form of self-governance in contemporary society has created such an elitist class, who have become self-appointed spokespersons of the communities whom they hold in contempt for the lack of practicing the belief they deem worthy of pursuits. Most of the top constitutional offices in society (decision-making bodies) have degenerated into interest trading centres for want of character of the occupant. Conventionally, powerful zealots (designated competent authorities) assume it to be their birth right to negotiate the interests of the powerless, on whose behalf they hold power; have violated the spirit of democracy while worshipping its form. Society appears to have lost its moorings in seeking certificate of merit and character from unscrupulous and characterless power maniacs.

It is most appropriate to recall the prophecy of Maharshi Aurobindo, " ...both rights and duties are European ideas. Dharma is a Bharatiya conception in which rights and duties lose their artificial antagonism created by the world-view of the world which makes selfishness the root of action and regain their deep and eternal unity. Spirituality is India's only politics. I have no doubt we shall have to go through parliamentary period in order to get rid of the notion of western democracy.........by seeing in practice how helpless it is to make the nation blessed".

Borrowed Vision and Failed Mission

Every society has a guiding vision which determines the mission at the individual and collective level. Unfortunately, since independence, India has adopted a policy of using foreign language as a medium of transmission and generation of knowledge; inspite of having indigenous languages of her own. English being a mother-tongue of pirates, who had an inglorious history of colonizing the globe, has a tendency to colonize the mind of its users. Mahatma had warned way back in the early 20th century by stating "Europeans have made it their religion to enslave the rest of the mankind." Today, English is perceived as a language of the educated in India; one fluent in its usage is assumed to be knowledgeable, an innocent belief of the ignorant; a privilege that was granted to Sanskrit in ancient India. Language proficiency as a measure of knowledge has crucified the wisdom of individual and society as a whole.

ekma, sat\ ivap'a bahuqaa vadint e

This axiom of Sanskrit implies that "Though truth is one, the wise believes it to be manifested as many". In essence, it conveys that the entire phenomenal diversity is rooted in noumenal unity. The entire universe is a manifest form of consciousness.

Goal of Education

Entire education system in ancient India was modelled on search for truth either in individual or collective life. Age, gender and languages are all variables that need to be put to use for unsheathing the truth that is at the bedrock of existence and ever present in the cavity of the heart of each and every living being.

To educate means to train the mind and its abilities. The dictionary meaning of mind is an ability to be aware of things, to think and reason, feel concern about, remember and be careful (about) which originates in the brain; content of mind in the form of information, analysis, synthesis and its application determines knowledge potential of an individual. In such a belief system, consciousness is conceived as an emergent property of molecular interactions in the brain, which can be decisively altered by specific input of chemicals e.g. pain relievers, anesthetic and psychedelic drugs. By implication consciousness is identified with being aware, mind, and knowledge. The question of establishing casual relationship amongst them is outside the domain of reductionist science. Principles and techniques of science can be applied only to those attributes which are quantifiable, reproducible and mechanistic. Love, beauty and truth being qualitative attributes that infuse vitality to life form gets automatically devalued when evaluated from scientific parameters.

The quest for truth is a fundamental requirement to be knowledgeable. In other words, to be aware about one's ignorance is an essential qualification for acquiring knowledge. Each and every life form carries in its being a species of 'Truth' unique of its own, whose manifestation contributes to the diversity of existence. In this scheme, knowledge of the truth, liberates the soul that keeps suffering from the bondage of flesh, which conveys the attribute of knowledgeable as

saa ivaVa yaa ivamautyao È

Root Problem

The genesis of an institution lies in the propagation of an ideal. Unfortunately over the period, survival of an institution becomes primary over that of an ideal. Knowledge as a weapon for domination by making it an object of negotiable instrument act for trading is a philosophy of the Occident, whereas knowledge as a means of severing the bondage of ego is a lifestyle of the Orient, where formal literacy is optional. The concept of knowledge in Oriental and Occidental societies generates a polar opposite understanding and as a result the standards used to measure the competency of knowledgeable also vary.

Since the Renaissance in the West, Truth is assumed to be conceived in the form of concepts or axioms in the minds of intellectuals which explains the forces operating in nature and can be put to use for social benefit. The one who conceives such a concepts is the owner of it and can be granted monopoly rights for personal economic benefit by the government of the day. Such an objectification of truth has transformed knowledge into a commodity item that can be marketed as a utility product by branding it in a variety of forms. The emergence of the concept of API as an indicator of competency of academicians is a brain-child of such a mindset. It is analogous to determining the quality of voice by measuring its decibel level.

This very idea is anathema to an Oriental who believes in wisdom contained in

> *ivaVa ivavaadaya QanaM madaya Sait: proYaaM piripDnaaya È*
> *Klasya saaQaao-ivapirtmaott &anaaya danaaya ca rxaNaaya ÈÈ*

Knowledge and money both constitute power, wicked use it to inflict miseries on others whereas relieving it is the way of virtuous.

Pirated Life

Egocentric life is a pirate's life. Ego's vision is myopic, when nurtured with care, it develops cataract and blinds the eye of the spirit. It is feverish giant butcher destroying the peace of the moment while engaged in fixing the future in the light of its limited past understanding. It is the usurper of the power of SELF without revealing its domicile as well as bonafide.

Unless one experiences an elementary distress as regards to the management of one's feelings, thoughts and actions, it is impossible to be aware of the spiritual sickness plaguing one's SELF. Contemporary HUMANOID assumes to have mastered the science of wearing the mask of civility while bearing mental stress and severe heartburns. Life is set on PYRE while living in fulfilling infinite aspirations doled out by spin doctors and dream merchants of the day.

Spiritual anguish is a reflection of ignorance about the SELF and knowledge about non-self. Doubts, fear and guilt forms an occlusion complex in the mind. It is a compulsive obsessive disorder for an ego to audit everyone's performance except itself. Ego severs ties with the SELF/spirit/consciousness and assumes responsibility that is not its own. In fact, ego is a prodigal son of biblical fame, who by a single act of denial voluntarily disgraces the very foundation that sustains its activities.

Hunger for truth, love and beauty constitute the universal need for the SELF. Whereas appetite for pelf, power and position reflects personal wants of ego. Thus, ego is the only toxicant that needs to be detoxified to access the bliss of self with the grace of a master. Master is one who has cured the SELF off the egoism. The only way to approach the master is with silent mind and open heart. The ultimate goal of education is to initiate the pupil into the life of the spirit.

Search the Researcher

Everything such as ideals, items, individuals and institutions in the universe is liked and loved for the SELF, where is the wisdom in pleasing the whole universe while ignoring the self? In fact, self never changes in life; it is the image one carries about it that keeps changing. Constitutive traits are age, gender, degree and designation independent. Acquired characters keep playing hide and seek with the self, which are purely circumstantial and are egocentric. They are the root of conditional lethality.

Each and every encounter in the life-stream generates an image in the mind that is stored in the memory bank as thought deposits in the form of experience. Search for the experiencer, depositor and withdrawer leads to real knowledge. Science that explores conscience destroys nescience (ignorance of self) whereas science that suppresses conscience inflames nescience and makes one an EGOIST. Arrogance, hostility and boastfulness are the attributes of ego whereas humility, homeliness and silence are the introduction to the self. Ego is at the base of all the errors in life. It conceives one's own errors as minor and insignificant and that of other's as major and significant. Grace of an enlightened master alone can invert such wisdom that is self-deceiving.

Acquisition of knowledge for sharing with the underprivileged is the integral ideal of unacademic institution whereas the concept of selling knowledge for self-glorification amounts to academic prostitution. Awareness about the contribution of multitudes in flowering one's personality leaves no space for arrogance of intellect. For such an individual humility is not a virtue but a necessity. Selfishness is **SYSTEM** nurtured whereas selflessness is self cultured. One whose self esteem is based on other's opinion is a vagrant (homeless) beggar.

Teacher versus Enlightened Teacher

Professional teacher is a groomer of personality traits by inculcating and reinstating the value of selfishness who lays an utmost emphasis on diligent exercise of intelligence to outsmart or out compete fellow colleagues in the discipline of one's choice i.e. arts, commerce, science or any other variation thereof. Degrees of masters and doctors are conferred by academic institutions while nurturing a slavish mentality. Innocent citizens are transformed into ECOZENS i.e. money generating trans-national entities. How can one rate the credit worthiness of intellectuals whose loyalty is for SALE!

An enlightened teacher is a broomer of personality traits who demonstrates by his/her own conduct the values of cooperation and equality, for whom comparison is poison and competition is a death of spirit and becomes an embodiment of selflessness contributing to the overall harmony and peace in the surroundings.

In other words, a professional teacher is a partially reduced species, still conscious of one's colourfulness as reflected as images in the eyes of those craving for infinite shades whereas enlightened teacher is completely reduced species devoid of any colourfulness. His/her radiance is beyond the visible range as the identity crisis demanded by those obsessed with colour is completely absent. One who has knocked out his/her superiority complex is by default or by design of nature immune of its inverse. The contemporary education system is the principle cause of psychological AIDS. AIDS stands for acquired identity deficiency syndrome where self compromised individuals and immuno compromised rats represent identical twins. Teaching is an art of SELF unfoldment and science of self (ego) destruction.

Be Conscious of Consciousness

The practice of teaching is an occupation and not a profession, an ART and not a scientific trade, a calling and not a corporate business, an obsession in which head and heart work in unison to supplement the diverse needs of willing students, who alone define according to their innate predispositions. Teacher is a psycho-catalyst for the blossoming of the spirit of all those intensely willing yet doubting to explore them for fear of conventional stigmatism.

To the extent one makes others self-dependent to that degree alone one is a teacher. Anyone trying to influence others in a way that confirms his or her image of them is a politician. Scientific reason is an instrument to prove to others that the opinion one holds is the best fit under the prevailing circumstances and all those who follow its ways are nearer to truth, knowing pretty well that in this relative world, there is no absolute truth. Since the entropy of the universe is progressively increasing, reductionist science has accepted the destruction of universe in precept before its adherents accomplish this in practice.

All of us are fellow travellers in the kingdom of God playing diverse roles which we have voluntarily opted for self-expression. The destination at which we find ourselves posted is the consequence of choices exercised enroute in the stream of life current. Unfoldment of our intimate urges at a specific age and stage under consideration contributes to the fragrance of existence which is conventionally labelled as CULTURE. Any friction of an embodied soul with the conventional mould generates the tension that needs immediate attention before it assumes the form of inferno and consumes the spontaneous manifestation of blessed **Being**, as aptly described by Nisargdutt Maharaj; "Be aware of being conscious and seek the source of consciousness". Otherwise, the fragrance of life is lost to confirm the prevailing sickness in the name of GLOBAL trend by locals. Never let yourself be trapped into sound-bytes of vocals.

29

Knowing Publication

Competencies for Academic Writing and Publishing

Minaxi S. Bhagwat and *R.G. Kothari*

Introduction

Publishing research paper/s or article or book is now becoming the benchmark for the professional growth of educational professionals and also it is accountable for their academic performance. Then it is obvious, weightage gained for their performance is intend to make them responsible/sensitised about the social aspects of dissemination/sharing of their own intellectual/academic work and thoughts among other intellectuals, professionals and the community.

Writing is considered by some academics as hard work (Boice, 1990; Silvia, 2007) and it requires adequate preparation. Sometimes, students/experts expect that inspiration will just appear and make their writing magical. Writing a paper or article requires proper sense of planning to organise the text/content in the right direction in order to make it a meaningful manuscript before going to a publication house. So thus it is expected for a writer to understand the importance of publishing and also have a proper knowledge about publication terms and procedures. Here, this paper is concerned with particular academic writing and academic publishing as it is observed that generally many scholars wish to write/disseminate their academic ideas/thoughts but they are lacking or do not have proper knowledge for academic publishing.

Significance of Academic Publishing

Writing for publication as proposed with an academic instance is referred to as academic publishing. In higher education, such writings are undertaken by the students, scholars, academic professionals or experts. However, Stoilescu and McDougall (2010) stated that publishing academic work will make a difference when applying for an academic job in a research-oriented position. As a novice researcher, there are serious challenges in designing research and reporting it adequately. Although students lack the experience in reporting research and are not always being trained in academic writing, there are ways to be successful.

Students should view the doctoral dissertation as a great opportunity to write academic research articles (Schniederjans, 2007). Students are experts in their area of study. They have worked for years reading articles and performed original research in this topic. Despite these advantages, there are not a great percentage of doctoral students publishing from their dissertation (Dunleavy, 2003; Francis and Mills, 2009; Goldsmith *et al.*, 2001). We know that doctoral dissertation is quite different from an academic research article (Bolker, 1998; Kamler, 2008; Luey, 2005).

To develop the culture of academic publishing, it is essential to develop awareness from the higher education level. In India, formal academic writing/scholarly writing begin mostly with master level programmes in the form of dissertations. Perhaps, dissertation writing is quite different from professional writing for publications. As the trend is growing for publication too, students and scholars have to gain the knowledge of academic publishing. 'It takes time to learn and produce successful writing in academic journals. Therefore, students should locate adequate journals that are interested in accepting the themes and methods of their research' (Knight and Steinbach, 2008).

Knowledge of academic publishing comprises aspects like current trends in academic writings, format for academic writing, expectations of addressing audiences, future aspects concerned with the written work. Academic writing is a skill that can be developed through practice, reading habits and social exposure.

Basics of Publication

Publication means dissemination or the medium to reach the masses/society/audiences. Due to global networking, it is reduced the physical meeting of the people but the advent in technology like internet, mobiles, media are responsible for connecting people. Media is the best medium to address the masses and available in the form of print, web, audio and video. Here, the concern for the print media and web media (e-form/online/offline) is considered.

Meaning of Periodicals, Magazines and Journals

A periodical is any publication that comes out regularly, periodically or occasionally. The Journal of Anthropological Research and the phone book are all periodicals.

A magazine is a periodical with a popular focus, i.e. aimed at the general public, and containing news, personal narratives, and opinion. Articles are often written by professional writers with or without expertise in the subject. Magazines use vocabulary understandable to most people, and often have lots of eye-catching illustrations.

A journal is a scholarly periodical aimed at specialists and researchers. Articles are generally written by experts in the subject, using more technical language. They contain original research, conclusions based on data, footnotes or endnotes, and often an abstract or bibliography

Scholarly Journals

Mainly there are three types of Journals generally found in libraries such as: (i) Scholarly, also known as peer-reviewed, academic or refereed journals, (ii) Trade or Professional Journals, and (iii) Popular Journals.

The purpose of scholarly journals is to disseminate new findings and the results of studies, experiments, theories, etc. These journals and the articles/academic-papers in them are usually written/edited by professors or researchers. The audience is usually professors or researchers in particular academic fields, though it may also include professionals in those fields. They may also review and critique these studies and findings. Articles/academic-papers are submitted and go through a review and editing process which can often be quite lengthy (often a few months or more). The articles are reviewed by a panel of "experts". These are often other professors who are familiar with the subject being written about. Thus, they are sometimes called "peer reviewed". Thus a article/paper may undergo a series of reviews, revisions and re-submissions before finally being accepted or rejected for publication. Also "Journal", "Transactions"," Proceedings", "Review" or "Quarterly" may appear in the title of the journal. These titles often refer to an academic discipline or specialized field of study. For example, Journal of Teacher Education, Anthropological Quarterly.

An academic paper typically belongs to some particular category such as: (A) Research paper, (B) Case report or Case Series, (C) Concept paper—these are done to gain funding for carrying out research or employment or admission to an academic programme, (D) Position paper/Vision paper, (E) Review article or Survey paper, (F) Species paper, (G) System paper, (H) Technical paper, (I) Technical note, or (J) Theory research paper.

Open-Access Journals

Open-access journals are scholarly journals that are available online to the reader "without financial, legal, or technical barriers other than those inseparable from gaining access to the internet itself". The publisher of an open-access journal is known as an "open-access publisher", and the process, "open-access publishing".

Peer Review

Peer review is a central concept for most academic publishing; other scholars in a field must find to be work sufficiently high in quality for it to merit publication. In other words, peer review is a control process whereby editors and other experts (peers) evaluate a manuscript for publication. The process also guards against plagiarism. Failures in peer review are sometimes scandalous.

ISSN—International Standard Serial Number

The International Standard Serial Number (ISSN) is an eight-digit number which identifies periodical publications as such, including electronic serials, and is used for serial/periodical publications such as magazines. The ISSN is a numeric code which is used as an identifier, followed by two groups of four digits separated by a hyphen. It has no signification in itself and does not contain in itself any information referring to the origin or contents of the publication. The ISSN is linked to a standardized form of the title of the identified serial, known as the "key title", which repeats the title of the publication, qualifying it with additional elements in order to distinguish it from other publications having identical titles.

On a printed serial, the preferred location for printing the ISSN is on the upper right-hand corner of the cover. It should always be preceded by the letters ISSN. Other good locations are the masthead area, the copyright page, or in the publishing statement where information about the publisher, frequency, and other publication facts are given.

ISBN—International Standard Book Number

The International Standard Book Number (ISBN) is a unique identifier for books, intended to be used commercially. The ISBN system was created in the United Kingdom in 1966 by the booksellers and stationers WH Smith and was originally a nine digit code called Standard Book Numbering or SBN (still used in 1974). It was adopted as international standard ISO 2108 in 1970. From January 1, 2007, ISBNs are thirteen digits long. ISBNs are assigned to monographs ("books"). An ISSN can be assigned to a series of monographs as such; and an ISBN will be assigned to each separate book of the series.

h-Index

The *h*-index is an index that attempts to measure both the productivity and impact of the published work of a scientist or scholar. Sometimes it is refered as research performance indicator. The index is based on the set of the scientist's most cited papers and the number of citations that they have received in other publications. The index can also be applied to the productivity and impact of a group of scientists, such as a department or university or country, as well as a scholarly journal. The index was suggested by Jorge E. Hirsch, a physicist at UCSD (University of California, San Diego) as a tool for determining theoretical physicists' relative quality and is sometimes called the *Hirsch index* or *Hirsch number*.

Graph 29.1: h-Index of Publications

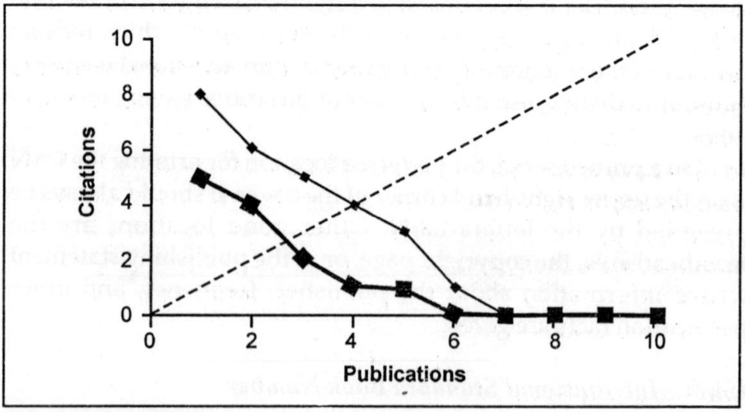

Source: Azrul, 2011.

The meaning of the h-index is that, a scholar with an index of *h* has published *h* papers each of which has been cited in other papers at least *h* times. Thus, the *h*-index reflects both the number of publications and the number of citations per publication. The index is designed to improve upon simpler measures such as the total number of citations or publications. The index works properly only for comparing scientists working in the same field; citation conventions differ widely among different fields.

Impact Factor

The impact factor (IF) of an academic journal is a measure reflecting the average number of citations to recent articles published in the journal. The impact factor was devised by Eugene Garfield, the founder of the Institute for Scientific Information. Impact factors are calculated yearly for those journals that are indexed in the *Journal Citation Reports*.

In a given year, the impact factor of a journal is the average number of citations received per paper published in that journal during the two preceding years which can be calculated below.

A = No. of citation in year N for papers published in year N-1 and N-2
B = No. of citable papers in year N-1 and N-2
Impact Factor for year N = A/B

While Planning for Academic Writing/Publishing

Prior and proper planning is required while one decides to do academic writing. Novice writers are expected to go through numerous literatures, articles, research papers etc., for the reviews and than have to start planning for writing. Some suggestions and measures are briefed here below.

Planning for the Manuscript

Writing manuscript either for your article or research paper or any other academic writing, certain suggestive measures need always to be kept in mind as briefed here.

For any writing, originality and depth are the two requirements for publication. Academic writing is expected to contribute new knowledge for the community. Thus, scholars have to involve their expertise, experience and interest in their writings. An article must have some theme or story. For the research paper, topic should be unique and there should be a logical reason to study it. Read and follow all the guidelines for manuscript preparation listed by/for an individual journal. Most journals have very specific formatting and style guidelines for the text body, abstract, images, tables, and references.

Write in a precise and accurate way. Avoid long sentences; the reader may find them difficult to follow. Short papers are more likely to be read than long ones. Avoid unnecessarily long paragraphs. Break up your paragraphs into smaller, useful units. All references used as sources of information in your research paper should be mentioned to strengthen your paper and also to avoid your work being considered plagiarized. Write a clear and concise abstract. Try to give only what is necessary in a couple of sentences or less. The reader has to understand the study rationale, the methods used, and the study findings. Many researchers will only ever read the abstract of your paper so it must contain the most pertinent information. Before submitting to publication, show it to peers, experts or colleague in terms to get feedback/reviews/corrections/comments.

Selection of the Journal

Each discipline has its own list of highly regarded journals, which are ranked according to their 'impact factor'. But the most common mistake to be made is not knowing the body of research in which an article fits. It is essential to look at journals that have published articles on a related topic previously. This is an encouraging sign that the proposed paper/manuscript may appeal to the journal editors. The journal impact factors are important. This gives some idea of the quality of the journal and how difficult it will be to get the paper/manuscript accepted. Also to look at average time to publication as well as average time to acceptance/rejection notification. Some journals highlight their rapid processing times as an impetus for authors to submit their work to those particular journals. Some journals charge fees for manuscript processing or colour figure reproduction for accepted manuscripts. One has to be familiar with the costs associated with publication before submitting the work. Johnson and Mullen (2007) suggested also targeting middle level journals. These journals deal with a lower rejection rate, somewhere between 25-75 per cent. They are willing to publish any suitable professionally written piece of work or any reasonable academic contribution and give authors a fair credit. In addition, some of these journals might have a faster review process so that the article might get accepted for publication in less than six months. Following are the websites where one can find the list of various Indian Journals for education, teacher education and educational researches.

- http://www.imd.gov.in/doc/indianjournal.pdf
- http://www.ncte-india.org/publications.htm
- http://www.teindia.nic.in/journals.aspx

- http://www.sagepub.in/about/imprints.asp
- http://www.aiaer.net/pdffiles/journalswebsites.pdf

After selection of the journal, manuscript/paper/work has to pass from the stages as:

(i) Submission, (ii) Peer Review, (iii) Re-submission, and (iv) Final Changes before Publication.

Thoughts on Encouragement for Academic Publishing

The objectives for publishing academic research is to disseminate intellectual thoughts/innovative ideas and it should reach the intellectuals/experts/practitioners and the targeted population also. But is it reaching to targeted people? Who are the targeted people/ population? Reaching to what extent? Also,

Concluding Comments

In addition, experts have suggested measures to make the publication process more efficient in disseminating new and important findings by evaluating the worthiness of publication on the basis of the significance and novelty of the research finding (Armstrong, 1997). Academic writing in higher education is expected with the research papers and research articles and dissemination of such work can proceed through journal publications. As of now academic publishing is encouraged by making paper publication as one of the performance indicators of career growth for educational scholars/professionals. Then, it is essential for them to be well versed with publication terms and strategies. Such guidance may help them to become the best academic writers and also to get insight for:

(i) publication numbers do matter but quality of ideas is more important; and
(ii) **to publish where their knowledge is more needed/ required.**

References

Armstrong, S.J. (1997). "Peer Review for Journals: Evidence on Quality Control, Fairness, and Innovation". *Energy and Environment*, 3: 63-84. http://marketing.wharton.upenn.edu/ideas/pdf/armstrong2/peerpaper.pdf. Cited on Wikipedia: Academic Publishing

Azrul, M.A. (2011). On the Importance of Academic Publishing. Retrieved from http://www.uniten.edu.my/newhome/uploaded/admin/research/publications/2011/On%20the%20Importance%20of%20Academic%20Publishing%20rotated.pdf

Boice, R. (1990). Professors as writers: A self-guide to productive writing. Stillwater, Oklahoma: New Forums Press. Cited in Stoilescu & McDougall (2010).

Bolker, J. (1998). Writing your dissertation in fifteen minutes a day: A guide to starting, revising, and finishing your doctoral thesis. New York: Henri Holt. Cited in Stoilescu & McDougall (2010).

Difference between a periodical, a journal, and a magazine. Retrieved from http://libanswers. umflint.edu/a.php?qid=213617 on 14/02/2013

Dunleavy, P. (2003). Authoring a PhD: How to plan, draft, write, and finish a doctoral thesis or dissertation. New York: Palgrave MacMillan. Cited in Stoilescu & McDougall (2010).

Francis, K., and Mills, J. (2009). Doctoral dissertations by publication: Building scholarly capacity whilst advancing new knowledge in the discipline of nursing. *International Journal of Doctoral Studies*, 4, 97-106. Retrieved from http://ijds.org/Volume4/IJDSv4p097-106Francis269.pdf. Cited in Stoilescu & McDougall (2010).

Goldsmith, J.A.; Komlos, J., and Schine Gold, P. (2001). The Chicago Guide to your academic career: A portable mentor for scholars from graduate school through tenure. Chicago: University of Chicago Press. Cited in Stoilescu & McDougall (2010).

ISSN: all about ISSN. Retrieved from http://www.issn.org/2-22636-All-about-ISSN.php

Johnson, B., and Mullen, C. (2007). Write to the top: How to become a prolific academic. New York: Palgrave, McMillan & Digital Printing. Cited in Stoilescu & McDougall (2010).

JournalPrep (n.d.). How to Write and Publish an Academic Research Paper. Retrieved from http://www.journal prep.com/en/101-tips.php

Kamler, B. (2008). Rethinking doctoral publication practices: Writing from and beyond the thesis. *Studies in Higher Education*, 33(3), 283-294. Cited in Stoilescu & McDougall (2010).

Knight, L.V. and Steinbach, T.A. (2008). Selecting an appropriate publication outlet: A comprehensive model of journal selection criteria for researchers in a broad range of academic disciplines. *International Journal of Doctoral Studies*, 3, 59-79. Retrieved from http://www.ijds.org/

Volume3/IJDSv3p059-079Knight84.pdf. Cited in Stoilescu & McDougall (2010)

Luey, B. (2005). Handbook for academic authors (4th ed.). New York: Cambridge University Press. Cited in Stoilescu & McDougall (2010).

Schniederjans, M. (2007). A proposed Ph.D. student bill of rights. *International Journal of Doctoral Studies*, 2, 1-8. Retrieved from http://www.ijds.org/Volume2/IJDSv2p001-008 Schniederjans22.pdf. Cited in Stoilescu & McDougall (2010)

Scholarly, Trade and Popular Journals. Retrieved from http://www.ithacalibrary.com/sp/subjects/jnltypes on 14/02/2013

Silvia, P.J. (2007). How to write a lot. Washington DC: American Psychological Association. Cited in Stoilescu & McDougall (2010).

Stoilescu, D. and McDougall, D. (2010). Starting to Publish Academic Research as a Doctoral Student. *International Journal of Doctoral Studies*, Volume 5, 2010. Retrieved from http://ijds.org/Volume5/IJDSv5p079-092 Stoilescu299.pdf.

Wikipedia: *International Standard Book Number*. Retrieved from http://en.wikipedia.org/wiki/ISBN on 14/02/2013.

Wikipedia: Academic Publishing. Retrieved from http://en.wikipedia.org/wiki/Academic_publishing on 14/02/2013.

Wikipedia: h-index. Retrieved from http://en.wikipedia.org/wiki/H-index on 14/02/2013.

Wikipedia: Impact Factor. Retrieved from http://en.wikipedia.org/wiki/Impact_factor on 14/02/2013

30

Competencies in a Good Researcher

Madhavi Dharankar

Introduction

Quality of research, especially at the doctoral level, is always a concern. It is many-a-times far from the acceptable level of rigour. When a volume of say 400 pages is read, one does not really get a feel of reading the result of well-documented study. At times there are gaps in the understanding by the researcher or there are inconsistencies within the report while at times there are flaws in putting across the total experience. All these direct towards the competencies of a researcher as a scholar. Such competencies have the impact at various stages right from the inception of the research through the conduction of the research till the presentation either in written or oral form. What are the competencies that a researcher is expected to either possess or develop before taking up the major and significant responsibility of researching at a higher level?

Research is an essential part of higher education. PG programmes like PG Diploma School Management or masters' degrees such as MA, MEd, M Com, MBA, MSW, etc., expect the learner to be a researcher partially while the research-oriented degrees such as M Phil, and Ph D are completely woven around research. Depending on the level of the programme the rigour would vary but the basic expectations from the role of a researcher remain the same.

Comparison of Competency with Some of the other Terms

Before deliberations are made on the various research competencies, the term has been discussed in comparison with the other related terms such as skills, capacity, etc.

Competency: The knowledge, skills and beliefs in one's repertoire is referred to as "Competencies" that a person possesses. Competency is defined in terms of what one knows, believes and can do. Competence is a collective noun and has no plural, whereas "competency" does occur in the plural. If one possesses competency, it does not necessarily mean that one is able to perform, but if one is performing, it certainly means that one has the needed competency. Thus competency is covert. If one possesses a competency, it cannot be observed unless and until one 'performs'. Competency can be possessed at various levels ranging from beginners to masters' levels. A competency comprises of skills, attitudes and knowledge.

Capacity: Capacity is the ability to do a certain thing.

Skill: Skills forms one component of a COMPETENCE. For example—I might be having very good interpersonal skills or people skills, but I will not be competent to join a company as HR professional unless I possess adequate education/experience (knowledge) and the right temperament/behaviour (attitude).

Why Research Competencies?

Research is considered to be the highest level of contribution to the discipline. Even in terms of academic achievements, contribution in the form of research is supposed to be of the highest level. Any research needs funding. So even in terms of the financial aspect it is an expensive affair. Hence, it is very crucial to underline the research competencies needed in a researcher before one takes up such a responsibility. The various reasons for deliberating on research competencies are discussed further.

- *Rigour*: Tick mark kind of research is of no use to the researcher himself/herself or even to the funding agency. Unless the researcher studies the problem with the fullest competencies, the rigour in the research will not be maintained.

- *Genuineness:* The findings of the research are used for the policy-decisions by organizations, by the Government. Unless such research is handled with high level competencies, it will not give genuine results and thus the policy decisions based on such research will be of no use in the long run.
- *Authenticity*: The research conducted earlier is used by future researchers for referencing and reviewing. Unless they are authentic, the base becomes weak. Even for this purpose it is essential to conduct the research with the competencies needed.
- *Utility:* The action research are especially conducted in order to solve the real-life day-to-day problems. Unless such research are conducted with the fullest capacities, they are of no use even for the researcher himself/herself.

Mapping of Research Competencies

An attempt has been made here to map the competencies needed at the various stages of the research. Five stages of research are taken into consideration here:

- Before the topic is finalized
- Before conducting the actual research
- During data collection
- During data analysis
- Report Writing
- Defending the research

The details of competencies needed at each stage are discussed in detail below:

- Before the topic is finalised:
  - ➢ Broad-based knowledge acquisition
  - ➢ Develop a problem statement and purpose in a focused area of inquiry.
  - ➢ Critical review of the literature and comprehensive theoretical knowledge and in-depth understanding. Employees/students or any other person, who is going to conduct research, must demonstrate the ability to

synthesize and critically review a body of literature that is more comprehensive than what is expected for a standard.

- ➢ Framing a research questions. The success of the research mainly will depend on the research question. Therefore, this ability/competency is vital for research. All the research conductors must demonstrate the ability to correctly identify a researchable questions.
- ➢ Use effective search strategies and critical evaluation of the scientific literature
- ➢ Synthesize the literature in a focused area.
- ➢ Evaluate theoretical/conceptual frameworks for applicability in designing a study.
- ➢ Identify, critique, and apply strategies for conceptualizing and/or operationalizing research variables.
- ➢ Write a research grant proposal.
- ➢ Analytical approach to defining scientific questions
- ➢ Design of scientifically testable hypotheses
- ➢ Concept mapping
- ➢ Heutogogical competencies

- Before actual research begins after the proposal is defended:
  - ➢ Develop instruments for effective research. The person, who wishes to conduct a research, must demonstrate the ability to design an instrument for collecting data. This competency includes the identification of existing instruments, the ability to adapt existing instruments for new modalities and to create a new instrument etc.
  - ➢ Identify and critique research methods for appropriateness in a given study.
  - ➢ Utilize a research design that is consistent with the problem statement, purpose, and theoretical/ conceptual framework.
  - ➢ Use sound and consistent methods to ethically conduct data gathering activities.
- Data collection related competencies
  - ➢ Students/employees/scientists must have document related competencies with primary data collection

including activities relating to data coding and data entry.
  - Ethically conduct research and adhere to standards of scientific integrity.
  - Develop a systematic approach to data management including data entry, cleaning, tracking, and maintaining confidentiality.
  - Interpersonal skills are needed during data collection, especially when the data goes much beyond the technical formats. Skills such as style, tone and non-verbal cues, negotiation, performance reviews/ feedback, difficult conversations/minimizing conflict are crucial.
  - Networking helps in wider data collection
  - Project Management competencies such as time management—establishing priorities and planning the project timeline help.
- Data analysis related competencies:
  - It's needed to have document related experience with scientific and systematic experience with analyzing primary data they have collected as part of a supervised research project.
  - Utilize appropriate data analysis techniques consistent with the purpose and design of a study.
  - Interpret and synthesize the findings in light of the existing literature and theoretical framework, and identify relevance for practice and future research.
  - Interpretation and analysis of data
- During writing report:
  - Writing for publications
  - Disseminate papers through selected peer-reviewed outlets including abstracts, presentations, and publications.
  - Maintaining internal consistency through all the chapters
- During defending the research:
  - Speaking logically
  - Presenting your research
    - Posters

- Conferences/seminars
- PowerPoint presentations

Specific Competencies

- **Collaborative research:** If the research is a collaborative endeavour, then the following competencies are needed.
  - Leadership Skills
  - Creating a vision and setting goals
  - Running meetings
  - Delegating responsibilities
- **Qualitative research:** This brings in even higher level of responsibilities on the part of the researcher. The competency to look into the details, to read between the lines, to deal with words, to read the diagrammatic representations as well as to express with diagrams are much crucial for qualitative researches. Visual literacy in short is much needed.
- **Mixed method designs:** The researcher adopting the mixed method design needs the competencies of both needed for quantitative as well as for qualitative research. In addition to this the researcher needs the competency to merge the data and also to identify the points of explanation and expansion of the results of quantitative and qualitative analysis individually.

Concluding Remarks

Merely identifying the research competencies needed is not sufficient. The problem does not end here. A set of further questions begin from this point. Some of these questions are—Can attempts be made to groom the prospective researchers for such competencies? Is there any scope to judge the level of competencies reached by a researcher? Can the evaluation criteria be evolved so as to underline these competencies at a more formal level? The quest for excellence will have to be at all the various levels—society, university, research institutions, guide and most importantly the researcher himself/herself. Unless an attempt is made in this direction, the products of the research efforts will remain on the racks of libraries.

References

Hase, S. and Kenyon, C. (2001). *From Andragogy to Heutagogy.* Retrieved from 16.3.2012 from http://www.psy.gla.ac.uk/~steve/pr/Heutagogy.html

Novak, J. and Gowin, D. (1984). *Learning How to Learn.* NY, USA: Cambridge University Press.

Research Competencies for Doctoral Students. Retrieved on 23.2.2014 from http://nursing.unc.edu/current-students/student-handbook/research-competencies-for-doctoral-students/

Research Competency. Retrieved on 23.2.2014 from http://youremployment.biz/competency/research-competency/#sthash.VtmAzplF.dpuf

http://wiki.answers.com/Q/What_is_the_difference_between_competency_and_SKILLS

31

Doctoral Skills and Competencies

Dr. Pushpalata Sharma

Introduction

The Ph.D. is rooted in the birth of the European University system in the thirteenth century, when a doctorate was considered a license to teach, rather than a recognition of research expertise or achievements.

The traditional euro-centric Ph.D. objective as characterized by Park (2005) was the production of "a piece of work that changes the course of human knowledge". However, there is a shift occurring in the perception of the role and utility of doctoral education. In Salzburg (Feb. 2005), the Salzburg declaration report agreed to the statements that doctoral education's core component is the advancement of knowledge through original research. It states that the contempory Ph.D. is no longer to be regarded as the necessary training and gateway to a career in academia alone but must involve a knowledge and skill development experience that has relevance and application to wider area. Thus the focus has almost inperceptibly shifted from the Ph.D. as product with a focus on content to the Ph.D. as a procer or stop in the training of a researcher where the focus is on competencies developed (Park, 2005).

All researchers are working and living in a highly competitive rapidly changing and complex world and it is no longer enough to be a good researcher. To a certain degree, researchers also need to be team leaders and managers. Consequently, they need communication and presentation skills.

Research contends that competencies are not developed in a random adhoc manner but tend to be occurred in a quasi hierarchical fashion over time (eq. Peddler *et al*, 2007; Buckley and Monks, 2008). Competencies are complex and dynamically interactive clusters of integrated knowledge of concepts and procedures; skills and abilities; behaviours and strategies; attitude, beliefs and values; dispositions and personal characteristics self-perceptions; and motivation that enable a person to execute a professional activity with myriad potential outcome (Rubin et al., 2007:453). Brown and McCartney (1995) added that Higher order skills are those upon which competencies are based; these being the ability to learn, adopt, anticipate and create, rather than simply demonstrate one's current abilities i.e. developing a proposal, collecting data, making a logical argument, applying knowledge and communicating ideas.

Sufficient challenge is necessary; gaining self insights and 'unlearning' old habits this is described as a process of personal transition which can include painful and confusing phase before clarity, confidence and new skills are enriched.

The higher order skills i.e. openness to new approaches to thinking and doing and the opportunity to test newskills and approaches in an applied setting (Buckley and Monks, 2004, 2008). Golde and Dore (2001) state that in addition to setting boundaries and objectives, Ph.D. students must be adept at grasping the informal and tacit expectations put on them. This requires an amount of self-knowledge, mental-ability and self-efficacy (More-Craft *et al.* 2002) and include sense making, analyzing, imagining, designing and other challenging intellectual activities.

The **Meta-abilities (or Competencies)** as described by Butcher *et al.*, are:

Cognitive Abilities; the key thought process required to 'read' situations which can be used to understand and resolve problems or issues (e.g. paradoxical thinking), and include:

Cognitive complexity—ability to take multiple and integrated perspectives, to recognize and hold conflicting concepts in mind; ***Cognitive flexibility***—the ability to shift perspectives, remain openminded and consider possibilities, ***Visionary abilities***—ability to think with a long-term perspective, envisage a strategic direction; ***Clarity Achievement***—the ability to use information effectively, sort, prioritise, and analyses data; ***(Perceptual acuity)***—the ability to notice and interpret what is happening in interpersonal interactions; ***Emotional resilience:*** Self-control and self-discipline; the ability to manage emotions appropriately; ***Personal resilience;*** the ability to cope with pressure and diversity; 'bounce back;' the ability to view one's self both positively and critically, ideally and realistically; ***Personal drive***: Motivation and ambition for responsibility, the ability to motivate one's self and others, take personal risk.

There is a large body of literature that has identified the skills and attributes that Ph.D. students should, in theory either possess prior to understanding their course of study, or develop throughout the experience of acquiring their doctorates (Cryer, 1997). He states that universities have a responsibility to help doctoral scholars to become aware of the skills that they can offer to their scholar. The study found that students were largely unable to indentify and discuss their key skills and attributes. The lack of a standardized vocabulary hampers attempts to discuss the research by scholars (Detament *et al.*, 1991).

In Australia, Borthwich & Wissles (2003) compiled a report on a study commissioned by the Department of Education, Science and Training under its Research Evaluation Programme. They highlighted the variation in the terms used, stating that misunderstanding of the terms, generic skills and transferable skills, should be incorporated.

Doctoral Competencies

Four key competencies are needed to be developed at the doctoral level.

- Become a scholar practitioner
- Become a critical thinker
- Become a researcher
- Become a professional communicator

Your growth in each area will come in stages tied to the three tracks.

- Track 1; obtain and comprehend knowledge.

- Track 2; Analyse and apply knowledge.
- Track 3; Synthesize and evaluate knowledge.

For example, you develop a programme plan that outline your approach to mastering the four competencies you also use Track 1 to learn about resource available to help you with each competency, such as writing. In Track 2 and 3, you assess your strength and weakess in each competency and work to fill in the gaps.

Become a Scholar -Practitioner

You come in Track 1 as a practitioner you have a significant body of practical knowledge related to your field. To complete your Ph.D. work; you must transform into a scholar practioner, which means you also understand academic theories and can use them to enhance your everyday work.

Track 1: Ask better question
Seek knowledge
Accept feedback
Track 2: Gain Competence
Practice theory
Broaden context
Track 3: Contribute to literature
Embody highest ethics
Use in practice

Become a Critical Thinker

Developing this competency means learning to analysis and judge information you must be able to break down information and recombine it into new ideas, detect bias in research, and use data to make high level decisions.

Become A Researcher

To complete your Ph.D. work, you have to generate original research. You get success by deepening your knowledge of research methods, refining your ability to analyze data and broadening your understanding of statistical software systems.

Become a Professional Communicator

At the doctoral level you are expected to be a master communicator. That means being precise and fluent in your writing, adhering to the American Psychological Association Publication guideline and seeking critical feedback.

According to Stephen Simmons (2005) *"Learning through writing is where the true synthesis occurs, and there's a lot of writing in this programme, when you're writing you're forced to assemble and really publish your thought processers and conclusions. I believe it's a better way of learning."*

In the last few years, there have been many changes in the rules relating to Ph.D in India. According to the new rules, most universities conduct an entrance exam. i.e Pre Ph.D test, in search for a competent researcher. After clearing the test candidates need to appear for an interview by the available supervisor/guide. The registered scholars have to undergo six-month coursework. The coursework includes oral presentation at a seminar and a written examination from the syllabus prescribed for the coursework. The student is required to pass an oral exam (presentation of the research proposal) and a written examination related to research methodology. Students who have failed in the qualifying examination will be allowed to retake it during the next regularly scheduled exam period. Any student who fails in the exam in the second time will not be allowed to continue in the Ph.D. programme. Only qualified candidates shall face the RDC meeting, here their research proposals are finalized. The students are required to give a presentation of the research proposal at the beginning, submit their progress, give a pre-submission presentation and finally defend the thesis in an open defense. Although the UGC has imposed Ph.D coursework and Academic Performance Indicators but still there is lacunue which needs to be fulfilled if we want genuine, competent, dedicated, simple, honest, cultured scholars.

Ph.D scholars should be able to independently identify and solve problems in a scientific manner, derive objectives, propose possible solutions, evaluate proposed solutions, implement effective solutions, and contribute to the advancement of the society.

The question remains as to how these competencies can be acquired and where and when the competence development takes place, one being that these competencies need to be part of a structured training programme. The structural training programme i.e. the six months course work has been implemented in the research programme, but to what extent is the course work running successfully? There is a shortcoming in the course work programme as to what extent are the research scholars seriously attending the course work programme and to what extent are the faculty members undertaking the course work seriously during their duties.

- Those scholars who are in service have to submit a permission letter to the research centre for attending the course work, but the scholars who are giving their service in private colleges are not regularly relieved to attend the course work.
- The candidates who have been appointed as assistant professor under statue 28 and have given their services in any college for two years are exempted from course work.
- There is shortage of research guide in some of the states, hence the norms required to become the guide is not being followed.

Hence these **shortcomings** can be removed if some amendments are made by the UGC which are universally followed in all the universities so that a systematic platform can be maintained regarding the following:

- Criteria for selection of Ph.D. scholars should be the same in all universities.
- The course work syllabus should be designed by UGC which must be followed in all the universities. Only twenty per cent changes can be incorporated in the course work.
- Criteria for selection of research guides should be universally the same in all the universities.
- Research guide can guide in not more than three universities with a maximum of total nine candidates.

Designing the Course Work Syllabus

The course work programme should be one of the important parts of the Ph.D work which needs to be redesigned as:

Conclusion

- *Language Competency:* It is the responsibility of the universities to encourage the doctoral scholars to become award of their communication skills. English is a scientific language. The research scholars must have excellent skills within both spoken and written English.
- Ph.D. candidates must demonstrate proficiency in an appropriate language. Students are required to submit as part of their plan of study, a proposal that indicates following:
    - ➢ What the language or research skill is?
    - ➢ How his particular proficiency will contribute to the student's development as a scholar?
- The scholar should be well versed in accepted method of collecting and analyzing data in a given field, capable of reporting findings accurately and able to advance knowledge in a given field.
- Student needs to demonstrate both a mastery of certain basic literature and their readiness to write a proposal. This will address to the levels of competency (general and specific).
- **Generic skills and additional transferable skills** should be incorporated in the programme. **Generic skills** are those that relate to successful completion of the research project. **Additional transferable** skills include advanced computer literacy, familiarity with the internet, to negotiate access to resources, to find information from specialist libraries or archive.
- **Research Tool Plan** is intended to help each registered scholar to identify research skills and competencies needed to further individual scholarly aspirations. It makes sense to think ahead so as not to arrive unprepared at the thesis stage.
    - ➢ After completing the course work, each student should consult their guide/appropriate faculty advisors and write a short Tool Plan of about four to

six pages spelling out areas of research competency he or she aims to develop while in a Ph.D programme.

- The research Tool Plan should address the following questions:
  - What are your major areas of interest?
  - What skills do you have already, and what additional or new competencies will you aim to develop to be prepared to do excellent research? How these particular skills relate to your areas of interest?
  - What specific courses or workshops have you attended for deepening skills of the relevant kind? Do you need to learn about additional options?

Guidelines for Research Tool Plan

1. Ph.D students should develop research related skills.
2. All students in the programme should complete the introductory seminar on the field of his interest to learn about various ways in which scholars define questions.
3. Each student should develop research related skills and competencies best suited to his/her individual interests. These may be skills and language competency, advanced statistical analysis, field work technique, survey design, interviewing, developing standardized tool, case based research, philosophy of social science, qualitative and quantitative analysis and so forth. Such skills will contribute to their Ph.D research work and prepare the research scholars to do additional research in one or more kind in his/her subsequent career.

Hence if the course work is conducted by the research centre with passion and dedication, and if the research scholars competently do their research work with dedication and honesty, it is but natural that the researcher's competency from all the angles can be incorporated. The scope of Ph.D degree should be broadened and that the scholars should feel that they able to pursue a variety of careers.

References

Borthwick, J. and Wissier, R. (2003), "Postgraduate Research Students and Generic Capabilities: Online Directions".

Boyatis, R.; Stubbs, E.; and Taylor, S. (2002), "Learning Cognitive and Emotional Intelligence Competencies through Graduate Management Education".

Brown, R. (1993) "Meta-competence: A recipe for reframing the competence debate" *Personnel Preview,* Vol. 22, No. 6, pp. 25-36.

Buckley, F. and Huley, J. (2001) "Change in the nature of the university: the quality regime and it's effects on the university teaching environment".

Finian, *et al.* (2009), "Doctoral Competencies and Graduate Research Education: Focus and Fit with the Knowledge Economy?"

Kodwani, Amitabh Deo (2009) "Competency Mapping". Paradigm Institute of Management Technology, Vol. 13, Issue 2, pp. 117-118, 2 p.

Naqvi, Farah (January 2009), "Competency Mapping and Managing Talent." ICFAI Journal of Management Research, Vol. 8, Issue 1, pp. 85-94, 10 p., 1 Chart.

Sahu, R.K. (2009) Competency Mapping (Ed. 1) New Delhi: Excel Books.

32

Gen-Y Researchers Need to Think and Act Globally

Arti Bhatti

Introduction

We are living in challenging times as we are in a phase of transition to a new knowledge-based society. Some educational resources are now fully accessible through different media formats via information and communication technologies (ICT)-through Web tools and search engines, including personal websites and those of formal educational institutions, libraries, information centres and civil society organisations (communities, associations, affiliations). There are advances in technology worldwide and hundreds of thousands of new resources published each day on the Internet. We see the world has changed dramatically and accordingly the academicians and researchers too have changed. Due to intervention of ICT in every sphere of learning, any information is just one 'click' away. In such a scenario, researchers will have to be able to "think and act globally". They will need to be increasingly multicultural, as agile in the academic world as in business, and able to engage in dialogue and interactions with the researchers in countries all over the world. Along with the core competencies that the researchers need to acquire, they must always be open to innovations and must be able to use open available resources in a just and apt manner. Rather than just confined to one locale the Gen-Y (Young Generation) researchers need to consider themselves a part of the global society, need to think, innovate and implement accordingly.

Competence and Competency

Competence refers to a state of being well qualified to perform an activity, task or job function. When a person is competent to do something, he or she has achieved a state of competence that is recognizable and verifiable to a particular community of practitioners.

A competency, then, refers to the way that a state of competence can be demonstrated to the relevant community. According to the International Board of Standards for Training, Performance and Instruction (IBSTPI), a competency involves a related set of knowledge, skills and attitudes that enable a person to effectively perform the activities of a given occupation or function in such a way that meets or exceeds the standards expected in a particular profession or work setting. The structure and assessment of competencies may differ from one community of practice to another and even within a community. To facilitate a common understanding of competencies in the context of globalization, some specifications have been elaborated. Typically, competency is divided into specific indicators describing the requisite know ledge, skills, attitudes and context of performance.

According to NPA Core Competencies Committee (2007-2009), competency has been defined as "an acquired personal skill that is demonstrated in [one's] ability to provide a consistently adequate or high level of performance in a specific job function." These competencies are meant to serve primarily as: (1) a basis for self-evaluation by postdoctoral scholars and (2) a basis for developing training opportunities that can be evaluated by mentors, institutions, and other advisors.

For any particular research topic, three levels of learning outcomes have been described. They are: (i) Be familiar with: At this level there is a basic understanding but little or no practical experience (I have read about it). (ii) Have knowledge of: At this level there is a sound theoretical knowledge but limited practical experience (I have read about it and understand it). (iii) Be competent at: At this level there is sound theoretical knowledge and understanding of the topic, together with sufficient practical experience to be able to complete/carry out the task concerned independently and without assistance (I have read about it, understand it and can do it consistently to a satisfactory standard).

A research competency is a description of this third level and specifies the knowledge and skills required. It does not describe how they may be acquired, although it is useful to provide this information in a competency document. However, it should be borne in mind that there are usually many ways in which a specific competency can be acquired.

Principles Underpinning the Development of Competencies

Competencies can be acquired through a number of means but the principles underpinning competency development are common to all areas of research. They are:

- Competencies can be acquired through multiple means. Knowledge alone is unlikely to allow an individual to achieve competency. Other experiences that complement training should reinforce the acquisition of competencies.
- A single curriculum is unnecessary to define the acquisition of competencies. Individuals will have experienced opportunities that are unique, and the programme to help them achieve competencies should be tailored to their specific needs.
- Those involved in the development of curricula should identify the target audience and level of competence to be achieved on completion of training. These should be specified in a training contract.
- The competencies for research will in part be common with other existing competencies developed for adoption during the course of research. The competencies should be developed in lieu of the global world requirement and underlying concept of globalization.
- The competency framework should be monitored and updated to meet the demands of globalized world.

Domains of Competencies

Competencies have been grouped into five domains. They are:

- Practical skills
- Problem-solving, thinking and communication skills
- Personal attitudes and professional ethics
- Dissemination
- Roles and functions

Research is a systematic attempt towards attaining new information or adding to the existing one. The researchers should be able to understand the processes involved in research and be able to critically appraise the science that underpins their practice. The rationale for the selection of these topics is based on three concepts. The first is the logical process of the scientific method, namely the identification of a problem; the formation of a hypothesis; deductive reasoning, data collection and analysis; and the derivation of a conclusion. The second is the utilization of a framework using the concepts of structure, process and outcome to complete the scientific method and the adoption of current good practice. The third is the importance of dissemination, and the skills required to write a research paper.

Domain A: Practical Skills

This domain is divided into five competencies. They are:

- Find and use resources
- Use library and information technology effectively
- Recognize and know when to use primary and secondary resources
- Observe and record behaviour
- Demonstrate basic computer competency

Domain B: Problem-Solving, Thinking, and Communication Skills

This domain is divided into five competencies that deal with the individual's ability to critique, communicate, and identify shortfalls in existing information. They are the ability to:

- Understand the difference between subjective and objective information
- Recognize when information provided is sufficient

- Evaluate when the basis for conclusions is laid out completely and clearly
- Generate research questions by recognizing gaps in knowledge
- Use oral and written communication to express ideas effectively

Domain C: Personal Attitudes and Professional Ethics

This domain is divided into three competencies that cover personal attitudes and professional ethics. The competencies are the ability to:

- Demonstrate an appreciation of the necessity and value of research.
- Demonstrate an awareness and adherence of ethical principles underpinning research
- Design and implement research studies that evaluate performance of earlier and ongoing research.

Domain D: Dissemination of Research Findings

This domain is divided into two competencies which deal with the dissemination of research findings and the ability to influence clinical practice. They are:

- Demonstrating the skills required for publication of research reports.
- Changing clinical practice based on outcome studies and other research

Domain E: Roles and Functions of a Researcher

This domain is divided into six competencies. They are to:

- Engage in activities that contribute to the development of a body of knowledge
- Design and implement a series of studies that address a significant issue.
- Write research funding applications to major funding bodies.

- Offer help and support to other researchers.
- Access paper and on-line journals and try to get work published in major journals.
- Contribute to the existing knowledge

The Competencies Needed in a Researcher Today and Tomorrow

A survey was conducted in eight countries by APEC/DELOITTE in 2010, with an aim to find out which competencies would a future generation researcher need. The eight countries studied were—France, Germany, Finland, Netherlands, the United Kingdom, Switzerland, Japan and the United States. This study addressed a wide audience: Ph.D. students, researchers and research personnel, recruitment and career management professionals in every type of organization (laboratory, business, university department, etc.), professors, newly qualified researchers, and executives keen to exercise their talents in the research world. Twenty competencies expected by everyone involved in research in all of the studied countries, in both private and public sectors are:

1. Scientific knowledge
2. Ability to learn and adapt
3. Ability to formulate a research issue
4. Capacity for analysis and grasp of sophisticated IT tools
5. Ability to work in an interdisciplinary environment
6. Ability to incorporate existing knowledge
7. Ability to work in a team
8. Ability to develop a network
9. Communication skill
10. Ability to assess
11. Language skills
12. Business culture and management skills
13. Project management skills
14. Ability to manage and steer teams
15. Awareness of the pertinence of the research and its impact on creativity
16. Open-minded approach
17. Motivation/Involvement
18. Adaptability
19. Ability to self-assess

20. Ability for innovations and creativity
- Scientific competencies
  - ➤ Scientific knowledge
  - ➤ Ability to learn and adapt
  - ➤ Ability to formulate a research issue
  - ➤ Capacity for analysis and grasp of sophisticated IT tools ✓
  - ➤ Ability to work in an interdisciplinary environment ✓
  - ➤ Ability to incorporate existing knowledge existantes
- Project and team management skills
  - ➤ Ability to work in a team
  - ➤ Ability to develop a network ✓
  - ➤ Communication skills
  - ➤ Ability to assess
  - ➤ Language skills
  - ➤ Business culture and management skills
  - ➤ Project management skills ✓
  - ➤ Ability to manage and steer teams
  - ➤ Awareness of the pertinence of the research and its impact on the environment ✓
- Personal aptitudes/interpersonal skills
  - ➤ Creativity
  - ➤ Open-minded approach
  - ➤ Motivation/Involvement
  - ➤ Adaptability
  - ➤ Ability to self-assess

(✓ Key competencies required for the future, * In the 8 studied countries (France, Germany, Finland, Netherlands, the United Kingdom, Switzerland, Japan and the United States)

Source: APEC/DELOITTE Study 2010.

Globalization and Changing Trends

Globalization is a combination of ideas, practices and technologies. It is something more than modernization, westernization and the liberalization of markets. It includes economic, political, cultural and social dimensions. It has brought the entire world into a small pocket. The event or a research happening in one part of the world reaches to other parts in no time. The researchers have to be aware that in this world of globalization, they have to develop global competency, apart from core competency listed above.

Globalization can be defined as the "intensification of world-wide social relations which link distant localities in such a way that local happenings are shaped by events occurring many miles away and *vice versa*" (Giddens, 1990) and "All those processes by which the peoples of the world are incorporated into a single society, global society" (Albrow, 1990).

To think and act globally the following criteria should be borne in mind by the mentors, policy-makers and stakeholders and researchers must try to understand their needs and try inculcate them.

- *New ways of conducting research*: The researchers must think and practice upon reinforcing multidisciplinary and interdisciplinary approaches. Everywhere, the emphasis is on the need to innovate. Multidisciplinary approaches encourage research at the interfaces between disciplines, ideal breeding grounds for new ideas.
- *Development of new tools influencing how research is done*: This is the era of IT. Everywhere in all the fields one can notice, breakthrough innovations in technology (the latest generation of DNA/gene sequences, for example) and in IT capacity (modelling and simulation tools, Web-based collaboration tools, open source software) are changing the face of research in certain disciplines.
- *Cost effectiveness*: Researchers should keep in mind the cost effectiveness of their research, though in most of the market driven companies, for innovative practices, budget is not an issue but the cost effectiveness of the entire project needs to be thought of and well planned. All involved in research must be aware of the importance of markets and the need for strict controls on spending. The tendency is more pronounced in some countries than in others, and also depends on the nature of the research (public or private) but is inevitably accompanied by:
    - The need for regular "evaluation/approval" stages for on-going research (and also for researchers).

- ➤ The need, on the national level, to develop a higher education system that aims, beyond excellence per se, at performance as a means of winning new markets.
- ➤ The need for researchers, over and above their scientific expertise, to be familiar with and adept at finding funding sources for their projects, and able to adapt to sometimes abrupt shifts in research priorities.

- *Innovation*: Over the past decade, innovation has become integral to universities, alongside the core mission in education and research. According to Prendergast (2013), "Innovation can be defined as the creative interaction between business, science and the citizen". He added, "The most innovative research happens at the interface between disciplines. I think science, arts, and the humanities will interact, whether in performing arts, or gaming technologies and visualization". He also clarified that clustering of great innovation doesn't just happen by magic. It needs to be strategized for, planned for, activated and incentivized. Researchers must be ready to innovate either when they are in fields of science and technology or while working with human subjects. Innovation is the key to unlocking many of the challenges that education is facing today. UNICEF has declared this year 2013-2014 as the "year of innovation for education of the girl child", which indicates the importance of innovation. It has also suggested some of the innovative practices that can be followed. Such suggestions are the outcome of years of research in different parts of the world, amongst different cultures and geographical situations.
- *Cultural developments:* Due to the global culture and easy convenient moves and opportunities possible, there a landscape of persons who constitute the shifting world in which we live: tourists, immigrants, refugees, exiles and other moving groups and people. Technology has developed a borderless society of knowledge and dissemination of information was never so simple as it is now. Oommen (1998) talks of the cultural impact of

> globalization and the "Birth of a New World Society". According to him, the consequences of globalisation could be discerned through four interrelated processes—homogenisation, pluralisation, traditionalisation and hybridisation. The process of homogenisation occurs due to mixing of cultural patterns and institutional arrangements initiated by the revolution in transport and communication as noticed by eating habits, erupting on international educational institutes, parliamentary democracy, western technology. Pluralisation concedes and commends the co-existence of a variety of crossbreeding of the traditional and the modern, the local and the global gives birth to hybridization which creates new cultural elements and social patterns which are neither traditional nor modern, neither local nor global. This leads to the resurrection of roots, a search for identity, a process of traditionalisation accompanied by revivalistic syndrome.

The Gen Y researcher has to understand and respect the changes occurring in the society and proceed accordingly.

Conclusion

Research, researchers and their contribution in today's society, is not just confined to themselves or to their institution, instead in this global world, their practices, findings and suggestions can be noticed and acknowledged by people sitting in any part of the world. In such a dynamic and cross cultural situation, where the influence of globalization is felt in every aspect of human life, researchers have to develop skills and competencies to match to the existing and upcoming diverse, modern, plural and yet traditional society. Apart from scientific competencies, project and team management skills, personal aptitudes/interpersonal skills, they have to also capitalize on global skills like working in cross cultural diverse environment, abilities to use IT skills, understand the need and future demands of a society, attempts to practice and implement innovations and still maintain the local traditions and the traditions of the society.

References

Albrow, (1990) as in Christine Monnier (2010). "Accelerating Social Change". Retrieved from: globalsociology.pbworks.com/w/page/14711303/What%20is%20Globalization.

APEC/DELOITTE (2010). "Skills and Competencies needed in the research Field: Objectives 2020". Retrieved from: http://www.deloitee.com.

Giddens (1990) as in Christine Monnier (2010). "Accelerating Social Change". Retrieved from:globalsociology.pbworks.com/w/page/14711303/What%20is%20Globalization.

Gray, C. (2007). "The Research Competencies Frame work". U.K.: The Royal College of Surgeons of England. Retrieved from: http://www.fgdp.org.uk/_assets/pdf/research/research%20competencies.pdf.

McGreal Rory, Kinuthia Wanjira and Marshall Stewart. (eds) (2013). "Open Educational Resources: Innovation, Research and Practice". Vancouver, Canada: Commonwealth of Learning and Athabasca University. Retrieved from: www.col.org.

National Post doctoral Association (NPA) Core Competencies Committee (2007-2009) Retrieved from: http://www.nationalpostdoc.org/competencies, on 01-03-2014.

Oommen (1998) as in Pandey, M.P. (2011). "Globalisation and social transformation in India: Theorising the transition" in: *International Journal of Sociology and Anthropology*, Vol. 3(8), pp. 253-260, Retrieved from: http://www.academicjournals.org/ijsa/PDF/pdf2011/Aug/Pandey.pdf.

Prendergast Patrick. (2013). "Open Innovation2.0" Dublin: Trinity College. Retrieved from: http://horizon2020projects.com/pr-knowledge-innovation/higher-education-in-open-innovation.

33

Meta Analysis of Educational Research in India

The Way Forward

Bibhuti Narayan Biswal

Introduction

In the world education arena India has one of the largest higher education system and has been witnessing rapid growth in its number of institutions and enrolment in the last few decades. The number of universities has grown more than six times in the last four decades which is above 700. Student enrolment in higher educational Institutions (HEIs) has grown 12 times in the last four decades. India has more than 35,500 colleges with one-third of the colleges having been set up in the last five years only. Germany in higher education has reached close to 18 per cent in 2011-12. India ranks second in the world in terms of enrolment of students in higher education institutions. On the global front only two Indian higher education brands featured in the QS World University Rankings 2011-12 of the top 500 global universities. Out of the 48 countries studied, India ranks last in the U21 rankings of national higher education systems. Similarly, in the Shanghai University ranking of World-class Universities, only three universities, namely—Indian Institute of Science (Bangalore), IIT (Kharagpur) and Calcutta University figure in the world's Top-500 for the year 2004. Only the Indian Institutes of Technology at rank 50 and the Indian Institutes of Management at rank 84 from India figure in the 2005 London Times Higher Education Supplement (THES) ranking of world's top 100 universities. In terms of the number of researchers and technicians engaged in R & D activities, India has merely 119 researchers, whereas Japan has 5,287 and the US has 4,484 researchers per million of population.(*UNESCO Institute of Statistics from WDI (2006)).*

India's 12th Five Year Plan (2012-2017) notes that the four main priorities of education policies have been access, equity, quality and governance. Though it gives priorityto these four areas, but places the greatest emphasis on improving learning outcomes at all levels. We must realize that our nation's fate is not to be measured in terms of the strength and size of the army and arsenals, but in terms of world of future knowledge through number of world class institutions that germinate, innovate and incubate new knowledge and new technology. Therefore centres of excellence, excellent departments, research institutions, colleges, work in tandem to realize the potential of India's huge human capital which seems missing in the present system of higher education. Our higher educational institutions are vulnerable to adapt to include, knowledge/technology generation, technology transfer, innovation, creativity, patent and IPR, spinoff of new technology based firms, corporate development, new knowledge creation through sustained research and lifelong education in their visions and missions due to which they are tagged as mediocre institutions and producing mediocre students (Biswal, 2013). Therefore continuous research of high quality can only accelerate our educational development in the country which in turn has larger impact on our economic development.

The term 'research and scholarship' usually refers to uncovering or generating new knowledge, or solving particular practical or theoretical problems. Research and development activities are aimed at making scientific discoveries and inventions that are commercially attractive (Harman, 2006). In other words educational research is a method, process and system for the addition and advancement of human knowledge, which opens new doors in the field of education for the larger welfare of mankind (Kumar, 2014). Owing to this attribute research is essentially connected to the process of education. The standards of academic research are low and declining (Agrawal, 2006). Some of the problems of the Indian higher education, such as—the unwieldy affiliating system, inflexible academic structure, uneven capacity across various subjects, eroding autonomy of academic institutions, and the low level of public funding are well known.

Types of Reserach and its Relevance: Decade-Wise

Higher education in India has expanded rapidly over the past two decades. This growth has been mainly driven by private sector initiatives. There are genuine concerns about many of them being substandard and exploitative (Agrawal, 2006). Educational research too has grown in multifold manner. For instance the numbers of doctoral degrees awarded in science and engineering in India is a little over 6,000 doctorates, compared to 9,000 in China and 25,000 in the US. It increased rapidly from a little over 1,000 in 1990 to over 9,000 in recent years in China. In comparison, there has been a modest increase in India (UGC, 2005).

As far as nature of research is concerned, it is of three types namely: pure research, applied research, interdisciplinary research. The OECD (2002) defines pure basic research as experimental and theoretical work undertaken to acquire knowledge without looking for long-term benefits; strategic basic research is defined as experimental and theoretical work undertaken to acquire knowledge in the expectation of useful discoveries; applied research refers to original work undertaken to acquire knowledge with a specific application in view; and experimental development is the systematic work, using existing knowledge gained from research or practical experience, directed to producing new materials, products or devices. Interdisciplinary research refers to an integral method of research wherein disciplinary knowledge converged into new branches of knowledge having wider applications. During 1970-80 there was more emphasis on pure/basic research that accelerated achievement in our educational goals. However, 1980-90 witnessed more interdisciplinary research like evolution of ICT. Post-globalisation, GATTs, WTO phase witnessed more applied and interdisciplinary research in India.

Gap Between Demnd and Supply

The growth of higher education in India has been phenomenal. Starting with 1950-51, there were only 263,000 students in all disciplines in 750 colleges affiliated to 30 universities. This has grown by 2005 to 11 million students in 17,000 degree colleges affiliated to 230 universities and non-affiliated university-level institutions. In addition, there are about 10 million students in over 6,500 in vocational institutions. The enrolment is growing at the rate of 5.1 per cent per year. However, of the degree students only 5 per cent are enrolled into engineering courses, while an overall 20 per cent in sciences. The demand for professional courses is growing rapidly. On the other hand the gross enrolment ratio (GER) of higher education in India is roughly 6 per cent (Kaul, 2006). This will need to be doubled in the next decade. This involves thousands of crores of Rupees of investment. There is a serious mismatch of demand and supply. The size of demand as it is projected, clearly indicate the need for new institutions imparting quality education in subject areas of contemporary relevance and job opportunities. Quality can be ensured only if there is sufficient competition among institutes to attract talented students and provide choices and innovative subject combinations, ample opportunity for research and innovations.

Title

Meta analysis of educational research in India in the past four decades: the way forward

Rationale

- Most public higher education institutions funded by State governments and States have limited role in maintaining quality standards which has resulted in poor quality research work in our departments.
- Due to poor monitoring system, the Central Government, the State governments, largely statutory government controlled bodies like the UGC, professional councils and the universities (particularly the affiliating the afflicting universities) and the voluntary accreditation agencies create a multi-layered burdensome regulatory system trying to achieve often conflicting objectives thereby allowing institutions of dubious quality to operate in our country.
- Due to poor public funding, dilapidated infrastructure of

our departments and weak regulatory mechanism, the quality of research has suffered a lot.

- World demographic dynamics shows that in another 20 years countries having advanced economy will face severe problems in skilled manpower whereas India's 45 per cent of population will be in their twenties in the same period which may usher in the future leadership role for our young mass which need to be nurtured well through quality research programmes in our HEI's.

Objectives

The major objectives that is aimed for the study as are under:

- To know about the Higher Education and Research (HER) in India.
- To trace the growth of HER in India since four decade.
- To determine the strategy to promote research in higher education.

Variables

Independent Variables

Research on educational administration

Dependent Variables

Research on curriculum reform, research on evaluation, research on professional development, research on learning environment

Review of Related Literature

Higher education plays an important role in supporting a nation's R&D efforts. It provides skilled human resources for the R&D system. It is often the lead player in the public research arena. Academic research through universities forms an important component of the technological base of a country. The institutional framework for research and development in India can be divided into two broad categories: Fundamental and applied research. The institutions involved in educational research in India are: UGC, ICSSR, TISS (Mumbai), ISI, ICHR, CSIR, TIFR, ICPR, ICMR, ICAR, UNESCO, British Council etc.

The World Bank Study (2000) has identified the following issues related to the higher education in India: Over-centralization and lack of autonomy and accountability, resource constraints and wastage, poor quality and relevance in many institutions, difficulties in retention of science and technology personnel in education, poor technology and infrastructure support, limited access and regional disparity.

The paper of **Naik (2012)** presents in brief, the need and importance of research based innovative world class universities and colleges, so as to keep India globally competitive. India needs professionals of world class standard, with higher imagination who can take it to greater heights on the international plane. Students need nurturing to become pace setters, technology pioneers and industry leaders. Institutes have to be ahead of time, to do this. They have to have research and innovative character. Conventional institutes in the absence of research base are unfit for the purpose. They produce, by and large, mediocre graduates, who produce only soldiers at best for multinationals. There is huge energy in Indian youths, yet too few become leaders in industry and technology on the global plane, because that is not what present institutes are teaching students to become. The number of world class institutes is now different, it will be producing mediocre graduates by world standards to manage its national and international affairs. India is then destined to lag behind in the brain race. The paper identifies strategies which contribute to make an institution world class. The strategies are grouped as governance, academic, administrative, financial etc. They are however tough to deliver and essentially call for political will.

Williams *et al.*, (2007) conducted research on "Closed book, invigilated exams *versus* open book, open web exams: An empirical analysis" whose abstract is as follows. The paper reports on the latest findings of an on-going research project evaluating the effectiveness of 'open book, open web' (OBOW) examinations. An assessment instrument used in a growing number of higher education institutions around the world, the OBOW examination model under consideration in this project is distinguishable by its firm commitment to the notion of authentic assessment, and the harnessing of the information and communication technologies to bring the 'examination paper' to life. The results of previous research undertaken have indicated that the OBOW approach receives the strong endorsement of students on a number of fronts, not least the quality of the learning outcomes. Scepticism remains, however, on the part of some traditionalists within educational circles who argue for the retention of invigilated examinations as this is the only means of ensuring that a student's work is their own and theirs alone. This paper opposes this position, presenting the case for an examination instrument that is more in keeping with modern learning theory.

Desiraju (2008) conducted a review study entitled "Science Education and Research in India" with an objective to identify the problems associated with science education (i.e. research and teaching, science and engineering, curiosity and courage), role of IITs, Central Universities, IISERs, State Universities, Research Institutes, Administration and bureaucracy, Non-governmental Involvement etc. Major findings of the study reveals that: Many aspects of the Indian scientific development are extremely unsatisfactory, lacking in both quality and quantity. Although the outreach of teaching and research programmes has increased considerably, populist political themes are favoured and special institutions have been created where research is undertaken independent of the university system. This article reviews the present scene in science education, and identifies the major problems and the challenges confronting the institutions involved in education and research. It suggests that the government should restrict itself to broad policy issues rather than be involved in day-to-day affairs and the university should be re-established as the primary agency for education and research.

Mustafa (2008) conducted a study on "Constructivist Approaches to Learning in Science and Their Implications for Science Pedagogy: A Literature Review". This paper draws attention to the literature in the areas of learning, specifically, constructivism, conceptual change and cognitive development. It emphasizes the contribution of such research to our understanding of the learning process. This literature provides guidelines for teachers, at all levels, in their attempt to have their students achieve learning with understanding. Research about the constructive nature of students' learning processes, about students' mental models, and students' misconceptions have important implications for teachers who wish to model scientific reasoning in an effective fashion for their students. This paper aims to communicate this research to teachers, textbook authors, and college professors who are involved in the preparation of science teachers. This paper is divided into two major parts. The first part concentrates on a critical review of the three most influential learning theories and constructivist view of learning and discusses the foundation upon which the constructivist theory of learning has been rooted. It seeks an answer to the question of "What are some guiding principles of constructivist thinking that we must keep in mind when we consider our role as science teachers?". The second part of this paper moves toward describing the nature of students' alternative conceptions, the ways of changing cognitive structure, and cognitive aspects of learning and teaching science.

Banerjee (2006) studied "Mathematics Education research in India: Issues and Challenge". The major findings are: Higher education has largely been a neglected area as far as mathematics education is concerned. The Indira Gandhi National Open University made some efforts to collect data on a bridge programme (the Bachelors Preparatory Programme, BPP) that they had launched to allow access to the undergraduate degree programme for people who had no formal high school leaving certificate. Feedback collected over a 3-year period suggested the need for curricular revision so as to meet the needs of the students (such as simplification of content, basic mathematics with emphasis on mathematical thinking and comfort with dealing with mathematical language) (Sinclair and Varma, 2001).

Avalos (2011) studied "Teacher professional development in Teaching and Teacher Education over ten years (2000-10)". The first part synthesises production referred to learning, facilitation and collaboration, factors influencing professional development, effectiveness of professional development and issues around the themes. The second part, selects from the production nine articles for closer examination. The paper concludes by noting how the production brings out the complexities of teacher professional learning and how research and development have taken cognisance of these factors and provided food for optimism about their effects, although not yet about their sustainability in time. The traditional "master" role of teacher educators and researchers is revised in a number of the studies reviewed. We read about partnership experiences between university professors and teachers in formal courses where roles and role-playing were investigated in order to further more productive engagements in learning and change. Other partnerships such as those generated by external researchers working with teachers as co-researchers contributed to modify the traditional separation between academia and the professions.

Sample and Population

The researcher has collected seven related research on higher education and research in India and abroad which is of paramount importance for the topic of search. They were taken for the meta analysis through purposive sampling technique. The researches on higher education and research constitute the population for the present study.

Methodology of the Study: Keeping in view the framework of the topic, the researcher has selected seven research studies so as to draw out the findings on various objectives that is being set.

Data Analysis: The researcher analysed the seven studies purposively to find out the suitable outcome which the study is aimed at.

Major Findings

Independent Variables

Research on educational administration: Over-centralization and lack of autonomy and accountability, resource constraints and wastage, poor quality and relevance in many institutions are the major road blocks for HEIs (The World Bank Study, 2000). The government interfering in day-to-day affairs of the university rather than looking into broad policy issues are the primary agency for degradation in quality of education and research in our country (Desiraju, 2008).

Dependent Variables

Research on Curriculum Reform: Conventional institutes/ universities in the absence of research base curricula produce, by and large, mediocre graduates, who produce only soldiers at best for multinationals. There is huge energy in Indian youths, yet too few become leaders in industry and technology on the global plane, because that is not what present institutes are teaching students to become (Naik, 2012). There is acute need for curricular revision in our universities so as to meet the needs of the students (Banerjee, 2006).

Research on Evaluation: The assessment methods in our HEI's are still rote based which does not promote independent thinking and creativity. Therefore, dynamic method of assessment is the need for our HEI's such as Open Book Open Web (OBOW) which is distinguishable by its firm commitment as an authentic assessment that brings the 'examination paper' to life. The Open Book Open Web (OBOW) approach received the strong endorsement of students on a number of fronts, not least the quality of the learning outcomes (Williams, 2007).

Research on Professional Development: The traditional approach of teaching in our HEIs lacks collaboration, innovations, incentivisation. A strong partnership between university professors and students promotes more productive engagements in learning. Partnerships such as those generated by external researchers working with professors as co-researchers contribute significantly to the traditional separation between academia and the professions (Avalos, 2011). Continuous professional development of faculty members needs immediate attention.

Research on Learning Environment: Research about the constructive nature of students' learning processes, about students' mental models, and students' misconceptions have important implications for teachers who wish to model scientific reasoning in an effective fashion for their students (Cakir, 2008). Thus enabling learning environment in HEIs seems vital for our universities/colleges rather than pursuing political and personal intentions.

Strategy to Bridge the Gap

Promotion and enhancement of research and innovation is a key focus area of the Twelfth Plan, to align research with the national development agenda and better serve the needs of industry and society. The Government must plan to invest more than 2 per cent of the country's GDP in research activity during the Twelfth Plan (from 1% at present). The increased investment may be used to develop institutions and create centres of excellence in research and research training. The 'National Initiative for Excellence in Social Sciences and Humanities' would be launched to encourage humanities as a choice for students and improve quality and research in this discipline (FICCI, 2012).

Quality Concerns

Research universities that are able to participate in research and teaching in multiple disciplines should be promoted. A legislative framework for setting up "Universities for Research and Innovation" should be considered immediately. The Government intends to have 20 such universities, which are either created or converted, by the end of the Twelfth Plan. The creation of 20 Centres of Excellence (CoEs) as a long-term investment in selected areas of national importance is expected to attract and retain research talent. In addition, centres of training and research should be established in frontier areas of science and technology, social sciences and humanities.

Futuristic Perspective

In order to promote research climate in our institutions good quality, market based e-learning courses and Internet cafeterias with programme structures that are relevant to the Indian context need to be set up urgently. Our Libraries must be equipped with computers that support high speed internet connectivity. To bridge the digital divide we need all night net libraries or late night accessibility at least, on payment basis. Saxsena *et al.*, (2010) referred favourable conditions for research in Indian universities/ colleges as: good library with ample reference material including online journals/open access journals, vibrant academic atmosphere, sound infrastructure facility, well equipped labs, adequate funds for the research project, learned faculty member having passion for research, sense of pride and feelings for national development through relevant research.

Value Aspects

Human values should be the guiding parameters for governance, planning and research -development processes at higher education institutions. It is desirable that human values should permeate and form part of the teaching in all disciplines and subjects. Alas! Our higher education research system suffers from degraded morality which emerges from the core intention of neglecting one's own duty and responsibilities (Kumar, 2014). Haste and shortcut in most research works leads us to pedestrian, unexpected and unusable results. Personal gains are the sole intention of our research work. Therefore, healthy attitude for educational research in line with 3P (Purity, Patience, Perseverance), 3H (Integration of Head-Heart-Hand), 3C (Commitment, Collaboration, Care), 3D (Determination, Dedication, Discrimination), 3W (Work, Worship, Wisdom) principles need to be cultivated in our higher academia.

Research Competency Framework

The Research Competency Framework (RCF) deals with generic research skills which a researcher should possess before jumping into it. Such RC-framework must be tailored to meet the individual needs of each researcher. It encompasses 6 domains namely: Personal attitudes and professional ethics, practical skills, problem-solving, thinking and communication skills, roles and functions, Dissemination, Core Value System etc., which are depicted as follows (Fig. 33.1).

Recommendations

1. UGC must try to improve technology infrastructure—high bandwidth connectivity and campus networks to enable technology to improve teaching, learning, research and governance of higher education system.
2. Restructuring of accreditation system to make accreditation effective in addressing quality concerns and NAAC must work in neutral manner.
3. There should be regular monitoring and evaluation of teaching and research in the Universities and other Institutions of higher learning. A Monitoring and

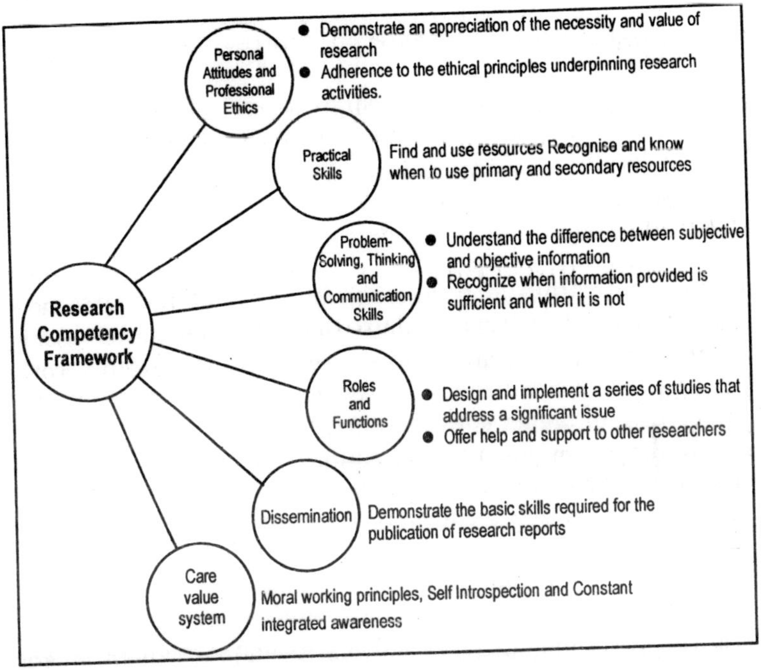

Fig. 33.1

Evaluation (M&E) Unit should be set-up at State level preferably attached to Chancellor's Office; and for its effective functioning, a Statistical Cell should be set-up in each University in the State, under the over all supervision of the M & E Unit.

4. A special effort would be made to strengthen international research linkages and leverage the 22million Indian Diaspora as a powerful asset for research innovation and entrepreneurship.
5. Encouragement of private funding of research by evolving a system of incentives, introduction of research assessment exercise, setting up a research portal regarding the issue of research coordination and maximum use of existing research infrastructure and experimental facilities. NAAC to set up a Research Grants Portal for monitoring and Co-ordinating research.
6. Government of India and Indian multinational corporates

must work together to set up more research and innovation driven universities.

7. Inter-disciplinary research teams within the higher education institutions must be encouraged at institutional level.

Epilogue

Higher education and research now act as indispensable component of cultural, socio-economic and sustainable environment development and sustained growth of our country which needs a fine balance between quality and quantity. The importance of higher education is growing gradually due to its role in the preparation of skilled human resource. Skilled human resource is the very basis of any progressive country, as we know. At present, the higher education in India is passing through a transition phase in order to compete with other countries and witnessing several opportunities and challenges. Quality research endowed with high moral premise and spirit of evolving new knowledge-technology-process-theory-patent seems imminent for our higher educational institutions.

References

Agarwal, P. (2006), Higher Education in India: the need for change, working paper no. 180, Indian Council for Research on International Economic Relations.

Avalos, B., (2011). Teacher Professional Development in Teaching and Teacher Education over Ten Years, *Teaching and Teacher Education*, Vol. 27.

Banerjee, R. (2006), Mathematics Education Research in India: Issues and Challenges.

Biswal, B.N. (2013). Formidable Issues of School and Higher Education: A Critical Analysis, *Edusearch*, Vol. 4, No. 2, pp. 1-8.

Cakir, Mustafa. (2008). Constructivist Approaches to Learning in Science and Their Implications for Science Pedagogy: A Literature Review, *International Journal of Environmental and Science Education*, Vol. 3, No. 4.

Desiraju G.R., (2008). *Economic and Political Weekly*, June 14. Janapath, Bapujee Bazar, Bhubaneshwar.

Harman, G. (2006). Research and Scholarship. In: Forest, James J. F. and

Altbach, Philip G. (eds.). *International Handbook of Higher Education.* Springer. Dodrecht, The Netherlands.

FICCI Higher Education Summit (2012), *Higher Education in India: Twelfth Five Year Plan (2012-2017) and beyond.*

Kaul, S. (2006) Higher education in india: seizing the opportunity working paper no. 179 Indian Council for Research on International Economic Relations.

Kumar, R. (2014), Quality Assurance in Education and Research, *Bhavan's Journal*, Vol. 60(15).

Naik, B.M. (2012) India desperately needs research based, innovative World class universities and colleges to nurture leaders for tomorrow How to go about? Abstract vol. of International Seminar on Higher Education in the year—2020, VNSGU, Surat.

OECD. (2002). Frascati manual. Paris, Organization of Economic Cooperation and Development.

Saxena, V.; Kulsrestha, S.; Khan, B., (2010), Higher Education and research in India, *International Journal of Educational Research and Technology*, Vol. 1(1), pp. 91-98.

UGC (2005). Research Handbook: Towards nurturing research culture in higher education institutions in India. University Grants Commission, New Delhi.

UGC report on higher education India: Strategies and schemes during Eleventh Plan period (2007-2012) for universities and colleges.

U21 Rankings of National Higher Education Systems 2012 report, QS top universities website,

University Grants Commission (2003) Higher Education in India: Issues, concerns and new directions, University Grants Commission, New Delhi.

World Bank Report No. 20416-IN: Scientific and Technical Manpower Development in India, August 30, 2000.

Williams, J. B.; Wong, A. (2007). Closed book, invigilated examsversus open book, open web exams: An empirical analysis, *Proceedings ascilite Singapore 2007: Concise paper.*

34

Resolving Dilemmas in Collaborative Research

A Road Map for Cultivating Wholistic Research Culture

J.N. Baliya

Introduction

Research as an activity engages optimal mental processes and therefore for effective outcomes of any research activity collective wisdom would be a significant move in this regard. Collaborative research appears to be growing in popularity. It is also being actively supported by governments and organisations. The decision to perform research with partners instead of individually influences the research process as well as its outcomes. Collaborative research may be conceptualized as a research effort done by research groups from different disciplines (interdisciplinary collaboration), either belonging to the same country (national) or to more than one country (international) or it may be a parallel research effort by groups from different countries applying the same protocol across various locations or a combination of the above. Collaborative research, mainly from complementary groups within one country, happened in the past. However, increasing globalization, characterized by the facility in communications and exchange of information, is already followed and is likely to continue by an impressive increase in the number, size and diversity of collaborative research projects. This phenomenon is widely recognized; however its characteristics, benefits, drawbacks and efficiency are seldom the objectives of systematic investigation

Realistic thinking always leads to the fact that the outcomes of researchers will only have an impact to the extent that it is conducted in a collaborative manner. In other words, the more organisational people are involved in research, the more confident in and committed to the results they are. In the centre of the philosophical argument is the view that one can only learn about a social world from the people in it. Researchers should take teachers, perspectives and ideas seriously rather than treating them as "subjects" or "objects" of their research. And finally, the political rationale states that researchers have a moral obligation not just to study, but also to act in the interests of those they study.

Recent literature on the topic includes a number of cases of collaborative research efforts between schools and universities' departments of education, ranging from small and informal ones, such as a university faculty member collaborating with several teachers to help them improve their practice, to large, complex and very formal ones, such as state-wide and even national networks of universities and schools sharing research tools and data, disseminating research results, and designing and implementing reforms. The nature of inquiry universities and schools get engaged in also differ from case to case. In general, partnership studies focused on one or more of these three aspects: inquiry into the partnership process, inquiry into professional development, and inquiry into professional practice (Hunkins, Wiseman, & Willams, 1995). Inquiry into the partnership process, a systemic study of patterns, promises, and pitfalls of current partnerships, can substantially contribute to the success of the partnership in the future. For example, one school-university partnership decided to analyze patterns of interaction between the partners assuming that interactions are the basic units of collaborative activity (Wiseman & Nason, 1993 in Hunkins, Wiseman, & Willams, 1995). The analysis revealed that most discussions focused on the partners' self-interests, with only a few instances of discussion that focused on differences between partners' institutions. The study demonstrated to the participants that members of partnerships need more understanding of the nature of their interactions in order to improve their ability to be mutually supportive in partnership function.

Who are the Research Collaborators?

Direct co-operation between two or more researchers is the fundamental unit of collaboration. At the most basic level, it is people who collaborate, not institutions. However, we often talk about collaboration at other levels—between research groups within a department, between departments within the same institution, between institutions, between sectors, and between geographical regions and countries. Indeed most policies are aimed at fostering collaboration at these higher levels rather than inter-individual collaboration. Two or more heads of departments, institute directors or even heads of state might sign a formal memorandum-of-understanding (MoU) that commits their respective departments, institutions or countries to closer cooperation on scientific matters. Again, uncertainty surrounds the concept of 'collaboration'. How closely do two departments, institutions or countries have to work together before the activity is considered to be a collaboration? How formal does the agreement to work together have to be to constitute a 'collaboration'? For example, to qualify as an inter-institutional collaboration, does the collaboration have to be formally sanctioned by the institutions' management or is informal cooperation between individual researchers in the different

Table 34.1: Different levels of collaboration and distinction between inter and intra forms

Level of Collaboration	*Intra*	*Inter*
Individual		Between individuals
Group	Between individuals in the same research group	Between groups (e.g., in the same department)
Department	Between individuals or groups in the same department	Between departments (in the same institution)
Institution	Between individuals or departments in the same institution	Between institutions
Sector	Between institutions in the same sector	Between institution in different sectors
Nation	Between institutions in the same country	Between institutions in different countries

institutions a satisfactory criterion? Must it involve two or more researchers working at two (or more) institutions? Or could it consist of just one researcher working part of the time at one institution and part at another? All these issues need to be looked into to sustain a climate of collaboration in research studies.

Sometimes, however, a collaboration cannot be clearly classified since it may appear to belong to both an *intra*-and an *inter*-category. For example, consider a collaboration that involves two domestic institutions and one foreign institution. This is clearly an *inter-institutional* collaboration. However, from one perspective this collaboration constitutes an *international* collaboration (domestic and foreign), while from another perspective it can be considered a mixture of *inter-* and *intra-national* collaboration. Thus, we see that a collaboration can be either *homogeneous* (i.e., unambiguously either the *inter* or the *intra* form of collaboration) or *heterogeneous* (i.e., a mixture of the *inter* and *intra* forms of collaboration). The need to distinguish between the two types will vary depending on the problem under investigation.

The Challenges Associated with Collaborative Research Culture

Collaborations among researchers can take many forms. In a sense, there is a continuum ranging from the classic partnership between two faculty members at academic institutions, to situations such as the use by one researcher of another's resources such as a piece of equipment, a biological strain, or a database. Collaborators have expectations as to what the nature of the research relationship should be, including the rights and responsibilities of each party. Sometimes, the term "collaboration" may have different meanings to the collaborators and others who may be directly or indirectly involved. If these differences are not identified early in the relationship, and resolved through clear communication, they can become contentious when researchers' interpretations vary concerning emerging issues such as the access to and use of the data generated, or the ownership of intellectual property. Many of the cases described in the literature lacked one or more of the ideal characteristics presented above. The reason is the complexity and difficulty of the collaborative process. In almost all cases, the authors, who were also the participants in the research partnerships they described, write about multiple challenges and tensions they had to face.

Besides enhancing personal productivity, collaboration appears to offer authors another advantage when it comes to a paper being submitted for publication. Gordon found a significant relationship between levels of multiple authorship for papers submitted to a leading astronomy journal, and their frequency of acceptance for publication. According to Gordon, one reason for this is that the degree of technical competence displayed in the multi-authored paper can be enhanced by overlaps existing in areas of specialized competence, and the opportunity for cross-checking and pre submission 'internal refereeing' which this provides for.

The most common challenges are:

- Difference in agendas and expectations—Academics are required to do "research" and to write "research papers", and school-based practitioners are required to do "professional development". So, while academics want to engage in deep discussions based on observations and theories, educators expect an efficient PD package or something they can apply in the work;
- Lack of research knowledge and skills—Though teachers are expected to work alongside academics as co-researchers, they may feel like subordinates because they are considered or consider themselves lacking necessary research skills and knowledge;
- Ethical concerns—Academics wanted teachers to examine theories and situations to develop new understandings; teachers perceived academics as dominant and considered them as assessors of their teaching practice;
- Time constraints and methodological concerns—Different participants have different time expectations: the challenge is to find a way to compromise on project timelines that protect research rigour while also providing timely results. It also takes a lot of time for new partnerships and trust to develop;
- Lack of recognition—Universities often do not encourage applied research, while school organizations do not always see research as a way to cope with problems. School

teachers rarely receive extrinsic rewards for participating in collaborative research;

- Political and financial instability—Unlike tenured university faculty, school boards are not stable over time. Publicly elected school boards can change their policies and programmes with the turn of an election. Additional instability occurs as the district and the school experience shifting levels of state and local financial support. When educational financing goes down, a district may decide to discontinue funding collaborative research projects (Davies, Edwards, Gannon, & Laws, 2007; Gaskell & Flessa, 2007; Hunkins, Wiseman, & Willams, 1995; Mitchell, 2001).

What Factors Support Collaborative Research Climate?

Numerous authors have studied the phenomenon of collaboration. However, while a wide range of factors apparently contributing to collaborative activity have been identified, few specific reasons have been clearly established to explain how and why it occurs. Collaboration can take various forms ranging from offering general advice and insights to active participation in a specific piece of research. These collaborative contributions can also vary in level from the very substantial to the almost negligible. Sometimes a researcher may be seen as a 'collaborator' and listed as a co-author simply by virtue of providing material or performing a routine assay.

The following factors supporting collaborative research may be considered:

- flexible research design that would accommodate the demands of both parties
- willingness on the part of both parties to experiment with different research roles
- adequate allocation of time and resources
- mutual interest
- clear expectations
- shared goals
- respect and trust in the other party
- long-term commitment on the part of university researchers and school and district personnel

- support and recognition from the administration
- shared power and ownership of the research project

What Meaningful Strategies be Used to Advance Collaborative Research?

The literature suggests that the following strategies can be helpful in overcoming some of earlier identified challenges and building successful research partnerships:

a. Implementing Reward and Recognition Systems

- University tenure and promotion processes need to be adapted to take collaborative/applied research into account;
- Top school and district administrators should demonstrate their full support of research partnerships;
- Intrinsic rewards of collaborative research for teachers such as professional expertise, increased knowledge and efficacy, enhanced collegial interaction, and strengthened positive attitudes toward teaching, should be emphasized.

b. Dealing with Time Constraints

- Schools can use pre-service teachers to support in-service teachers' research activities;
- University students can be paired with teachers to serve as research assistants;
- Sharing of tasks in research teams can decrease time commitments for teachers.

c. Dealing with Lack of Experience and Training

- For teachers not familiar with research techniques graduate study opportunities or workshops can be offered at the partnership school campus;
- Collective design, analyses and interpretation of data help engage different perspectives of practitioners, students and academics in ways that encourage critical reflection, collaborative learning, and mutual critique.

d. Disseminating Knowledge

- Academics and teachers can contribute articles to journals and conferences;
- They can also report findings to school boards, local educational groups, and peers or build them into professional development and graduate study;
- Teachers should also apply newly created knowledge to their instructional practice.

e. Appropriate Financial Support

- School boards should emphasize long-term commitments to the research partnership by allocating sufficient funds and supporting the partnership's agenda.

f. Regular Communication for a Sustained Collaboration

- Regular and *ad hoc* meetings should be explicitly built into the research process to signal to individuals that the process is their responsibility and that the partnership requires their personal time and attention (regular meetings); and to provide opportunities to deal with emergent issues, to change direction if necessary, or to check on current needs or perceptions.
- There should be constant communication between the participants. This can be achieved through meetings, exchange of discussion papers and memos, telephone and email conversations, forums, and access to shared online databases.
- Creating liaison positions for large and complex partnerships can help improve communication between the parties and coordination of activities.

While summarizing my paper, I would like to conclude by saying that collaborative research has some positive effects on teachers' sense of agency such as increased self-confidence, enthusiasm for and enjoyment of teaching and learning. Positive outcomes for teachers' professional development, such as extended pedagogical content knowledge and improved teaching and research skills, were also observed. As a result of participation in collaborative research, teachers may achieve transformative understandings about themselves and their profession. Collaborative research helps develop professional communities and trusting relationships. It also provides teachers with opportunities to assume new roles and exhibit leadership. Although there have been many studies of collaboration, little has been published on what exactly is meant by the concept of 'collaboration' or on the adequacy of attempting to measure it through co-authorship. Likewise, little consideration has been given to distinguishing different forms of collaboration or to analysing the additional costs it entails.

References

Ainscow, M., Booth, T. and Dyson, A. (2004). Understanding and developing inclusive practices in schools: A collaborative action research network, *International Journal of Inclusive Education*, 8(2), 125-139.

Ancess, J., Barnett, E. and Allen, D. (2007). Using Research to Inform the Practice of Teachers, Schools, and School Reform Organizations, *Theory Into Practice*, *46*(4), 325-333.

Baumfield, V. and Butterworth, M. (2007). Creating and translating knowledge about teaching and learning in collaborative school-university research partnerships: An analysis of what is exchanged across the partnerships, by whom and how', *Teachers and Teaching*, *13*(4), 411-427.

Davies, B., Edwards, J., Gannon, S. and Laws, C. (2007). Neo-liberal Subjectivities and the Limits of Social Change in University-Community Partnerships', *Asia-Pacific Journal of Teacher Education*, 35(1), 27-40.

Gaskell, J. and Flessa, J. (2007). *Researching Effective Schools in Toronto: Politics and Partnership*. Paper presented at the AERA Conference, Chicago, IL.

Hunkins, F., Wiseman, D., and Willams, R. (1995). Supporting Collaborative Inquiry. In R.T. Osguthorpe (Ed.), *Partner Schools: Centres for Educational Renewal* (1st ed.). San Francisco: Jossey-Bass Publishers.

Lang, L. (2001). Searching for Collaborative Balance: Negotiating Roles in School-University Partnership Research. In M. Richards, A. Elliott, V. Woloshyn, & C. Mitchell, (Eds.). *Collaboration Uncovered: The Forgotten, the Assumed, and the Unexamined in Collaborative Education.* Westport, CT: Bergin & Garvey.

Levin, B. (1993). Collaborative research in and with organizations. *Qualitative Studies in Education, 6*(4), 331-340.

Mitchell, C. (2001). Negotiating Agendas in Collaborative Research. In M. Richards, A. Elliott, V. Woloshyn, & C. Mitchell, (Eds.). *Collaboration Uncovered: The Forgotten, the Assumed, and the Unexamined in Collaborative Education.* Westport, CT: Bergin & Garvey.

Ross, J. Rolheiser, C. and Hogaboam-Gray, A. (January 1999). Effects of collaborative action research on the knowledge of five Canadian teacher-researchers. *The Elementary School Journal, 99*(3), 255-275.

Schulz, R. and Hall, C. (2004). Difficulties in promoting inquiry in teacher education partnerships: English and Canadian perspectives, *Journal of Education for Teaching, 30*(3), 255-269.

Tikunoff, W.J., and Ward, B.A. (1983). Educational organizations as loosely coupled systems. *Administrative Science Quarterly*, 21, 1-19.

35

Quality of Educational Research and Pedagogy

An Exposition

Mouchumi Deka

Introduction

In a rapidly changing global business environment, research, innovation and highly skilled employees are key to maintaining the competitive advantage of organizations. Educational research in India is of fairly recent origin and it is still in its infancy. It is because of the fact that the study of education as a subject at the University stage did not begin seriously until the forties. Although the need for educational research was acknowledged for the first time in 1913, by Government Resolution on Educational Policy. After independence in 1947 a systematic effort to develop educational research was made in India. The research programmes in education received great stimulus in the first decade after independence by the establishment of national and state organizations for the development of elementary and secondary education, educational and vocational guidance, and research in curriculum and textbook development and evaluation procedures. Certain organizations helped to spread research programmes by starting Extension Service Departments. The organizations like NCERT, ICSSR and UGC, financed certain research project for improving curriculum, methods of teaching and techniques, evaluation etc. Quality research should contribute to knowledge and human welfare. It should be a deliberate effort not a flash of intuition, though it starts with a sudden spark of ideas. Quality research should be a creative process that can question authority and must objective and free of bias.

Rational of the Study

Educational researchers have come to the consensus that, educational research must be conducted in a rigorous and systematic way, although what this implies is often debated. There are a variety of disciplines which are each present to some degree in educational research. These include philosophy, psychology, sociology, anthropology etc. The overlap in disciplines creates a broad range from which methodology can be drawn. Educational research attempts to solve a problem. Research involves gathering new data from primary or first-hand sources or using existing data for a new purpose. Research is based upon apparent experience or empirical data. The quality of research includes its fundamental merit and academic impact which includes the originality of research by researcher and its impact on the development of the same or related discipline areas. The broader impact is an assessment of value through use, i.e. the extent to which research is successfully applied—that is recognition by qualified end-users that quality research has been successfully applied. Educational research helps to construct curriculums, to prepare new text books, to adopt new theory or to adopt a new method of teaching.

Objectives of the Study

Following are the objectives of the study:

1. To study the present scenario of quality research and pedagogy,
2. To study the problems in conducting quality research,
3. To suggest some measures of quality research.

Methodology

In this study a documentary survey has been made. The present scenario of quality research and pedagogy and problems of quality research has been analyzed and some measures which will help the researchers to accomplish a quality research have been suggested.

The Present Scenario of Quality Research and Pedagogy

In the present day, many new changes have been taking place in the field of knowledge due to scientific and technological development. Research methods and procedure have been improved with the aim of attaining more objective and reliable information. Many new methods of data collection and analysis were devised. The scope and field of educational research have greatly expanded. Researches is being conducted all over the world for determining the effectiveness of different aspects of the curriculum, teaching methods, evaluation, guidance, administrative practices and planning. There are some points that highlight the present scenario of educational research such as:

- In India there are around 50,000 people studying for doctoral degrees and around 40,000 people employed as researchers. These people have high level technical skills and are also likely to have experience in effective communication, project management and team working. This experience will have been built up through a mix of training, individual study and practical work experience.
- In India, in science education and research, inspite of relative huge increase in funding and being the major technical manpower supplier for IT and global research community, successfully undertaking Moon mission and so on
- Now a days, all the universities had started M. Ed, M A, M. Phil, Ph. D courses. In India extensive research work has been done in all dimensions. A lot of highly sophisticated work has been conducted on relevant issues. The researcher also faces challenges in the field of education.
- The organizations like National Council of Educational Research and Training (NCERT), State Institute of Education, National University of Educational Planning and Administration (NUEPA) etc. were established in the country to promote and coordinate educational research at different levels of instruction.

- Many journals like Indian Educational Review, Indian Journal of Education, Journal of Higher Education, Journal of Education and Psychology, Indian Journal of Applied Psychology, Journal of Psychological Research, Journal of Educational Planning and Administration etc. and other periodicals were also started to publish information and articles relating to research findings in the field of education in the Indian context.
- The Education Surveys separation oversees planning, design, operations, statistical analysis, reporting and dissemination for elementary, secondary, vocational, post-secondary and library surveys. The division ensures the preservation of statistical quality and maintains liaisons with department officials, federal agencies, state and local education agencies, and post-secondary institutions; and statistical, education and library associations; and other individuals and groups concerned with national elementary, secondary, vocational and post-secondary statistics.
- Since, 1944 and uptil now only 225 philosophical studies have been carried out on education. But this review has been taken from the first survey to sixth survey of educational research. However, there are lots of studies that have been carried out in the educational field.
- The University Grant Commission, the Ministry of Human Resources Development, the Indian Council of Social Sciences Research, the National Council of Educational Research and Training and some other organizations provide financial aids to research workers in education and other related fields to undertake and accomplish useful research. Many Universities already started pre-Ph.D course work to search for competent researchers.
- Recently, highly appreciable research work has been made on profitable horticulture farming practiced in polyhouses. There is a change in the agricultural trends in almost every state where youngsters now make the best use of easily the latest technology and expertise for remunerative farming.

But still it is observed that research quality is not satisfactory compared to other countries with less interest where research work casually. Moreover, there are very few institutions in India who are giving quality inputs so as to inculcate learning skills amongst students. Research in India compare to developing/developed countries needs substantial improvement. Institutions must look into constantly updating in order to help students adapt with the changing scenario. If such developments take shape in its true sense in our country students would be attracted to pursue quality research. Efforts should also be taken to guide students to develop a good quality research. Institutions should also inculcate multitasking abilities amongst students, foreign languages, advanced IT knowledge so that they can perform better in the chosen field. Student exchange, cultural exchange should be encouraged and various ways and means should be found to enhance students interest level. UGC and other organization also should provide sufficient funds, schemes to the institution for enhancing overall support.

The Problems in Conducting Quality Research

Educational research improves the quality of education and ensures access to equal educational opportunities for all individuals. It conduct basic and applied research on the teaching and learning process; the economic, social and policy contexts of education; and other areas defined as high priority. Educational research collects and analyzes statistical data on the current condition of education and project education trends. It demonstrates, disseminates and adapts new knowledge and practices in various educational settings. Therefore, great efforts should be made to improve the quality of research. There are some major problems which have been discussed as follows:

1. Repetition of Topics

This is one of the most important elements of research. Repetition makes duplication of research which decreases the research quality. To improve the standard of Ph. D research, topic allotment should be original and there should not be duplication or any repetition of any research work being done presently at other Indian Universities. However, the problem arises when the same topic is registered at two or more Universities at the same time, whether knowingly or unknowingly. Unfortunately, there is no Central Registration Agency which can provide data before registration of a particular topic whether same topic or same topic in a modified form is being pursued at some other University or not.

2. *Improper Evaluation System of a Ph.D. Thesis*

The evaluation system of a Ph.D. thesis is the root cause of our terribly low standard of research. Unfortunately, many students who have no aptitude for research, are first admitted to a Ph.D. programme and worse still, acquire the degree dirt cheap because the thesis are sent to their supervisor's friend/colleague/ contemporary for evaluation. In some Universities, the supervisors themselves suggest the names of Ph.D. examiners. The supervisor always looks for safe examiners, and if he does not know any, he takes the help of his colleague(s) to procure the names of such safe examiners. Some examiners even dare to evaluate the Ph.D. thesis, which is not at all related to their field of specialization. This disastrous approach is the main cause of our mediocre Ph.D. degrees as the supervisor is not bothered about the rejection of the thesis. One can find such thesis in our libraries, which do not deserve to be there at all.

3. *Hiding Identity of Supervisor and Candidates*

Some universities hide the identity of the scholar's right from Matriculation exam to M.A. Examination, kept secret from the examiners. However, it is strange that in such an important examination like that of Ph.D. and M.Phil, the identity of candidates is not kept secret from the examiners of Ph.D. Sometimes it is seen that the names of supervisors is boldly printed on the title of thesis/dissertations. As a result, most of the examiners do not evaluate the thesis/dissertation but write reports/award grades proportionately to the status of the supervisor. Generally, if supervisor happens to be a Dean/Chairperson, his candidates get excellent reports for Ph.D. thesis and awarded highest grades for M.Phil dissertations. Therefore, while sending Ph.D. thesis/ M.Phil dissertations for evaluation to external examiners, identity of both supervisor as well as candidates should be kept secret.

4. Lack of Specialized Teacher and Organization

In the absence of specialized teacher and institution, the bulk of research is being conducted by the students. Most of the research is confined to training colleges which have very inadequate facilities for research and few competent people to guide it.

5. Lack of Credibility and Dependability of Data

An important issue to consider with research is how to ensure credibility and dependability of the data. Poor credibility and dependability is one of the main problems in conducting quality research. To increase the amount of data, larger samples may be needed to achieve data. In addition, multiple interviews may be necessary to obtain enough rich data.

6. Lack of Effective Communication Skills

Improper communication skill is another main problem of quality research. Quality research requires effective communication to optimize participant responses. First, a researcher needs an accountable and respectful attitude. Second, researchers need to understand the communication challenges. Acquiring knowledge about the topic may help in communication. The researcher must also be open-minded, be flexible to deal with the unpredictability of the situation. An effective strategy to confront communication challenges is required for good research.

7. Lack of Regulations of Funds

The amount of scholarships given to researchers are low. Students suffer due to financial problems and it hampers research work. Expenditure on educational research has been negligible. Proper funds are not available and there has been considerable duplication in research work.

8. Lack of Additional Services

Services like documentation, computation, consultation etc have not been developed. Some research has been done and remained in the archives and the administration has not used its findings for the formulation of policies.

9. Spending Money on Non-Performing Institutions

Spending money on non-performing institutes and universities is one of the main limitations of a quality research. Because of these, bias scholars are produced. Many students who have no aptitude for research, are first admitted in Ph.D. programme and with poor quality acquires the research degree.

10. Lack of Scholarship and Other Facilities for Ph.D. Scholars

Due to inadequate money researcher can not do proper research in their areas as they have to visit places for data collection, and hence, level of accountability among the scholars also decreases. Other facilities such as improper physical infrastructure like laboratory and library, no internet connection in computers in libraries, communication problem, hostel facilities for researcher etc.

There are Some Measures of Conducting Quality Research

1. Establish a Cell for Information about Ph.D Topic

In order to improve the quality of research work for Ph.D. programme, UGC should be pursued to create a cell where information from all the Indian Universities regarding registrations of topics in a particular subject for Ph.D. is available at the initial stage of research. As soon as higher Board of Studies of a University clears a topic, it should be sent to UGC and only after clearance from UGC, student should be finally registered for Ph.D.

Alternatively, universities can also take some initiative of their own in this direction by setting up a Cell in their Libraries where all the information regarding registration of topics in a particular subject of all the Universities is collected from internet and websites of different Universities and also by requesting them personally. Information so received should be then fed in the computers and supplied to the Chairperson of the Department concerned, much before the process of registration of Ph.D.

candidates begins. This single step will prevent repetition of topics to a large extent.

2. *Evaluation System of a Ph.D. Thesis*

Something serious has to be done with the evaluation system if we really want to improve our standard. Firstly, the supervisor should not be involved at any stage, in selecting the panel of the examiners. This will make the supervisor work harder and take the Ph.D. thesis of his student more seriously. Secondly, there should be a centralized system of evaluation. The UGC can play a major role in this direction. It should build a data bank of all specialized serious and good workers in the country who can act as examiners of a Ph.D. thesis. The Universities should send the Ph.D. thesis to the UGC, from where it will be mailed to at least two examiners by masking the names of student, supervisor and their affiliations. Alternatively, universities can have their own data bank and pool of examiners from where the Vice-Chancellor can pick names of any two examiners in a particular subject without bringing it to the knowledge of Chairperson or Supervisor. The evaluation should be strictly on merit. At times rejection of a Ph.D. thesis would serve the purpose because either the supervisors will start taking things seriously or they will stop guiding any Ph.D. student. It is better to produce only a few good quality theses than to have a number of weak theses.

3. *Video Recording of Viva-Voce of Ph.D. Candidates*

To improve quality of higher research, video recording of *viva-voce* of Ph.D. candidates is a must. If the *viva-voce* of the Ph.D. candidate is excellent, then the video recording of such a *viva-voce* will help future candidates for Ph.D. to learn and to improve their own performance.

4. *Appointing Eminent Educationist*

Eminent educationists should be appointed broadly to promote educational thought and set-up research. The universities and research organisations should contribute in a big way to the development of educational research.

5. Specialized Training System

Good and specialized training for research work and services for data processing, statistical analysis and consultation should be provided by universities and other research institution.

6. Financial Help by Organization

The NCERT, ICSSR, UGC and other organizations played a significant role in increasing awareness among the researchers. Material help in the form of financial assistance and equipment is provided to the researcher.

7. Improvement of Pedagogy

The purpose of quality research is to develop new or improved pedagogy to achieve well-specified learning goals or objectives, based on a well-specified theory of action appropriate to a well-defined end user, creation of measures to assess the implementation of the solution, and collection of data on the feasibility of implementing the solution. Emphasis must be given to the pedagogy so that they can develop the basic skills and perform well in the world, across the globe.

8. Good or Proper Proposal for the Research Work

The proposal should include a strong theoretical and empirical justification for development of the proposed strategy. If the theoretical basis rests on evidence related to individual features or components, the proposal should provide a compelling rationale for how combining these features or components into a new intervention is expected to achieve the intended outcomes.

9. The Proposal should include a Description of the Initial Concept for the Planned Investigation

It includes a well-explicated theory of action or logic model. The concept and logic model should identify key components of the intervention i.e., the ingredients hypothesized to be critical to achieving the intended results and should describe their relationships, theoretically, and operationally.

10. Reduce Spending Money on Non-performing Institutions

Reduce the money spent on higher education and research for non-performing institutes and universities. Private institutes and universities must follow a minimum standard to give degrees. All institutes/universities should be graded and judged as per their performance and monetary support should depend on that. Introduce strict accountability of research in the institute or university.

11. Increase the Scholarship and Other Facilities for the Research Scholar

Increase the fellowship of researchers so that they can work independently and increase the level of accountability among them. Universities should improve other physical infrastructure like buildings, laboratory and library, internet connected computers in libraries etc. Arrange hostel facilities for researchers.

12. Provide Opportunity to the Scholars

Provide adequate opportunities for students in rural and semi-urban areas in the form of transparent information dissemination, transparent selection for fellowship/scholarships and recruitments. Facilities should be provided to the research scholar to go through those national and international study materials which help them a lot in their respective areas.

Pedagogical Issues in Research

1. In the context of the university, the teachers work is to be the authoritative carrier, producer and disseminator of worthwhile knowledge; in contrast, the student's work is to obediently absorb this worthwhile knowledge through learning to be critical but in a disciplined sort of way, and maybe one day—as a Ph.D. candidate—to contribute some fragment to it. The relations of pedagogy appear very top down. In this sense, supervision is a particular form of pedagogy in a larger scene of higher education pedagogies. Supervision is role in transforming the

student from reproducer of knowledge to producer, a transition that is challenging at many levels.

2. First, supervision is a pedagogical context of unusual intimacy and intensity between two (or more) unequally positioned people. In many cases supervision is conducted in privacy and sometimes the student does not have access to anyone else for guidance with their research. Even when they are not, they will usually be seen by the student to have influence beyond the context of the supervision itself. Two questions arising for the student out of this characteristic of supervision are, on the one hand, what counts as dependence and, on the other, how much ignorance to show the supervisor. Students are unused to showing a teacher their work-in-progress; many fear that any sign of incompetence or dependence will be used against them in the final examination. This fear springs from the very different institutional locations of supervisor and student—a difference with potentially far-reaching consequences.
3. The face-to-face quality of supervision is a very good pedagogy. They are the members of different social groups that structure our society. These kinds of power relations enter the intimate context of supervision in a very direct way: gender and cultural differences in communication affect the way meetings and other interactions go. Body language, as well as talk and written feedback, have greater significance when the supervisor and student work together over time and through a process during which the student usually experiences many ups and downs, surges and losses of hope and belief in him/herself.
4. The pedagogy of education should be such a way that the scholar gets opportunity to interact with other thinkers through seminars or workshops, video conferencing which help them a lot in their respective areas.

Conclusion

Quality research should be premised upon the principles of scientific inquiry i.e., empirical observations using systematic designs, the theoretical underpinnings and philosophy of science. Quality research most commonly refers to the scientific process encompassing all aspects of study design; in particular, it pertains to the judgement regarding the match between the methods and questions, selection of subjects, measurement of outcomes, and protection against systematic bias, non-systematic bias, and inferential error. Research has an important and growing role in the study of quality and safety. The rationale for establishing the quality research is the main challenge for the researcher. Problems occur when attempting to determine exactly how this task can proceed. It is evident that debate and discussion, together with systematic evaluation of the implications of adopting various methods for appraisal, are necessary to resolve many of the critical issues raised here. We have to prompt a design to stimulate appraisal of different dimensions of quality research. There is a need for future development in this area to focus on the distinctive study designs and theoretical perspectives that quality research can adopt and it recognise that many of the more important and interesting aspects of research may remain to be measured. The increasing percentage of quality research will certainly increase its scenario and students in turn will start adding value to the world and towards the growth of our nation.

References

Creswell, J.W. (2002). *Research Design: Qualitative, Quantitative, and Mixed Methods Approaches.* New York: Sage Publication.

Koul, L. (2008). *Methodology of Educational Research*. New Delhi: Vikas Publication House Pvt. Ltd.

Kothari, C.R. (2004). *Research Methodology: Methods and Techniques*. New Delhi: New Age International Publisher.

Miles, M.B. (1994). *Qualitative Data Analysis: An Expanded Sourcebook* (2nd Edition). New York: Sage Publication.

Woods, M.D. *et al.* (2004). The Problem of Appraising Qualitative Research. Retrieved on March 3, 2015 from http://qualitysafety.bmj.com/content/13/3/223.

Index